table of contents

foreword

In the spring of 1993, Roberto Goizueta asked me to come back to The Coca-Cola Company as its first ever chief marketing officer.

I would be in charge of a worldwide budget that exceeded $5 billion, and the very first question that crossed my mind was, "How am I going to be able to talk to consumers in an efficient way, while growing the business?"

There were a lot of things that contributed to the success we ultimately experienced, or, should I say, to the success of the team that I assembled. I was able to hire the best marketing people in the world and also to get the best partners in the world. The only way that we were going to grow the business from nine billion to fifteen billion cases in only three short years was to bring together the very best in every area of the business.

Packaging, as a key component of brand design, had always attracted me. I believe that it is the most efficient way to talk to consumers–and I also believe that it has been misused and mismanaged over the years.

In 1985, during my first tenure at The Coca-Cola Company, on the heels of the introduction of New Coke and at the beginning of the one-hundred-year anniversary of The Coca-Cola Company, I got a phone call from the corporate department of the company asking me to develop a new graphic design so we would have something to show the bottlers at the 1986 celebration of the anniversary. I was shocked at first because I believe that packaging should not be show-and-tell but an expression of identity that should really be put to work for the brand. But I lost the argument, and the packaging was redone. All of the brands of The Coca-Cola Company were reduced to a single design. It was a political design created for the wrong reasons, not for the right causes.

When I came back to the company that August (1993), after a seven-year hiatus, I immediately started looking for people who "got it." In the design arena, I was introduced that fall to Marc Gobé in Paris, and the very first two questions I asked Marc were, *Do you get it?* and, *Can you help me?*

- Do you understand the importance of graphic design as a selling tool?

- Can you help me take the incredible power of the design and the iconography of the logos of The Coca-Cola Company to help us sell more product?

Marc impressed me with his emotionalized approach to brand design, a concept ahead of its time. Over the next three years, the aid that Marc gave me was instrumental in helping us take the volume of The Coca-Cola Company from nine billion to fifteen billion cases a year. It was not only in the design of the graphics of the bottle or the can, which is what all graphic designers do, but more in Marc's great understanding of the role of hidden assets like the trucks and the uniforms and all of the visual expressions of a brand.

Millions and millions of Coca-Cola impressions are in the streets every day, as trucks, for example, travel up and down in front of consumers . . . and we had never spent any time really designing them to sell.

When I went to Paris, Marc and his people showed me the design they had done for the Olympics in Albertville and the design they had done for Boucheron perfume. It was remarkable right away how they had used color–not only the traditional colors–and how they had used design–not the traditional designs–to really communicate the essence of products to connect emotionally with the consumers.

I have always believed that brand design in packaging is a critical part of marketing. It should translate the meaning of the brand for the consumers. Marc and his partner, Joel Desgrippes, understood very clearly that packaging could actually serve to translate the meaning of the brand to the consumers every day, on every shelf, in every aisle, on every truck, and in every vending machine all over the world. I could probably write a book about my experiences with Marc, about how much I learned from the color blue that Marc had used in creating a corporate identity for the Albertville Winter Olympics, for the Boucheron perfume bottle and store design, and later on in the redesign of Gillette's packaging. It was eventually a color that changed the refreshment appeal of Sprite.

I understood so much about the culture of The Coca-Cola Company and the brand's connection to the color red (that piece of equity and iconography that was critical to the development of our sales). So, it wasn't only what the word Coke or Sprite or Fanta would do, it was about using all of the elements of the brand–aggressively and with kick-ass creative.

I went with Marc to the fashion shows in Paris, and together we learned from the great designers of the world about how to use color, shape, and form to connect with consumers. At the time, I was probably one of the very few marketing executives from a consumer goods company who had bothered to go to a fashion show. Marc had assured me it would be time well spent; he was right.

In this book, Marc mentions briefly the '96 Olympics effort in Atlanta for Coca-Cola. It's mentioned in a modest way, but for us it was a significant change in managing something that traditionally had been done in a passive way, or rather, something that was done to sell the *Olympics* as opposed to selling Coca-Cola. Our brand presence at the Olympics ranged all the way from the Coca-Cola Olympic City design, to the package graphics themselves, to the uniforms, to what we put in the stadiums and what we put in the airport and train stations. As I write this, I have just returned from the Olympics in Sydney, and I appreciate even more how a proactive, purposeful design works to accent a marketing effort. In Sydney, it was obvious that many of the sponsors got lazy. It was a display of disconnected design that ignored an opportunity. Every day, I see in stores what I saw in Sydney: lazy design without vision.

What I learned from my work with Marc and Coca-Cola, more than anything else, was that imagination gives dimension to a brand; that it's not about where your company is right now, but about where you eventually want to be. Every day, through Z Group Strategy Consulting, I preach that an integrated brand strategy is the key to reaching your destination. And an integrated brand strategy is at the heart of Emotional Branding.

Emotional Branding is about building relationships; it is about giving a brand and a product long-term value. It is about sensorial experiences: designs that make you feel the product, designs that make you taste the product, designs that make you buy the product.

I believe that kick-ass creative is critical to the success of a brand, and no designer is better qualified to explain creative, integrated design identity than Marc Gobé. *Emotional Branding* will help you understand how great brands–from Stew Leonard's in rural Connecticut to multinational Coca-Cola–grow their businesses and attract loyal customers.

Sergio Zyman

preface

The confluence of the emergence of social media and the massive shift from fixed to wireless communication tools, the election of Barack Obama as President of the United States, and the greatest economic crisis of our lifetimes motivated me to update my first book, *Emotional Branding*. At no time in our recent history have we seen the type of powerful changes that will affect our society and our civilization from an economic, social, and business perspective. These are emotional times.

How will these changes impact our lives and our brands in a time of crisis? This book is all about answering this question. As online communication has given power back to the people, consumerism as we know it will change and force businesses to evolve to meet the demands of a newly empowered consumer. How brands will survive or thrive in this new environment depends on their willingness to meet the expectations of a people shaped by Twitter, Facebook, and other social media sites that have changed the media and privilege dialogue, engagement, and sharing.

The old way of pushing products people don't want will wane as new businesses are created that engage people with offerings that inspire. A new business model that emphasizes connection versus arrogance and inspiration instead of hype is taking its place.

We are leaving a world where consumers have seen car companies go bankrupt shortly after promising an "American Revolution" and have raised their voices after the iconic juice brand Tropicana changed its packaging from one of the most revered designs in the industry. This type of brand arrogance toward consumers is over, and this second edition of *Emotional Branding* will bring forth examples of changes that demonstrate how to close the gap between the logical approach of corporate cultures and the emotional world of consumers.

As a designer and filmmaker, I will look at the most important element of branding: people. Inspired by the videos I filmed for my Web site (*www. emotionalbranding.com*), I will capture in this book the emotions that shape demand and inspire marketers. Emotionalbranding.com was in Washington when the inauguration of Obama made history, and in Moscow uncovering why BMW built one of the largest billboards in the world right in front of the Kremlin. Emotionalbranding.com was in Liverpool discovering how a giant mechanical spider brings thousands of people out in soaking rain just to be stimulated emotionally; in Los Angeles speaking with street artist Shepard Fairey to find out why this form of art is such a draw for younger generations and how he feels to be the designer of the official Obama campaign poster. I will take readers with me to São Paulo to hear the chief marketing officer of one of the city's biggest banks tell me that graffiti art might be the only art a majority of the Brazilian population, who can't afford a visit to any museum, will ever see. I also talked with São Paulo's mayor, Gilberto Kassab, on why he tore down all forms of the city's outdoor advertising to fight what he calls "visual pollution." To my utmost surprise, I heard how marketers and advertisers were relieved by the mayor's decision.

For this book, I interviewed visionaries who are inventing new ways to bridge the gap between brands and people, but I also noticed when brands got it wrong. I want to know why some activists are motivated to cross the Pacific Ocean on a boat made of plastic bottles to protest against our out-of-control pollution and why kids under ten years old won't shop in stores that don't meet their expectations of sustainability. Finally, as more than 50 percent of the world's population now lives in urban environments, I focus on what impact this will have on our habitat and lifestyle and what this means in terms of our new consumption habits. Most importantly, this book looks at how people across all social categories get and consume information and how and why they connect with each other.

When I witnessed towers being erected in the favellas in Rio de Janeiro to help residents connect to the Internet, I realized that traditional TV will have a shrinking role in our future. The world is in movement and our planet is rapidly changing. There is so much we don't know and so much information we are missing through the traditional, overhyped media. This book, when combined with Emotionalbranding.com, starts a conversation that is hard to find anywhere else.

I show that a direct link between brands and people is being created on the Web, challenging traditional media. This new dialogue, based on new media whose impact could be compared to the invention of the mechanical printing press by Johannes Gutenberg, will transform our civilization and commerce as we know it.

When Alexander McQueen, the most compelling fashion designer of his generation, decided in October 2009 to stream his Paris runway show live to the larger public, it was evident that some walls were coming down. In a fifteen-minute interview before the show, McQueen justified his decision by saying that he wanted to bypass the traditional fashion print media that only interpret what he is truly about and the meaning of this work.

Ironically, at the same time that Alexander McQueen was online reaching out to a new crowd, a film documentary about Anna Wintour, the legendary editor-in-chief of *Vogue*, was hitting the screens to confirm the fact that indeed the fashion magazines have the power to make or break a fashion house. *Vogue* was seen in this film as the ultimate power broker between fashion houses and the American audience.

As both events happened simultaneously, you could not help but marvel at the coincidence and feel that a change was taking place in how some news, including fashion news, will be delivered in the future. The Internet as a new medium will eventually help challenge traditional forms of communication to connect brands and people directly, making the public the de facto decisionmaker.

I have updated the Ten Commandments of Emotional Branding, which are even more relevant today. I have focused again on three powerful generations–Baby Boomers, Gen X, and Gen Y–to explain why the smaller demographics of Gen X will hurt our economy for some time as their demographic numbers fail to replace the consuming habits of Baby Boomers retiring from the workforce. You will discover a completely new chapter on social media and an updated report on advertising and the challenges advertisers face.

As a designer, writer, and producer, I have always created ideas in the expanding frontiers of my imagination, relying on my most powerful intuitions and my relentless need to explore, discover, and study the margins of society to feed my insatiable curiosity. What I bring to brands is my ability to connect them with people and find the right language to reach the consumers emotionally. I want brands to see the world and its people with a new set of eyes. I want to help them see a smile, understand the power of a dream come true, and vibrate with people celebrating hope. And, most importantly, make them understand how good it feels when they do something right.

This book is about a dream.

acknowledgments

In revising *Emotional Branding*, I got tremendous help and inspiration from many amazing people who gave me time and all those ideas that guided me in this project. Some people I have met personally and interviewed on camera; some others I tried to meet but couldn't. Some never returned my calls . . . oh, well.

And then there are the books. As a designer and filmmaker, I have realized that what is important is not the starting point but the end result. Any creative endeavor, such as the design business or film business, needs preparation but can't operate within a strict process. You need a discovery approach that allows you to find the right angle in order to develop great ideas. The kiss of death is when somebody tells you that the only way to get to a result is by following a strict formula. Great ideas live in our imaginations, not in the rigid guidelines professed by some branding book. Branding is not a horse race, but a human journey.

So, I read and reread books that make me laugh, think, or cry–books outside the branding business, books that inspire my work, or stories that stimulate my mind.

My favorite is *Existentialism and Human Emotions* by Jean-Paul Sartre. "If I eat pink cake, the taste of it is pink," he said, going on to profess that to eat is to appropriate by destruction.

And you can't beat Anton Chekhov, who, in *The Cherry Orchard*, has one of his characters, Lopakhin, say, "Russians is what we are, we pay the Germans to make us French."

Other books give me a sense of what real leadership and integrity look like, such as Jon Meacham's wonderful book *Franklin and Winston: An Intimate Portrait of an Epic Friendship*. Roosevelt and Churchill's personal communications in longhand and via telegraph about every major decision during World War II have a human and emotional quality that demonstrate their love and respect for each other. Together, they spoke a language you do not find among executives anymore.

I could not put down either book by Barack Obama. In them, this great American shows so much intelligence and vision for his country so early in his life: "There is not a black America and white America and Latino America and Asian America–there is the United States of America," he wrote, exposing the fallacy of segmentation along racial lines.

Emotional Branding is the sum of many parts and cannot be reduced to a simple diagram. Iconic film director Sidney Lumet, in his book *Making Movies*, wrote that after intense planning and preparation there are some moments when intuition must rule. "When the magic happens, the best thing you can do is get out of the way of the picture. Let it tell you how to do it from now on . . . after proceeding with great control and preplanning. . . . I'd trust my momentary impulses on the set and go with them."

And then I enjoyed meeting such authors as Marty Neumeier of the bestselling *Brand Gap*, who invited me to the launch of his third book on design, *The Designful Company*. I indulged myself with Jeff Gordinier's *X Saves the World: How Generation X Got the Shaft but Can Still Keep Everything from Sucking*, a book so fun, so personal and sensitive, and so full of the American energy the world craves–as this European sees it. Jeff had organized a talk at one Manhattan bookstore with three other members of Gen X: Jeff Chang, the author of *Can't Stop, Won't Stop: A History of the Hip-Hop Generation*; Kara Jesella, coauthor with Marisa Meltzer of *How Sassy Changed My Life*, about the glory and fall of one of the most exciting magazines ever published; and Douglas Rushkoff, the author of *Get Back in the Box*, which includes his powerful thoughts on how social media is first and foremost about sharing. It was awesome.

I am also indebted to *How Obama Won* by Chuck Todd and Sheldon Gawiser, which gave me a sense of how targeted the Barack Obama campaign was, as it privileged the human factor over strict demographics. *Estée: A Success Story* by Estée Lauder made me cry, and *Raymond Loewy* by Laura Cordin made me shiver.

A talk by Beth Comstock, the CMO of GE, at a business group I attended energized me when she spoke of the success of Hulu, and a few executives at Weight Watchers showed me how commerce and people can live and benefit each other without taking advantage. Kevin Clark, a former IBM executive, and Christine Astorino, the founder and CEO of fathom, a Pittsburgh-based consulting group that brought life to that city's children's hospital, pushed the limits of my thinking.

Thanks to Peter Levine and Anneliza Humlen, two of the best branding thinkers I have met. Anneliza is now a partner at Emotional Branding Alliance, and Peter wrote again a new text on Generations. Thanks as well to the wonderful owner of MMC, Marina Maher, who gave me a new way to look at PR; and to Desiree Gruber of Full Picture, who is transforming communication as we know it with productions such as Modelinia. I want to thank Tony Hsieh, the visionary CEO of Zappos, for his interview, and in absentia Jeremiah Owyang (partner, consumer strategy at Altimer Group), who I could not reach. Both have a public profile on the Web that indicates how much transparency brand leaders will have to show in the future if they want to build trust in social media. I have also met such visionaries as Ric Jurgens, the president of Hy-Vee, who wants to make Iowa the healthiest state in the nation. Iowa rocks!

TV1's Selma and Sergio Motta Mello developed my Web site, Emotionalbranding. com, for me and helped me launch it in São Paulo with the presence of the city's mayor. Albert Levy, the globally known family doctor in New York City, always keeps me abreast of new ideas on how people react to life emotionally. George Fertitta, the president of NYCvisit, the internal advertising agency for New York City, gave me access to some of his team: Jane Reiss, Angela Tribelli, Jim Hanes, Melissa Velez Goldberg, and Willy Wong. This group, which works to make New York an ever more compelling place, is one of the best branding communication agencies I have ever witnessed. Many thanks also to the inspiring students I advised for the 2009 FIT Master's program in cosmetics and fragrance marketing and management: Bill Hughes, Kory Marshisotto, Marisha McEwan, and Alexis Stern.

I also had the great privilege to film inspiring leaders of politics, academia, and the arts: São Paulo Mayor Gilberto Kassab, on his decision to ban all forms of outdoor advertising; Gary Knell, the head of *Sesame Street*, which is by far the most admired American brand around the world; Alain Lambert, a French politician and former finance minister who can't back down from his principles, finding support for his ideas from hundreds of thousands of people through a most compelling blog that he manages with a passion; the team at Scenic, a multisensorial branding firm in New York; Philippe Apeloig, one of the leading typographic designers; and street artist Shepard Fairey, on why Barack Obama selected him to design the campaign's official poster. Executives at Lew Lara, one of the most innovative ad agencies in Brazil, gave us so many insights on advertising–with imagination, there is no problem that can't be solved. I had a great conversation with Patricia Soares da Costa, a journalist from Portugal, who connected me with Sara Batalha from Media Training Worldwide, who, in turn, helped me see social media in a new light.

I will forever thank the support Thomson Reuters gave me for my first Webinar– such a powerful medium–and the inspiring talk I had with Mike Cotter, who oversees global communications services there. I have a special thank-you for the team at Advertising Research Foundation (ARF). Bob Barocci, their president and CEO, and Joel Robinson, chief research officer, as well as Steve Rappaport, knowledge solutions director and one of the best kept secrets in the branding business, gave me their souls. They opened their doors and their hearts to me. At ARF, you can find the most advanced thinking in the power of social media, and I encourage anyone to join this group to grasp their relentless quest for truth.

I also thank my publisher, Tad Crawford at Allworth Press, for his continuous support. He recommended that I work with editor Melanie Tortoroli, who brought her writing skills, disciplined thought process, and unwavering commitment to this book. Joyce Hughes, my former public relations aid, is always an insightful sounding board. Finally, I can't finish without mentioning my film crew, which is hard at work on our next documentary on how branding visually impacts our environment. They include executive producer Chidem Alie, director Gwenaelle Gobé, and film editor Kinga Orlikowska.

I kept the foreword by Sergio Zyman, the powerful marketing and branding executive. It is a classic.

This is where I look for ideas and where I find powerful emotions.

Emotional Branding: Fuel for Success in the Twenty-first Century

What is this story about? What did you see? What was your intention? Ideally, if we do this well, what do you hope the audience will feel, think, sense? In what mood do you want them to leave the theater?
–Sidney Lumet, *Making Movies*

Over the past decade, it has become resoundingly clear that the world is moving from an industrially driven economy where machines are the heroes toward a people-driven economy that puts the consumer in the seat of power. A *New York Times* article a decade ago already made it clear that "over the last fifty years the economic base has shifted from production to consumption. It has gravitated from the sphere of rationality to the realm of desire; from the objective to the subjective; to the realm of psychology."[1]

Simple ideas, such as computers, have morphed from "technology equipment" into larger, consumer-focused concepts known as "lifestyle entertainment." Airplanes are less about transportation vehicles today and more about "travel organizations" that can enhance our lives in many ways through their elaborate bonus-point programs. Food is no longer about cooking or chores but about home and lifestyle design and "sensory experience." And the universities of tomorrow will be branded and will function as modular "knowledge banks," focusing on a new kind of flexible "lifelong, global learning" that caters to students from around the world, both on campus and far away, with differing backgrounds and agendas rather than the traditional youth-driven, highly structured undergraduate and graduate programs. In order to be relevant and survive, it is crucial that brands understand the vast changes afoot and compete accordingly. We are clearly operating within a completely different set of values today versus five years ago. Speed has replaced stability and intangible assets have become more valuable than tangible assets. The traditional supply/

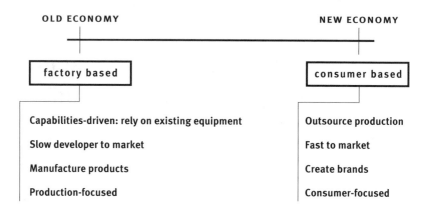

OLD ECONOMY	NEW ECONOMY
factory based	**consumer based**
Capabilities-driven: rely on existing equipment	Outsource production
Slow developer to market	Fast to market
Manufacture products	Create brands
Production-focused	Consumer-focused

demand economic models are being completely reevaluated. Corporations have realized that the new market opportunities are not based on squeezing costs and increasing profits around a set business model, but are above all in *growing entirely new lines of revenue with innovative ideas.*

A *Wall Street Journal* article titled "So Long, Supply and Demand" reaches this conclusion: "The bottom line. Creativity is overtaking capital as the principal elixir of growth. And creativity, although precious, shares few of the constraints that limit the range and availability of capital and physical goods."[2] In this new business atmosphere, ideas are money. Ideas are, in fact, a new kind of currency altogether—one that is more powerful than money. *One single idea—especially if it involves a great brand concept—can change a company's entire future.*

But what exactly constitutes a great brand concept today? In this hypercompetitive marketplace where goods or services alone are no longer enough to attract a new market or even to maintain existing markets or clients, I believe that it is the *emotional* aspect of products and their distribution systems that will be the key difference between a consumer's ultimate choice and the price that they will pay. *By emotional, I mean how a brand engages consumers on the level of the senses and emotions; how a brand comes to life for people and forges a deeper, lasting connection.*

By emotional, I mean how a brand engages consumers on the level of the senses and emotions.

This means that understanding people's emotional needs and desires is really, now more than ever, the key to success. Corporations must take definite steps toward building stronger *connections* and *relationships* and recognizing their

customers as partners. Industry today needs to bring people the products they desire, exactly when they want them, through venues that are both inspiring and intimately responsive to their needs. Welcome to the world of Emotional Branding, a dynamic cocktail of *anthropology, imagination, sensory experiences,* and *visionary approach to change*!

Emotional Branding provides the means and methodology for connecting products to the consumer in an emotionally profound way. It focuses on the most compelling aspect of the human character: the desire to transcend material satisfaction and experience emotional fulfillment. A brand is uniquely situated to achieve this because it can tap into the aspirational drives that underlie human motivation.

Brand Identity Starts at Home

A brand is brought to life for consumers first and foremost by the personality of the company behind it and that company's commitment to reaching people on an emotional level. Bernard Arnault of LVMH, the hugely successful luxury group that owns Dior and many other prestige brands, lives by this credo and has built his company around these ideas. He says, "What I like is to feel emotion . . . and I agree even more when I see the sales results."[3]

Given this new, emotionally driven paradigm, is it fair to say that consumers are thinking more with their hearts or guts than with their heads when choosing products, or that the public wants to be assured of a corporation's unequivocal commitment to it? I would answer yes to both of these questions. The largely uncharted territory of emotions—including how people feel about corporations or the corporate world at large—is an increasingly important part of the buying routine at a time when most products offer the same quality and are in danger of becoming mere commodities in an overcrowded marketplace. And today, with the advent of the Internet and its far-reaching effect on the business world at large, a distinct "win-win" opportunity exists to create a partnership between people and businesses that can lead to increased benefits for both. This win-win partnership model is fast becoming the new standard in business.

Learning from Rome, Thinking like Athens

According to Harold A. Innis, author of *Empire and Communications* (1950), the medium available for communications accelerates the success or demise of civilizations and ultimately transforms them. Innis compared the "oral" culture of ancient Greece to the "written" culture of the Romans to illustrate how these different types of communication produced two completely different civilizations. His is a theory that has become even more relevant in the twenty-first century, as we observe how the Internet as a new communications model is dramatically impacting and challenging the traditional routes of commerce. New online opportunities empower consumers and change the ways in which different commercial messages are consumed. We cannot underestimate the impact this technological revolution will have on our society and the changes it will bring about in consumerism, and thus we must first look to the historical ramifications of Innis's findings.

It is the ease by which papyrus, a light medium, allowed the Romans to communicate across the four corners of their vast empire that gave them the ability to build a centralized administration that could support expanding conquests and manage such vast territories. Reliance on this written, albeit not durable, means of communication thus fostered a civilization Innis called "Space." The Roman model of centralized rule is probably the most accurate analogy to the corporate world as we know it today: efficient centralized business models, supported by the speed of information provided by new technology, helped build a top-down, pyramidal form of decision making in which the few at the top hold all the power.

Ancient Greece, on the other hand, lacking the flexibility of a light medium, relied on a heavier and more permanent medium, such as parchment. The Greeks turned to the oral medium to communicate and administer a tradition, according to Innis, that emphasizes "Time." Sharing information orally carries stories that last for generations (think of Homer's *Odyssey*, which was in the Greek culture, some suggest, long before it was cemented in writing), but that information can reach only a limited audience. As such, the Greeks were limited administratively and in their territorial expansions. Instead, Greek oral culture forced decentralization and encouraged a practice of debates that stimulated long-lasting, innovative thinking. As a result, debates helped create the context in which ancient Greece became the birthplace of many successful yet experimental ideas such as mathematics, trigonometry, geometry, architecture, philosophy, and even science. The Greek culture of innovation was so strong that it has survived millennia and continues to influence all subsequent civilizations.

Today's analogy to the Greek oral tradition is social media and its elusive yet powerful platform for ideas to be played out by the many instead of the few in an ongoing public debate. No one with an influence in the realm of politics, ideology, the arts, education, or commerce can underestimate the impact this new form of interaction will generate. Social media and its instantaneous modes of communication will bring about the most innovative and breakthrough ideas for those who know how to understand its new philosophy.

Ultimately, the best-case scenario, as I interpret Innis's theory, leads me to believe that the greatest societies are those that manage to bring both the pragmatic Roman culture and the emotional Greek tradition together. "Space" and "Time," oral and written, innovation and realism.

The sheer size of the Roman empire required a cumbersome bureaucracy that relied more and more on written rules and procedures as well as the creation of fixed and written decrees. Rome became a rigid, centralized administration that ultimately opened the door to nepotism and bureaucratic corruption. In their book *The Story of Civilization*, Will and Ariel Durant sum up the failings of the Roman state: "The plunder from the provinces provided the funds for that orgy of corrupt and selfish wealth which was to consume the Republic in revolution." Corporations should learn from the Roman empire that when a culture loses its spirit of spontaneity and imagination, it deteriorates into a dogmatic and bureaucratic one, displacing all other forms of innovative thinking.

The Greeks, on the other hand, produced a society with more flexible, philosophical leanings and relied on less dogmatic thinking. The oral tradition gave people the freedom to become spokesmen for others and fostered an independent search for truth that separated science from myth. It brought the creation of a structure adapted to its needs; it brought change. Its flexibility even encouraged the introduction of mathematics and gave rise to philosophical speculation.

Brandbarians at the Gates

A new oral culture driven by the Web might mean the end of capitalism as we know it and the end of commerce as we have experienced it in the past. Our society is moving from a "Space" culture built on physical bigness into a radically changed one that privileges emotional interaction, or "Time." The pendulum is swinging, and the business system and infrastructure we have known in the past will have to transform. It will start on the Web. One thing is for certain: the monopoly of information by dominant media and the monopoly of brands by multinationals is over.

Amazon.com is an example of a change agent: it is a retail business that has no stores. The service is impeccable and, from an emotional perspective, it is one of those businesses you can completely trust; you can be certain your package will show up on your doorstep, and it most likely will be what you ordered. When you hear employees at Amazon talk about their business, their only language is people, service, ease of shopping, prices, and human connection.

With a warehouse somewhere in Kentucky, Zappos.com is a billion-dollar online business with a highly motivated staff and a focus on consumers that is unparalleled. In place of a central headquarters and an army of bureaucrats, Zappos has a new online business philosophy, a new type of culture, and a new type of leadership whose mantra is to focus on only one thing: people. As we'll see in chapter 16, Tony Hsieh at Zappos is fully involved in social media, in particular Twitter, as a way to better connect with people. The values he professes ("radical transparency") show that Hsieh is fully engaged in sharing his life and starting conversations with his potential customer base to gain their—our—trust. At Zappos, there is no dead weight and no expensive consultants required to keep the bureaucracy alive; everyone has a simple responsibility: to serve the people. A new philosophy is sweeping over businesses that privileges creation, imagination, and responsibility to the people.

Harold Innis might have seen the change of our civilization unfolding when he talked about the subversive relationship between those at the centers of civilizations and those on the fringes or margins. From an emotional perspective, this is a compelling thought at a time when we see an extraordinary shift in how our civilization consumes information and how we might be moving from one of *writing*, where the written word is law, to one of *talking*, as in social media, where the written word is an expression of people's emotions.

Before the Web became the amazing social movement it is today, executives in corporate empires saw Web sites and blogs as nice to have as long as they fit into the controlled environment they built for themselves, isolated as they were in the comfort of their palatial headquarters from reality and their customers. Even traditional media such as TV and large newspapers, flushed with their "monopolies of knowledge" and endowed with the supreme right to edit information for us, did not yet see a cause for serious alarm, for they controlled information and how it was delivered. Traditional brand empires could feel protected because they had an overwhelming financial power that helped them buy out competing empires and the ability to afford the most sophisticated technologies to help them consolidate their growth. Most importantly, their territorial monopoly on distribution and knowledge kept competitors at bay. The system privileged stale and self-serving processes over imagination and power over creation.

Social media and the leaders it brought with it is the revolution these brand empires did not see coming. Suddenly, newcomers could write their own technology language and bypass the traditional distribution systems by moving commerce online and creating new lines of business that did not exist before. Not unlike the Greek oral tradition, these newcomers used their connection with people and the access to their input to bring forth a more democratic and agile philosophy that brought people and their emotions into the fold. Ouch! These newcomers were about people, service, and bonding. How do you compete against this when your only defense is a bureaucracy?

From Social Media to Social Branding

It is scarcely possible for generations disciplined in the *written* and *printed* traditions to appreciate the *oral* tradition. With a shift in power from corporations to people and from controlled media to self media, how will armies of executives and consultants trained and disciplined in the written and printed culture's brand wars fare now that their world based on secretive strategic programs and cultural dominance has shifted toward poetry?

When NBC invested in Hulu, the online video service, they first rented big offices and brought in an army of consultants, futurists, and technologists to spearhead the business. But soon after, in came Jason Kilar, the new CEO, and out went the consultants. The fancy offices were replaced by a cheap rental with cheap furniture. His goal: to work with people who have what it takes to connect emotionally with others.

How prepared brands "in the center" are to manage this change will depend on their willingness to radically reevaluate their whole company culture. Do they have the people (like Kilar) who can handle such a change? Do they have a corporate culture that can breed those new executives? It is easier to be the cat observing the fish (consumers) in the aquarium than to be in the aquarium, especially if you are a cat. The Web that turned out to be a blessing for multinationals or businesses operating in large geographical areas might have also triggered a different type of revolution: the return to the Greek model, consumer democracy, and the end of all monopolies.

Brands that want to deal with this change need people with open minds, those trained to work in the Greek tradition and endowed with extreme creativity such as architects, designers, engineers, scientists who invent things, fundamental researchers who roam on the fringe of innovation, and philosophers who can speak about human emotions. Those who know how to speak the new language embedded in technology codes are speaking the language of the future, especially when they use it to better serve people. Artists with the know-how to emote in ways that challenge our reality and make us uncomfortable will be at the forefront of this new way of doing business, and I encourage corporations to start bringing those people in.

I don't know if Twitter is the symbol of a Greek revival in branding, but what I know is this: if companies notoriously known for their bad service (think telephone companies or banks) do not understand that there are millions of people on Twitter who have answers to every problem ready faster than those thousands of people in their call centers somewhere in India, these companies will miss a really big boat. The movement of information will be less controlled and more spontaneous, moving from, "Press 1 for a technical problem; for English, press 2 . . . ," to one built on users or professionals connected directly to consumers and backed by a community ready to pitch in with help–like your neighbor who is eager to supply you with salt when you are out of it.

The values of the emerging creative civilization based on dialogue and "Time" will gravitate around this new language. The opportunities given to us by the Twitters of the world will foster greater humanism and a renewed search for truth that could even inspire the rise of genuine leaders and genuine cultures whose philosophy will lead to the type of debate and discussion aimed at expanding people's reality. Social branding is that philosophy, and a fundamental search into what inspires people and brings them joy.

Traditional brands will increasingly be separated into those that can and those that cannot adapt or be invited by consumers to join their new social media. Thinking that social networks are just another communication channel like TV, another media platform the brand can rule and dominate, is far from people's reality.

Advertising as we know it (based on TV spots) will never be a substantial part of social branding unless the brand advertising has a substantial, passionate following, such as BMW or Barack Obama did. Old brands will have less and less space where they can advertise, giving new products more access to the consumer wallet. iPhone Apps, for example, has fostered new businesses with products that are adapted to the new medium. This is the opportunity social branding will provide: new products that allow people to better enjoy the medium. What brands will be included is not up to manufacturers but the people, and those in industries that dominate the landscape need to realize this. Money can't buy love.

CREATIVITY RULES

So, now that we have reached this time when corporations clearly need to fine-tune their focus on the consumer psyche and understand the importance of the constantly evolving trends in their consumers' lifestyles, how exactly do we professionals do this? In order to accomplish this feat of emotional connectivity, corporations have to "start at home" by developing a more humanistic and imaginative culture both in terms of how they conduct business and how they manage their employees. Wal-Mart founder Sam Walton put it another way when he said, "It takes a week to two weeks for employees to start treating customers the same way the employer is treating the employee."[4] The most important thing a company can do today is begin to foster a creative, caring business atmosphere internally. Courage, daring, and energy are contagious forces that can spread through a corporation and the rest of the world online at breakneck speed, if allowed!

Visionary Approach to Change (Connecting the Dots)

We are embarking on a new millennium with great eagerness and apprehension, convincing ourselves that the twenty-first century will be about humanity and spirituality. In the last hundred years, the speed of globalization led by industrialization and commerce was supported by faster transportation, cable communications, and now an instant connection to each other. The Internet has brought to our homes with vivid immediacy the contrast between innovative and retrograde ideas–social justice and injustice and the explosion of solutions and mixed opportunities of a global community.

The re-engineering business practices of the old economy that focused mainly on cost saving for increased profits and speculation for corporations completely destroyed what was left of the emotional contract that once existed between employees and corporations. And this lack of trust toward the established authority has also resulted in increased cynicism toward leveraging brands. Gone are the days of lifetime employment and lifetime brand fidelity–say hello to the age of individuality, where a new "me first" generation has understood the "art of the deal."

"You" Is Really "IT"! The Ascendance of the Individual

In their last issue of the twentieth century, the French magazine *L'Express* elected "you" as the person of the year 2000. On the cover of their magazine was a 3 × 5 mirror, which reflected the faces of all of their readers of different nationalities, races, religions, and creeds. The statement behind this cover is that people, individually, are the force that needs to be reckoned with in the century to come from a political, cultural, artistic, and business point of view. "You" is really "IT"!

Emotional Branding is a means of creating a *personal dialogue* with consumers. Consumers today expect their brands to know them–intimately and individually–and to have a solid understanding of their needs and cultural orientation. This is a greater challenge than ever before in today's increasingly complex marketplace, where we find global consumers with different values, origins,

and aspirations that reflect the ever-evolving mix of the current three most influential generations: Baby Boomers and Generations X and Y. Add to this picture the dramatic increase in numbers and spending power, and expanding social identities of women, ethnic (particularly Hispanic and African-American) and gay and lesbian populations in America, and you realize the challenge and opportunity existing today. In addition, the fact that we now live in a truly global market and are influenced daily by cultures from around the world has made our lives more exciting with an enlarged scope of opportunities and increasing expectations. The age-old human need for variety has new meaning in the rich mosaic of today's marketplace.

How do brands begin to meet this new, more refined and complex need for diversity? Emotional Branding navigates these choppy waters by enabling brands to carry on a personal dialogue with consumers on the issues which are most meaningful to them. The new model will be one of brands connecting with innovative products that are culturally relevant, socially sensitive, and that have presence at all points of contact in people's lives.

Most importantly, the biggest misconception in branding strategies is the belief that branding is about market share, when it is really always about "mind and emotions share."

SERVING THE WHOLE "YOU"

Since consumers are in the driver's seat, they will experience brands in a different way. People today feel empowered; they are more connected to each other and global events and feel capable of influencing the world with their beliefs and shaping part of their own future. We will see people seek and redefine for themselves the quality level of their life. They will fulfill their desires for themselves and for everyone around them by bringing an unprecedented personal and emotional dimension to their choices and decisions. The increasingly important "quality of life" concepts of hassle-free shopping, time management, stress reduction, connectivity, and heightened pleasure will profoundly affect consumers' overall receptivity to new product or marketing ideas. There is a new mandate of tailoring every aspect of business toward *serving the whole person.* Those brands that don't understand this will miss a big opportunity.

The biggest misconception in branding strategies is the belief that branding is about market share, when it is really always about "mind and emotions share."

The future of branding thus rests in listening carefully to people in order to be able to connect powerfully with them by bringing pleasurable, life-enhancing solutions to their world. In the future, traditional companies will not be able to rely on their brand history or dominance in classical distribution systems; they will have to focus on providing brands with a powerful emotional content.

This holistic, very personal experience that one can have with a product is, quite simply, the future of branding, and it will affect product distribution. As we can all see, modes of distribution are certainly changing at a rapid rate to help this transition—and this trend is only bound to continue. Many malls are currently victims of a retail glut phenomenon, in which too many similar brands at highly competitive price points are sold. However, the mall is in the process of being reinvented as a form of exciting and diverse community entertainment and a cultural center, such as the Easton Town Center Mall in Columbus, Ohio. The mall of the future will most likely be less about purchasing products than exploring them in a physical setting, while the Internet model is fast becoming, among other things, the ultimate "one-to-one" distribution machine. This means that retail environments will have to become places to build brand images, rather than just places to sell products. Stores will need to emotionally bond with consumers through retail design and merchandising strategies that incorporate imaginative features, offering the kind of entertainment and sensory appeal that cannot be found on the Web.

In the stores of tomorrow, buying will be outmoded as a sterile activity, and in its place will stand "the art of shopping," which is less about purchasing and more about experiencing a brand.

From Branding to Emotional Branding

In order to avoid dramatic price wars, which affect all commodity products lacking a strong image, corporations need to deliver tighter and more potent messages about their products. Over three thousand new brands are introduced each year, not including e-brands. What is the difference between Ralph Lauren's fragrance, Romance, and Estée Lauder's Pleasure, between one cola and another cola, between a particular sneaker and its competitor, among the many different kinds of jeans, coffees, or gas stations, or between one beauty Web site and another? In this ocean of offerings, all fighting for the same consumer dollar, the emotional connection is what makes that all-important, essential difference. The emotional element is what gives a brand both the foundation and fuel for future business strategies—consumer-driven strategies.

As a further illustration, just take a look at the Evian waterdrop-shaped millennium bottle. It is not just about water or luxury in the traditional sense. It is about seeing water in a whole new way through groundbreaking design, taste, home decoration, and the evocation of the sensory experience of a water drop.

Emotional Branding is the conduit by which people connect subliminally with companies and their products in an emotionally profound way. Google's innovation, France's romance, Gucci's sensual elegance, *Vogue*'s iconic glamour, and Tiger Woods's amazing drive and spirit reach us emotionally by striking our imaginations and offering promises of new realms. This strategy works because we all respond emotionally to our life experiences and we naturally project emotional values onto the objects around us.

Branding bridges the gap between the provider and the receiver—between authority and freedom. It is about trust and dialogue. Powerful Emotional Branding comes from partnership and communication. Building the right emotion is the most important investment you can make in a brand. It is the promise you make to consumers, giving them permission to enjoy the world of the brand. "What do you hope your audience will feel, think, sense?" Sydney Lumet is right, and branding might be more about creating narratives for the many than building flowcharts for the few.

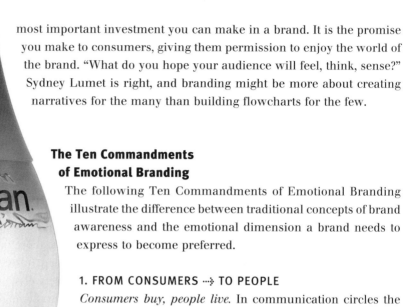

The Ten Commandments of Emotional Branding

The following Ten Commandments of Emotional Branding illustrate the difference between traditional concepts of brand awareness and the emotional dimension a brand needs to express to become preferred.

1. FROM CONSUMERS ⋯⟩ TO PEOPLE

Consumers buy, people live. In communication circles the consumer is often approached as the "enemy" whom we must attack. It's us (meaning manufacturers, retailers, and their communications agencies) against them. Terminology like "breaking down their defenses, decoding their language, and strategizing to win the battle" is, in my day-to-day experience, still commonly used. But why employ this tactic when there is a better way to create desire in customers in a positive manner without harassing or talking down to them? This can be achieved by using a win-win partnership approach based on a relationship of mutual respect. After all, the consumer is your best source of information.

2. FROM PRODUCT ⋯⟩ TO EXPERIENCE

Products fulfill needs, experiences fulfill desires. Buying just for need is driven by price and convenience. A product or shopping *experience,* such as REI stores' rock climbing walls or Apple's inspiring store environments, has added value and will remain in the consumer's emotional memory as a connection made on a level far beyond need. For established products to attract and retain consumer interest, it is critical that innovative retailing, advertising, and new product launches capture the imagination. The lines are drawn every day between newness and tradition, between what is expected and the excitement of change. Our curiosity and sense of adventure often wins out over the known. However, a product can be old and new at the same time if it continues to have emotional relevance for consumers.

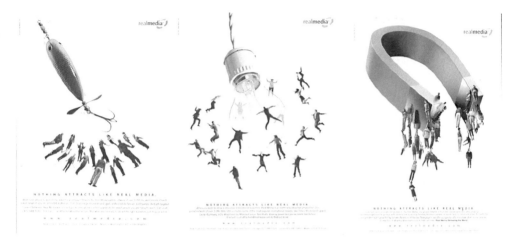

In depicting consumers as moths, fish, and metal shavings in situations of helpless attraction, these ads for a media firm aptly illustrate the mentality Commandment #1 seeks to counteract!

3. FROM HONESTY ⋯> TO TRUST

Honesty is expected. Trust is engaging and intimate. It needs to be earned. Honesty is required for business today. The federal authorities, consumer groups, and people in general have an increasingly rigorous standard for products as they impact the environment or our quality of life. Brands will be rated very quickly on what needs to be on the shelf and what doesn't. Trust is something else altogether. It is one of the most important values of a brand and it requires real effort from corporations. One of the most powerful moves toward building consumer trust was retailers' implementation of the "no questions asked" return policy some years ago. This strategy brings total comfort to customers and gives them the upper hand in their choices. A very smart decision, indeed.

4. FROM QUALITY ⋯> TO PREFERENCE

Quality for the right price is a given today. Preference creates the sale. Quality is a necessary offering if you want to stay in business; it is expected and had better be delivered. Preference toward a brand is the real connection to success. Levi's is a quality brand, but it has currently lost its preferential status. Victoria's Secret, a brand that has achieved an enviable and highly charged emotional connection with consumers today, is revolutionizing a new category and redefining the hosiery and beauty businesses. There is no stopping a brand when it is preferred.

5. FROM NOTORIETY ···> TO ASPIRATION

Being known does not mean that you are also loved! Notoriety is what gets you known. But if you want to be loved, you must convey something that is in keeping with the customer's aspirations. Awareness is obviously not the only criterion to successful branding. Beyond awareness, what does AT&T really mean on an emotional level to consumers? And is there really a difference for people between the well-known (and some would say infamous) brands Exxon Mobil and Texaco? But between Twitter and MySpace, the difference exists. The Barack Obama campaign lifted the candidate's genuine character to be loved by people beyond doubt.

6. FROM IDENTITY ···> TO PERSONALITY

Identity is recognition. Personality is about character and charisma! Identity is descriptive. It is recognition. Personality is about character and charisma. Brand identities are unique and express a point of difference vis-à-vis the competitive landscape. But this is only the first step. Brand personalities, on the other hand, are *special.* They have a charismatic character that provokes an emotional response. American Airlines has a strong identity, but Virgin Airlines has *personality.* AOL's identity is recognizable, but the unique and flexible graphic expression of Google's logo stimulates our imagination.

7. FROM FUNCTION ···> TO FEEL

The functionality of a product is about practical or superficial qualities only. Sensorial design is about experiences. Functionality can become trite if its appearance and usage are not also designed for the senses. Many marketers design for maximum function or visibility and not for the real experience of the consumer. Design is about responsible human solutions, based on innovation that presents a new set of sensory and subconscious experiences. Creating product identification by stressing product benefits is only relevant if product innovations are memorable and exciting to consumers. Toyota's Prius, Apple products and stores, and Gillette razors are brands that are focused on presenting responsible solutions, fresh shapes, or sensory experiences consumers appreciate.

8. FROM UBIQUITY ···> TO PRESENCE

Ubiquity is seen. Emotional presence is felt. Brand presence can have quite an impact on the consumer. It can forge a sound and permanent connection with people, especially if it is strategized as a lifestyle program. There is hardly a stadium, a player uniform, a concert hall, or an urban space of size (billboards, bus stops, walls, and even the inside of bathroom doors) around the world that has not been used to promote a brand. And then, of course, there are the T-shirts, caps, mugs, and so on. But how effective is all this clutter, really? Most brand presence strategies are based on the concept of quantity, not quality. The fear that a competitor might occupy the physical territory becomes the motivator, instead of a focus on inventive ways of making a real, lasting connection. A natural garden wall in Tokyo that surrounds a new real estate project is so much more inspiring for people living in Tokyo than a commercial barricade.

9. FROM COMMUNICATION ⋯⟩ TO DIALOGUE

Communication is telling. Dialogue is sharing. Communication, as conducted by many companies, is primarily about information–and information is generally a one-way proposition. Take it and like it–hopefully. The bulk of most budgets is still spent on advertising efforts that approach consumers with the B1 bomber approach: a massive, all-encompassing blanket advance at the target audience. Not only can advertising deliver more personal, targeted messages, but other media, such as digital communications, PR, brand presence, and promotions can also stretch the message much further to really speak to consumers where they "live." Real dialogue implies a two-way street, a conversation with the consumer. Progress in social branding now allows this evolution to take place and will finally help foster a rewarding partnership between people and corporations.

10. FROM SERVICE ⋯⟩ TO RELATIONSHIP

Service is selling. Relationship is acknowledgment. Service involves a basic level of efficiency in a commercial exchange. It is what allows or prevents a sale from taking place. But relationship means that the brand representatives really seek to understand and appreciate who their customers are. It is what you feel when you walk into an Apple store and find that the music, the décor, and the salespeople all speak the same language–the customer's! It is how trusting you are when buying from Zappos, Amazon, or eBay. Who does not feel special when someone in a store, a restaurant, or even an online merchant welcomes you by name? The emotional component of a true relationship is not always targeted to our personal needs. We are still, in most cases, just a number. Sometimes a big number, but still a number.

As we will see, the consumer train is leaving with or without brands. We are living in a challenging economy in which brands will be less defining as we look elsewhere to fulfill our need to demonstrate who we are and what we believe. We are more interested now in corporations we can be proud of and brands that make us feel confident and smart. Emotions that have defined brands superficially in the past are replaced by more important ideals, such as how that brand helps us affect our environment or impact the social nature of our world.

For corporations who want to adopt the "Time" model fostered by the oral tradition, it is the moment to create a personal dialogue with consumers. When corporate executives are limited in their creative pursuits by bureaucracy, they lose their brand's connection to the people. Change starts at home. Corporations need to leverage their inner talent and become their own center for intense interaction, cultural change, and innovation. They need to realize that their employees and online friends are their best ambassadors. The transparency and viral reach that the Web brings to any brand, coupled with its endless opportunities for connection and the sharing of ideas, will help make that difference. Who you are and how you engage people in promoting your brands will have a direct impact on how you will be perceived and taken into people's hearts.

This new edition of *Emotional Branding* will take you through a fresh understanding of a new marketplace and will offer solutions on how to help your culture connect with people in the most emotional of ways.

section 1:
relationship

customer, customer, customer!

It's the Twenty-first Century: Do You Know Who Your Customers Are?

The oldest Baby Boomers are roughly sixty-five years old, Gen Xers forty-five, and Gen Yers twenty-nine. New generations such as Gen X are taking on more responsibilities and Gen Y's large demographic is entering the workplace with quick success, particularly in social media. As they age, Baby Boomers are faced with the consequences of an economic climate that robbed them of their savings and the prospect of dealing with a new generational culture that is vastly different for them. Coupled with Gen X's lower demographic numbers and their own reduced capacity to spend, the economy will be hurt for years to come as a new buying power will not be there to pick up the slack from the Boomers. That's when the Baby Boomers will rediscover their old fighting spirit, but reduced expectations will be their new reality.

As the Baby Boomers fade from the scene, Gen X and Gen Y will have to pick up the slack. This generation has already put its president in the White House and is setting the tone for the future with social media, defining the race for technology invention, and spearheading ideas for a cleaner planet and better ways to do business. Traditional brands need to prepare. A new world is emerging. The combination of generational and complementary power between Gen Xers and the next youngest generation, Gen Y, will merge into what I am calling "**xY**" and will define how the world will be shaped.

1

A Generational Gap: Targeting New Emotional Criteria

Three major consuming populations inhabit the retail landscape today: the Baby Boomers (forty-six to sixty-four years old), the Gen Xers (twenty-nine to forty-five years old), and Gen Yers (ten to twenty-eight years old). These three population segments (plus or minus a few years and, for some, more of a state of mind than actual age) simply don't speak the same language. Baby Boomers respond to cues of achievement, status, and performance, while Gen Xers value imagination, creativity, and relationships, and Gen Y responds to fun, interactivity, and experiences.

From Aging Baby Boomers to "xY"

Born 1946–1964, Baby Boomers are used to challenging America's assumptions and fighting for what they want. This generation's sheer size has empowered it like no other American generation. In the '60s and '70s *their* mores, *their* music, *their* clothes, and *their* politics were the forces that restructured America. As they fought for women's rights and civil rights, Jimi Hendrix composed their new American vision via a psychedelic rendition of the national anthem they could call all *their* own. Then, exit bell-bottoms and braless babes, enter white picket fences. Haight-Ashbury and loose joints gave way to Wall Street and martinis. As Boomers marched into the boardrooms and back rooms of the '80s, they were suddenly fighting for success and affluence, and redefining success, materialism, and the "American dream" in the process.

Now, this generation finds itself presented with a new obstacle, unlike anything it has ever encountered before: LAF–Life after fifty. Boomers should have been LAFing all the way to the bank, but the world they helped build got taken away from them.

WHEN REALITY HITS

Curran Cadillac, the ultimate Baby Boomer brand, closed its doors after four decades in Westport, Connecticut. For the town's residents, it is like a bit of their lives was taken away. The family that owned the dealership were visible supporters of community events and causes. Gone! From an emotional perspective, the takeaway message is that in losing that Cadillac dealer, a staple and source of pride for the Westport community, Westport now understands that its once economically prosperous community might face harder times. At the same time, for millions of Boomers, the launch of the HBO made-for-TV movie *Grey Gardens* had their sexiest woman in the world, Jessica Lange, portraying an over-seventy-year-old-looking grandma, which broke the illusory mirror that Baby Boomers as a generation had tapped into some form of eternal youth.

As those emotional symbols pile up, Boomers will watch their spending, scale down on the next spa trip, and discover that they have to trade that Harley for a place in a (gasp!) retirement home. Their major spending is now *saving*. The Baby Boomer buying machine might rest for a long while, which is not good news for the economy.

No doubt that as in their previous exploits, Boomers will confront this change with vigor and finesse, co-opting the meaning of maturity and retirement and fitting it to their generation's idiosyncrasies. Well into the first quarter of the new millennium, Boomers will still comprise a dynamic and challenging demographic, and the brands that can provide an identity as versatile as the Boomers themselves stand to reap great success.

Boomers bring tremendous influence and have merited marketers' careful attention like no generation that preceded them. Boomers comprise eighty-one million people, 30 percent of the population, and once commanded 55 percent of the United States' discretionary income. In the past, marketers disproportionately devoted their promotions to young consumers based on the assumption that consumers captured early in life would remain loyal for years to come.

While targeting Generation "xY" could be the key to future success, market-ers cannot ignore the new needs of the largest generation. More and more Boomers will trade power for attention and success for affection. The biggest challenge for brands will be to help this group trade down with respect and sensitivity, giving them some of the luxury trappings of past years at a price they can afford in their golden years (as they have elected to call this new phase in their lives). They are incorrigible. The specific energy and concerns of the Boomers require a particular sensitivity and awareness on the part of brands. This generation will not bend to the strains of age or a reduced economical situation. Instead, they will revitalize and reshape what it means to be "mature." To the marketers of the twenty-first century, they have one thing to say: "You ain't seen nuthin' yet."

FOREVER YOUNG

Before we go any further, one thing must be made clear: Boomers are not getting older; they are reaching a youthful maturity. At this peak in their lives (one of many—whatever age a Boomer is is always the best age), they can look forward to indulging in the three big benefits of maturity: wisdom, health, and status. In their fifties and sixties, Boomers are anxiously indulging in treats with connotations of youth and adventure that reaffirm their youthfulness and energy. If fifty-year-old Boomers are exceptionally convinced of their youth, they may be right. As a group, they are healthier and more active than any previous generation of fifty-year-olds. Competitive careers, demanding families, and a slew of medical advances have kept this group remarkably fit. Furthermore, it is their youthful state of mind that enables some of the Boomers' highest achievements. By denying their age, they are more apt to undertake ambitious projects such as starting a new company or vacationing in rugged terrain (think Billy Crystal's character in *City Slickers*). Hence, their Peter Pan, "never grow up" mentality constitutes an empowering attitude. Brands must keep this in mind and, with the goal of further empowering this generation, devote themselves to providing personalized products and care which supplement this generation's youthful maturity.

Boomers bring tremendous influence and merit marketers' careful attention like no generation that preceded them.

A glance through any Boomer-oriented magazine, whether it be *Martha Stewart Living, Smithsonian, Newsweek,* or *Forbes,* will quickly illustrate the broad array of advertisers appealing to Boomers. One ad from the MasterCard "Priceless" campaign features the text, "Dinner for eight, Chez Marella, $475. One Happy Birthday card, $1.95. One leopard-print, peekaboo nightie, $45. Still being able to make her blush, priceless." The "still being able to make her blush" punch line implies that over the years, the couple has retained their vital qualities, including sexuality. Other appeals to the Boomers' desire to preserve youth include Charter Club's "Live the way you feel," or Tropicana's ad for grapefruit

juice, which depicts a woman in her early forties drinking juice atop a Harley, while her sexy older gentleman companion straddles another Harley in the background.

At the other end of the spectrum, the *Atlantic* magazine, a Boomer favorite, keeps them relentlessly aware of the reality that the world in the second decade of the twenty-first century will not resemble the one they have known—one that promised decent retirement and well-earned pensions. The global economic situation is so bad that in an edition of *Departures*, the American Express magazine for platinum card holders (an A-to-Z guide of people, places, and ideas to know), warns: "Now it's about simplifying, getting back to fundamentals, rebuilding." You bet! "It's fitting that this year [2009] marks the bicentennial of Lincoln and Darwin's birthdays. This certainly is a Darwinian survival of the fittest moment, and it's ripe for some Lincolnesque inspiration." Can't agree more.

In the rush to meet the demands of aging Boomers, intelligent product and marketing design is key to attracting them without making them feel poor,

You think ruby red is a dainty color? Feel these bones, pal.

Here's a delicious new way to kick-start your day. New Tropicana Pure Premium Ruby Red Grapefruit Juice with Calcium has been revved up with FruitCal®, a better type of calcium proven to help keep your bones healthy and strong. In fact, one glass has more calcium than a glass of milk.

Perfect.

old, or infirm. Products that present themselves as panic purchases, catering to Boomers fleeing their fates, will flop. However, products with universal ergonomic principles will be met with success. Lifestyle innovations such as pens equipped with soft rubber encasing, door levers instead of doorknobs, and large, easily read dashboard displays are accommodating and pleasing to all consumers. Rather than marketing these innovations as aids for the elderly, they are presented as intelligent innovations for all. This is essential. For example, savvy hotel chains have begun refurbishing select rooms with features such as larger buttons on remote controls, bedside control panels for lighting and drapes, and carefully disguised bathroom railings. These rooms are marketed as the luxurious counterpart to traditional rooms, rather than "over the hill-friendly."

In addition to appealing to their playful, adventurous Id, Emotional Branding is about comfort, reassurance, and solutions for this group. Many of yesterday's brands attempted to scare consumers into buying their products. Today's brands romance the consumer and demonstrate understanding. The fashion industry's evolving affair with the Boomers provides another illustration. Women in their forties, fifties, and beyond have been making appearances throughout ads and runway shows recently. Dove cosmetics's campaign for "real beauty," for example, tapped into the talents of beautiful and mature women to showcase their products and deliver a subtle message to older audiences, saying, "These are for you." The Dove campaign showing a woman in her seventies with the headline, "Wrinkled? Wonderful?" is a wonderful approach, especially when depleted savings might not provide for pricey surgical beauty enhancements that Boomers may be tempted to indulge in.

At the same time, fashion designers are recognizing that Boomers' bodies are, of course, not shaped quite the same as a twenty-eight-year-old's. Recognizing this, Victoria's Secret, a company known for revealing lingerie, has accommodated its designs accordingly, but without sacrificing thir youthful image or fashion sensibility. Comfort has also become a priority for many Boomers. Brands that want to prosper in the coming decades must continue to appeal to these and the new tastes that Boomers will develop. Brands need to think about how their customers perceive their age and what products will enable the best of those feelings, as the cosmetic industry has done.

Emotional Branding is more than ever about comfort, reassurance, and solutions for this group.

The cosmetic industry will benefit from this landfall if they provide the "goods" at an old-fashioned price. Since the introduction of alpha-hydroxy acids that use natural ingredients to strip off layers of dead skin and provide a younger appearance, anti-aging cosmetics have taken off. Renova, introduced in 1997, is approved by the FDA to market itself as a wrinkle reducer. Any product that purveys a more youthful appearance is of strong interest, especially those that are relatively affordable. In marketing these products, those campaigns that emphasize physical and psychological benefits are more successful than those that focus on the problem being solved. For example, many men are concerned about aging because they realize they are competing in business with men increasingly younger than themselves. For these men, looking better may be part of feeling more confident in the workplace. If a brand can empower them in this way, then a brand should.

As the focus for less takes hold, we will see a corresponding shift from a desire to be forever young to acquiring well-balanced longevity. Boomers understand the connection between eating healthy food and paying attention to good nutrition and looking and feeling healthier. From an era of vanity that had no limits in terms of how many miracles you could get from expensive plastic surgery,

Women say it bothers them to see young, wrinkle-free women in ads for anti-aging products.

the Boomers are now following the advice of Dr. Paul D. Thomson, who in a recent *New York Times* article emphasizes the importance of less visible health programs such as training for heart and against muscle atrophy.[5] Older people lose muscle strength, so focusing on preventing atrophy is important for every activity from walking to opening a jar. The health industry is thus an area that has the potential to thrive in this economy, especially if it recognizes Boomer needs.

This generation will use its influence to the fullest to save themselves and the mess they have created. Unlike in the movie *Wall-E*, in which Earth's inhabitants leave robots to clean the Earth they have polluted, the Boomers will become the most vocal advocates of environmental issues, influencing their Gen-Y children and grandchildren. Daniel Goleman, author of *Emotional Intelligence*, also published *Ecological Intelligence*, a book that vocalizes exactly the radical thoughts of the Boomer generation. In an interview in *O, The Oprah Magazine*, Goleman says, "The real leaders are not the Al Gores, they're the moms."[6]

Let's face it. Boomers will try to keep their influence wherever they can, and they want brands to understand that they will continue to influence future generations and should not be ignored. On the whole, they have worked pretty damn hard at their jobs. Whether in the workplace or the social agenda, Boomers are known for having battled for what they have. Throughout their lives they have faced a highly competitive workplace as a result of their peers and, for twenty years now, a constant influx of younger workers. For all their anti-authoritarian noise in the '60s, this generation has developed a strong regard for status and achievement. Boomers are becoming increasingly adept at maximizing the quality of their limited and elusive free time by focusing on big ideas they believe in. Businesses of all kinds will provide this group with a new sense of worth and a life in which simplified choices do not mean downscaling will thrive.

The biggest draw for this group will be businesses they perceive as "genuine." They will come back to what's real and true, basic and simple. In this economy, it is invaluable knowledge in the hands of savvy marketers. It is not enough to say, "I sell computers." *Brands must develop much more sensitivity to the symbolic values surrounding their products and image that are open to constant repositioning or embellishment.* A computer brand possessing the aforementioned data will identify the potential for computers to simplify life and free up leisure time. It will clearly and carefully illustrate its product's capacity to process tax returns quickly and easily, thereby freeing up users' time to go picnicking at a bright and cheery arboretum. *Such approaches enable brands to highlight both the real, tangible, and psychologically oriented solutions they bring to life. In order to succeed, brands must carefully craft these psychic identities* as well as the more concrete qualities quantified in *Consumer Reports.* Besides, I don't really care about how much RAM my computer has as long as it gets the job done.

But what about the big change: retirement? This generation will bring their finesse to bear on this, as well. Even as they begin to downsize, Boomers will maintain remarkably active lifestyles. According to the U.S. Census Bureau, the number of Americans over sixty will jump to fifty million by 2015 and sixty-five million by 2030. Don't expect this tidal wave of elderly Boomers to crash on Florida's shores, though. According to a recent Gallup survey, 60 percent of respondents over fifty dream of retiring to a small town somewhere.[7] Projections indicate a disproportionate percentage of this group migrating to the Rocky Mountain States and southeastern states such as North Carolina. Generic retirement communities that have flourished in Florida are being forgone for small communities, pleasant main streets, and polite neighbors. Many Boomers will also supplement this lifestyle by reentering the workforce, whether out of boredom or a need for money.

Stew Leonard, the owner of the eponymous, iconic supermarket store, told the *News-Times* of Danbury, Connecticut, that with the recent economic recession, shoppers are still coming out but buying less and in smaller, packaged portions. With people eating out less frequently, he foresees that cooking at home will become the new trend and a necessity for many. He also notices "an uptick in the sale of fruit trees and vegetable plants."[8] This is a sure sign of growing self-reliance and maybe even the beginning of a new trend toward more consumers growing their own food in small plots of rented land, which now occurs in Europe.

It is time for marketers to show that they care at a time when consumers are challenged, so it is important to pay attention to this growing cooking-at-home trend. Cookbooks and online recipes, for example, will become very relevant and popular. Do-it-yourself advice on how to garden could be another interest-ing focus. The visual of the grandfather on his Harley will be replaced by a responsible grandfather in the garden. Retailers with a green passion will be flooded with new products packaged to sell to this marketing-savvy group and their new passion in life.

Understanding both these sides of Boomers—the desire to escape and downshift while remaining active and sustaining a healthy lifestyle—is vital for twenty-first century businesses. Products and promotions must sensibly cater to both halves of this mentality. Condescending branding strategies that connote easing them into inevitable elder oblivion will fail. The key is active and meaningful aging: the benefits of old age with none of the drawbacks. Free self-help programs organized by brands for this group in their neighborhood will appeal to the Boomers' sense of community and can promote brands in a most fun and memorable way.

Understanding how they see the Web is also important. As a generation, Boomers first saw the Web as a competitive tool for professionals in the business world who adapted to its global operations and used it to their competitive objectives. "Geeks for corporate success" was the mantra. This was not an emotional bastion of warm feelings.

AOL changed all this by bringing the power of a more personal communication model to the masses. Computers were aplenty; the public was plunging. It all came to bear symbolically with 1998's *You've Got Mail*, a Boomer movie star-ring Meg Ryan (b. 1961) and Tom Hanks (b. 1956) that scripted the values of the generation. First, their love of new inventions but hesitance to discard the past. For example, Ryan's character's writer boyfriend doesn't want to separate himself from his old typewriter. The movie's depiction of the technological revolution was moderately softened with a background of classic music from the '60s and '70s so as to maintain a certain level of comfort for our favorite couch potatoes. The movie also portrayed the Boomers' most important value, the preservation of anonymous connections: Hanks (NY960) and Ryan (Shopgirl) communicate through AOL screen names.

You've Got Mail was not only a Boomer romance but a technology "cyber-smorgasborg" of a movie that is emblematic of the way Baby Boomers first related to technology: they would control technology and not let technology control them. We all know now where AOL is in the pecking order of "cool" technology brands, and that IBM quickly downloaded its ThinkPad division to a Chinese group, Lenovo, out of fear that they might have to "Apple-ize" the brand. Still, for Boomers, the Web needs to let them keep to a certain level of privacy and the "club exclusivity" that they are used to.

With all this ambition and motivation, is there anything outside of death that will remain impervious to the Boomer influence? Actually, there isn't—and that includes death. As one funeral consultant reported in a *USA Today* article, "Baby Boomers are living like no other generation in the world, and they are going to die like no other generation."[9] The costly and conservative funeral based on stuffy tradition is giving way to a more intimate one marked by poetry, contemporary music, and post-funeral parties, among other innovations. Some individuals are opting to be buried with their pets, reports the *USA Today* article. Mobile lifestyles and environmental concerns will make cremations more popular, while those still attached to burial can be presented to the afterlife in personalized "art caskets." WhiteLight, a Dallas company, sells such coffins as "Fairway to Heaven," created for the golf nut. Another one of their coffins appears to be made of brown parcel paper and is stamped with red lettering, which reads, "Return to Sender." Boomer vitality and humanity is even applied to the final checkout.

Gen X to Gen eXcel: No Slacking Here

Let's clear up any remaining misconceptions about the so-called Generation X, born 1964 to 1980, starting with that annoyingly persistent misnomer "Gen X" and all that it conjures up. Sure, this generation got off to a rough start. Reared under the shadow of skyrocketing divorce rates, downsized parents, a sputtering American economy, the AIDS epidemic, and horrifying new social problems such as the invention of crack cocaine, they were the first latchkey kids, and they knew life wasn't perfect long before they saw the Challenger plummet to Earth in a ball of flames.

Generation X as a group is earnest and smart, and they make the most imaginative and visionary executives, but they still have an ambiguity about belonging to the mainstream. Jeff Gordinier explains it best in his book *X Saves the World: How Generation X Got the Shaft but Can Still Keep Everything from Sucking* when he writes, "That duality, that 'stuckness' between a desire for change and profound doubts about how to achieve it, would come to define the philosophy of X. If the Boomers had shot their way forward by trying to forge a utopia, Kurt Cobain was saving the world by steering his generation away from that delusion." If you understand their drive to change their world, you will understand the Xers. They are the generation that will truly have the most impact in this century.

Their sobering generation provided a fertile atmosphere for fostering their take-control, independent-minded, pragmatic mentality that, aided by a booming economy, has effectively shed all resemblance to 1991's dispirited and dejected "slacker." Douglas Coupland, who coined the infamous term with his novel *Generation X*, now says of the phrase, "It's almost retro now–it feels as far away as grunge."[10] Brands that continue to target the mythical thirtysomething slacker are on the wrong track. However, brands that tap into the energy and spirit of today's "eXcel" generation will be able to forge a long-lasting partnership with this generation, which is ready for some respect.

The eXcel generation clocks in at forty-four million members. At a mere 17 percent of the U.S. population, its numbers can't rival the mammoth Baby Boomer or Generation Y generations, each of which comprises about 30 percent of the population. However, they are a significant demographic as "influences." Conservative and sensible in all matters pecuniary, 71 percent regularly save a portion of their income and 54 percent have started a financial plan.[11] While their Boomer brethren frivolously cavort in their second, third, or fourth youth, Gen eXcel exercises maturity and prudence.

A NEW GENERATION CHASES ANOTHER

Jeremiah Owyang is a partner in customer strategy at Altimer Group. As a blogger who "discuss[es] how Web tools enable companies to connect with consumers," he has quite a large following. In addition to his blog (*Web-strategist.*

com/blog), you can find him on Facebook, Twitter, Technocrati, and Flickr, where he has thousands of personal and professional photos to share with you. At the writing of this book, he is ranked #500 on Technocrati—beating out over 100 million blogs. Google Analytics gives him 72,596 unique visitors, and his is considered a number-one industry analyst blog and is ranked #37 as a media and marketing blog. He has over 33,000 followers on Twitter.

Now it is clear that Jeremiah's life is all about business, and his exposure to potential clients is his main asset. The amount of news and comments that he writes daily makes a Boomer like me wonder how he can do anything else, including his billable work. But Jeremiah is emblematic of a new generation, Generation "eXcel," that has mastered the art of multitasking. His profile and his opinions on social spaces intrigued me a lot. Because he lives and breathes that space as a consultant gives him insight and ability to see the pitfalls that social branding can create. His personal profile is also a typical portrait of eXcel executives: open, real, and authentic. An interesting observation: Jeremiah was probably more visible and popular in the underground of the blogosphere than his company's president while he as at Forrester Research.

"PUNK'D"

"Punk'd" is the word by which Jeremiah's blog describes companies "that were blind-sided by the Internet, [that] didn't understand the impacts of the power shift to the participants, or how fast information would spread, or were just plain ignorant"—a good point for brands that just think of this medium as an another top-down communication strategy. In this section, you can find a list of wrongdoers, brands such as Exxon Mobil, CNN, Motrin, JCPenney, Louis Vuitton, Burger King, and Johnson & Johnson. On Jeremiah's blog, it seems nobody is protected. Hey, brands have gotten quite a nice run in faking the truth about their products, so it is hard for most to have to face the music (and a new reality in social media). But the best part about Jeremiah's personality is another trait of this generation: honesty and transparency in communicating via social media and the importance of building trust through truth. For example, after the departure of the chief marketing officer of Mzinga, a technology solution for social media, Jeremiah suggested that this executive's move may be covering bigger problems within the company. Realizing that his information was erroneous, he rapidly apologized for jumping to conclusions too fast, posting "A Public Apology to Mzinga" for all to read on his blog. His followers congratulated him on the courage he had to reverse position and accept his errors.

But most emblematic of Generation eXcel is how willing Jeremiah is to share his personal life with others online. On his blog, you can actually find Jeremiah's personal profile and statements about what he feels his strengths and weaknesses are—total transparency. Looking at Jeremiah's portrait, you can't help but think about this new "customer." How do they value brands? What do they expect to find in the brands they will buy? Most importantly, what will be said about those brands, and what will others comment on?

This generation views family life with prudence and caution. Like the pre-Boomer generations, they are averse to divorce but are not ready either to be part of the 50 percent rate of divorce the country experiences right now. However, the eXcels have tailored their own solution—wait until your career direction is set and your youth enjoyed. The median age for marriage is twenty-five among women and 26.8 among men. Furthermore, when they do get married, eXcels don't feel restrained by marriage and have expanded its meaning to be a more inclusive human proposition. Whether it is a heterosexual or same-sex marriage or just a union between people, they renovate the institutional trappings of a dwindling traditional family unit from within to make it more realistic for their lifestyle.

Brands with the flexibility to be appropriated by eclectic and individualized tastes will find in the eXcels a funky functionality that, by its mere unpredictability, is exciting. For example, while these budding family women and men aspire to own traditional style homes, they view these homes foremost as a symbol of their individuality rather than their status symbols, although more desire for status may well set in for this generation, as the eXcels' stock portfolios plump up over time. But for now, the eXcels are planning their homes with that mix of frugality and personality that is their trademark. Urban Outfitters has been particularly successful in appealing to their tastes. According to Melanie Cox, its creative director, "We sell a little bit of very inexpensive furniture and . . . [home] accessories. Our customer is somebody who has probably gotten a sofa from mom or dad, a table from grandma. None of it matches and [he or she] really wants to put his or her own mark on it by adding touches of personality and drawing it all together with some interesting things."[12] This generation has a sharp and discriminating taste that freely adapts and subverts existing fashions and brands while meeting hip fashions and individualizing. In other words, your basic postmodern portrait.

The eXcels have been a handful for stodgy human resource departments the nation over. These thirtysomethings have been quickly absorbed into the tight job market, and that's exactly where they've worked some of their most significant and exciting changes. They saw job security and corporate loyalty fly out the window during the layoffs of the early '90s, and as a consequence, they are the workers most likely to leave the company they are with if they receive a better job offer. They are unwilling to sacrifice their personal lives on the corporate altar. They expect a healthy balance between personal and private life, and thanks to the high demand for workers and what amounts to a veritable generational coup, they've successfully rewritten corporate rules to their favor. They favor work that offers variety and enhances their own skill set while allowing them to learn. Further complicating the situation for managers and human resources, they are entrepreneurial and want to direct themselves, if not work for themselves. They account for 70 percent of new start-up businesses. Supplementing the eXcels' independence and drive is also a yen for teamwork. Unlike the more competition-oriented Boomers, among whom solitary work was prevalent at this age, the eXcels are accustomed to collaboration and enjoy being part of a team. Being told what to do damages their morale, but being allowed to find their own solution and make their own mistakes is very rewarding for them. To top this all off, the eXcels seem to make pretty good bosses, and those that become bosses are likely to do so because they want to be a better boss to their subordinates than they themselves had. They are also equally accustomed to working for male and female bosses and show diminished concern for gender issues in the workplace, as in other realms. Wow! In another ten years, Gen Y may be thanking these folks for fixing the place up.

Businesses that understand the need of eXcels to be valued and appreciated will find eXcels to be a hotbed for creativity and flexibility, the two most valuable assets in the market today.

Brands definitely can't and shouldn't try to deceive these folk. Instead, businesses must provide accurate depictions in their media and appeal to the eXcels' individuality and their aspirations. Humor, particularly sarcasm, is a favorite of theirs. Anything irreverent has a good shot at stirring their sympathies and maybe, just maybe, their loyalties. Zippo's campaign to familiarize twenty-something consumers with their lighters also taps into the hip irreverence to which eXcels are highly responsive. Recasting the Zippo as an "ignition device" rather than a "cigarette lighter," the campaign's slogan is, "Use it to start something." The TV ads are right up the alley of the young eXcels and elder Gen Yers. In each ad, a character named "Zippo guy" encounters strange and challenging circumstances with his Zippo. In one ad, he tells the viewers, "According to recent studies, the ozone layer is rapidly depleting. The main cause for the phenomenon is the release of bovine gases. Igniting these gases early on will keep them from rising into the ozone. I will save the planet for the ages." Zippo guy is subsequently caught by two farmhands trying to light a cow's fart on fire. Crass? Tasteless? Brilliant? Yes, yes, and yes. Sure, Zippo could have explained the long history of their product and the refinement and personality embodied by its brands, and sure, that might have hit home with a Boomer, particularly with a few shots of James Dean with a Zippo. However, if you're going to try commanding one moment of an eXcel's valuable time, you'd better make it worthwhile. An amusing story with a great punch line and a good laugh is one way to do it. Offbeat, slightly off-color humor is often advised. For stumped and confused account executives, I suggest they sit down with my daughter and her friends and watch an episode of *South Park*. This show, hugely popular with Gen Xers, features irreverent cartoon characters who swear, fart on one another, and reference every bodily function known to *Homo sapiens*. By the end of the program, they will understand.

However, different brands will want to approach Gen eXcel in different ways, and traditional media should not be written off. As with all campaigns, Gen eXcel campaigns need to consider what each medium means to the consumer and how that medium and the content of its campaign adds to or detracts from the brand. A study conducted by BBDO New York of 104 adults revealed the media perceptions of this generation.[13] They described the Internet as a means of escape and mental stimulation as well as a way of gathering specialized information. They added that the medium gave them feelings of intelligence, accomplishment, and innovation. Users of the Internet were described as young and career-oriented. As an interesting comparison, magazine readers were described as—attractive! Feelings of luxury, creativity, and sexiness were associated with reading

eXcels have abandoned the typical hierarchical mentality in favor of equality—in other words, they expect others, even their bosses, to treat them as equals.

magazines, and magazines were seen as a source of current information and, for some, a personal reward. TV was described as a means of entertainment or relaxation at the end of the day and was largely associated with homemakers and families. Watching TV was said to impart feelings of happiness, comfort, and fun. Newspapers were seen as a means of gathering in-depth information first thing in the morning, and readers were perceived as middle-aged and, more often than not, male. Feelings imparted by reading the paper included security, stability, and respect. Radio was described as a background medium listened to in the morning or while doing other activities. It gave feelings of relaxation and youthfulness to listeners, and listeners were perceived as young and hip. Based on these findings, one would assume that newspapers would be an excellent medium for advertising "serious" products, like financial services, whereas TV would be seen as the place for products associated with fun; however, such findings only provide hints and background information on how advertising can and will function in these mediums. Many of the most successful campaigns will take into account these traditional expectations and uses regarding specific media and then subvert these expectations to grab the attention of bored eXcelers. Although seducing the eXcels is difficult, even for experienced and creative professionals, it can be done with a thorough knowledge of their life and lifestyles.

Campaigns that target the eXcels should strongly consider nontraditional approaches.

Recipe for a Gen-X Cocktail *by Peter Levine (a little shaken in 2009)*

Generation X grew up with television and pop culture references in their DNA. They were born between 1964 and 1980 and are now twenty-nine to forty-five years old. This fascinating generation makes up 17 percent of the population and is sandwiched between monster-size generations, the Baby Boomers and Generation Y.

THE GEN X RECIPE

1 PART SCOOBY-DOO. *Scooby Doo* was the first Saturday morning cartoon that was the "anti-Archie." It was not about a group of squeaky-clean, middle-class, white high school students. Instead, *Scooby Doo*'s title character was a mangy, talking dog, who was part of a gang of misfits that banded together to have adventures, get in trouble, and survive. This message was perfect for Gen X, and Gen X broke the rules because—in their minds—the rules got you nowhere. As a result, Gen X has been the generation of original entrepreneurs. Alternative music, independent film, cable television, and even the Internet owe a debt to this generation's new way of thinking.

1 PART JAN BRADY. Stuck between the beautiful, popular Marsha and the lisping, adorable Cindy, *The Brady Bunch*'s Jan was the misunderstood middle child who embodied the awkward heart and soul of Gen X. Jan was a symbol of the notion, "I may not be so awesome right now, but just you wait to see what I make of myself—I'll have the last laugh!" And make it this generation did. Generation X was the first age group in the U.S. to have four out of five members enroll in and complete college.

1 PART TEENAGE MUTANT NINJA TURTLES. These characters were flushed down the toilet and had to survive in the sewer on chemical waste—the perfect representation of the boom and bust times in which Gen X grew up. The Mutant Turtles developed tough skins for survival; Gen X was weaned on disappointment and saw collapse everywhere. From watching the first civilian, a schoolteacher, attempt to go into outer space and instead "blow up," to the scare of razor blades in Halloween candy, this generation got the underlying message, "you're screwed, and you'd better get used to it."

1 PART LUKE SKYWALKER AND PRINCESS LEIA. Even light years away, Gen Xers could identify with the overwhelmingly outnumbered youngsters of *Star Wars* who fought to save the Empire from evil with only their wits. Today, this generation is again marginalized. Attention is concentrated on Gen Y, the emerging youth and young adult population, and the Boomers, who face retirement. As a result, Gen Xers have gotten lost in the middle and gone underground as they begin married life and start families. But as Gen X changes careers a second or third time, their natural agility never aims to fix a game but rather to reconceive the game their way.

1 PART SUPERMODEL. Gen X grew up in the era of first-name model icons: Linda, Naomi, Christy, and Cindy. Looking amazing from head to toe was a new form of competition for this generation. Gen X became the generation to evolve the Boomer notion of "I want to be successful" to "I want to be rich and famous." They put the "I" into the equation, as in "self-branding." They initiated the concept of being *who* you are, not just the skills, finances, degrees, family, or social status you *have*, as the determining factor in your star power.

1 PART MADONNA. Simply put, she was not The Beatles, the idols of Boomers who took the nation by storm with a sound, look, and aura of an exciting import. Homegrown in the American Midwest, Madonna brought shrewd, ambitious savvy to the table. She set her own terms and broke any barrier she could just because she knew she deserved the adulation. Her music, artistry, and performance style were all a platform for herself. Gen X was built on small successes and course corrections that aggregate into an interesting life—not a calculated plan or strategy that has a determined end point.

In a lot of ways, Generation X embodies the true resilience of the American spirit. The Boomers can still experience devastating disappointment when things don't go according to plan. And Gen Y has proven to be the most coddled generation yet. But Gen X alone is the scrappiest of the three generations that comprise the consumer groups that marketers covet. Gen X has the ability to emotionally wake up and say, "Who do I want to be today?" They don't dwell on what may have gone wrong in the past. With a patient acceptance that that's just how things are, Gen X keeps moving. The best chapter still lies ahead.

Generation Y: Coming Right at You (at Warp Speed)

The seventy-six million members of Generation Y, born 1981 to 1999, compose a tidal wave poised to redefine America in general and branding in particular. The sweeping social changes that spawned a new world before the eyes of Generation X and the Boomers–the fall of Communism, technology's ubiquitous presence, a spiraling Dow Jones–have been the positive backdrop for their entire lives. They are the inventors of social media and, with the warm embrace their Gen X bosses will give them, this generation will accelerate a generational gap, albeit in a civilized way. This generation will break down the monopolies of businesses, media, and politics that their parents built by building new businesses that match their own generational expectations.

Although still evolving, this generation's emotional palette and passions are entirely unique and comprise a fascinating challenge for Emotional Branding. If the Boomers have fought to open the gates of discrimination and sexism, and Gen X watched in awe of the opportunities offered by those open gates, Gen Y is rushing out of the gates in amazing numbers. For a start, according to a survey by the National Campaign to Prevent Teen and Unplanned Pregnancy and *CosmoGirl.com*, 22 percent of this generation claims they have posted nude photos or videos of themselves online.[14] Gen Y women will also bring about the most defining women's culture the world has ever known and will knock down every taboo that could have existed around the battle of the sexes. Even in traditionally male-dominated arenas, Gen Y women are stepping up: Danica Sue Patrick, an American auto racing driver, won the Indy Japan 300 in 2008, becoming the first woman to win an Indy car race. This win made her an instant celebrity, and she has since published an autobiography, designed clothes for charity, and cavorted on the pages of *FMN* and the 2008 *Sports Illustrated* swimsuit edition.

New social media will be the battleground for this new generation of women. Gen Y women will take advantage of the new social spaces, which optimize their talent in sharing and connecting by allowing them private emotional spaces to share their private lives with others or the brands they trust. While some brands agonize over how to build a relationship with this generation of women online, others just have a knack for attracting young people generation after generation.

The *Playboy* presence on Facebook is a good place to see for this kind of insight. It has over one million "friends," and, surprisingly, those friends are not the expected old-timers on the prowl. No—the friends are mostly young men and women. In fact, one of my professional acquaintances, a Gen Y executive, is a friend of *Playboy* on Facebook. She explains her motivations for being a fan: "The magazine is a classic. . . . It's an old cliché. . . . but something that has lasted for as long as *Playboy* has impressed me. Longevity is what all businesses . . . are hoping for." You'll recognize in Jacquelyn the perfect Gen Y emotional profile. She does not want to change the world by taking down the previous generation's idols as the Gen Xers do, but rather relishes what some of the parent generation has done and feels comfortable with the belief that it is her—and her generation's—time to use that experience to foster her own identity. One thing is clear: don't judge Gen Y against yesterday's standards, or you will lose their support.

It will be worth looking at the Y generation as they approach an age to be a part of the workforce. A great example of the emerging prominence of this generation is Agustina Vivero, an Internet and television celebrity from Buenos Aires who was propelled to fame by a Web site that promotes Cumbia music, "a form of fusion of Latin Pop, salsa, and dance that is popular among Argentina's lower class."[15] There are many in this generation who, like Vivero, have used social media to propel themselves into stardom. And this generation craves fame—let's not forget this is the group that keeps Paris Hilton and Britney Spears relevant.

"The warp-speed generation" would be a fair title for this group. They are going faster and doing more than any previous generation. A study conducted at the University of Michigan found that 75 percent of kids' time is preprogrammed today. Soccer leagues, homework, and family responsibilities have eaten away at this group's free time—today's average twelve-year-old has less than three hours of free time a week, ten less than their 1981 counterparts had. What little free time they have is heavily multitasked like the PC software they are so adept at using. It's not uncommon for them to be connected to the Web while talking on the phone, eyeing the television, and listening to their iPod at the same time.

The activities that absorb them fully are done through demanding and concisely packed content. After all, this generation has been reared in the era of the sound and word bite. In trying to reach this generation, advertising needs to be brief and sans fluff. One popular ad campaign by Arizona Jeans, which was directed at this generation, featured teens mocking flashy ad campaigns and demanding, "Just show me the jeans."

Targeting this age group is complicated because they have a tendency to reject the "mainstream," and as soon as a brand becomes big it is in danger of falling into their disfavor. Success = sellout = bad. Hence, brands must walk a fine line between prominent exposure and overexposure.

Brands should never talk down to these consumers as "kids." These are the most adult teenagers since the birth of the "teenager" concept; by the time they reach twelve, they will have achieved a notable sophistication and awareness of the world. These latchkey kids have grown up with an unparalleled access to information coupled with an absence of omnipresent supervision. Consequently, they have developed responsibility and awareness early in life. Having witnessed the horror of school shootings, the placement of metal detectors at school, and the president of the United States lying about the reasons for war, they are aware of the hypocrisy and danger that prevail in public (and private) life. Similarly, the high expectations put on them by family, school, and friends have developed precocious maturity in a large body of this generation. It follows that branding strategies that underestimate the sophistication of this generation will fail. However, brands that respect the mature identity of these youngsters and supplement that identity are among the most successful. Surveys among teens have uniformly identified intelligence as an important value in their lives, and brands aimed at them should recognize and showcase their acuity.

"The warp-speed generation" would be a fair title for this group.

Gen Y demonstrates an unprecedented sensitivity to global issues, such as poverty, war, and environmentalism, as well as race, gender, or sexual orientation discrimination issues. The sense of empowerment and knowledge that marks this generation's outlook on life has also reshaped social activism, revealing not only their intelligence, but also their altruism. But unlike their Boomer parents, who challenged the status quo and took to the streets for change, this generation is more apt to volunteer. All their lives, this generation has been praised and told it could do whatever it wanted, and with that encouragement they have chosen to apply themselves to improving a screwed-up world. They hold civic responsibility in high regard, and where their Boomer parents fought to topple society, today's youth would rather improve it.

The television program *Sesame Street*, with its philosophy of appreciating differences in others, has had a big influence on this group. "You can't hate anyone if you know them," Gary Knell, the president and CEO of Sesame Workshop, told me. *Sesame Street* airs all over the world, encouraging kids to understand each other's gender, race, and religious differences. In South Africa, a five-year-old, HIV-positive Muppet named Kami helps kids understand the importance of not ostracizing those children with HIV that represent one in nine kids in the population. In Egypt, *Sesame Street* helps empower little girls to dream about being a doctor or a lawyer. This is incredibly visionary in a nation where only 10 percent of women embrace a professional career. In the U.S., with the prevalent issue of childhood obesity, *Sesame Street*, believing in prevention before intervention, advocates a balanced diet with none other than the iconic character Cookie Monster as spokesperson for this cause—a very smart choice. In Indonesia, one of the most populous Muslim countries in the world, *Sesame Street* shows children preparing for prayers and encourages girls to believe in their potential. *Sesame Street*'s model is smart and successful because it adapts its characters to local cultures and uses popular culture, including film and television celebrities and musicians, to help children learn important lessons and engage adults who watch with them.

Value-driven behavior among Gen Y is also linked to an increase in traditional values. Like their elder Gen Xers, Gen Yers have seen enough of divorce and strongly intend to avoid it in their lives. However, while they may not wish to emulate their parents' marriages, they still hold their parents in high regard. A survey by Yankelovich Partners in 1999 found that 94 percent of teenage girls consider their mothers to be friends. 80 percent claimed that their mothers understood them. Mothers and daughters alike characterized one another as intelligent, honest, and attractive.

Brands should never talk down to these consumers as "kids."

This fits into the overarching trend among these youth that exhibits integrity and respect for authority, as well as disdain for arrogance (seems like a diet of Bart Simpson and rap music may not be as subversive as was expected). Hence, when approaching this generation, brands should recognize that trashing their parents and other elder influences is a big mistake. There is also an interesting dichotomy between this generation's individuality and its conformity. Although, like most youth, they have a profound need to fit in with their peers and are keen on being part of the latest, most hip trends, they also consider themselves autonomous individuals and express a desire to customize fashions to meet their personal needs, regardless of the trend. This desire is matched by an increasingly fragmented market, ranging from the media to consumer goods, which caters to individualized tastes. And with the Internet at their disposal, they can freely and independently of their parents develop their own tastes. Whether it's Pokémon fan clubs or a passion for snowboarding, there is a broad cultural offering at their disposal. Increasingly, with the advent of mass-customization technology, they will be able to create their own product lines and further develop this yen for individual expression.

Bubble Yum has attempted to ally their brand to teens' individuality sensibility via the "Blow your own bubble" campaign, which stars a duck who sports a Mohawk, spiked collar, nose ring, and anklet. The nonconformist cartoon character blows bubbles that literally blow away all the other average, normal-looking ducks. Bubble Yum, whose Gen Y sales had been slipping, has found that twelve-to-seventeen-year-old males seem to identify with the foul fowl. The campaign has also reached into cyberspace, where screen savers featuring the duck are available for download.

This generation, more thoroughly versed in and accustomed to computer technology than any other, exhibits ease with the Internet, and it would seem that they would also be natural techno-shoppers. But for Gen Y, it is a means of staying connected that provides a feeling of empowerment–it is this feeling of empowerment that has proved one of the greatest draws. In particular, Generation Y enjoys using the Internet as a social space. Gen Y businesses have had marked success with Internet sites, but traditional brick-and-mortar retailers should not panic yet–this generation is nothing if not experience-driven. In what other ways can brands catch the attention of these youngsters who, perhaps more than any other generation, have "seen it all"? By approaching them directly and putting it in their face, on their back, in their hands or the hands of someone they admire, brands can intimately connect to this generation. Guerrilla marketing efforts are enormously successful with Gen Y. The advantage of this style of marketing is the ability to directly target clients and communicate with them in their own language without confusing adults. By selectively and personally targeting consumers, particularly the most influential and trendy members of this generation, this approach has an edge and appeal unmatched by other forms of marketing.

This is the main reason why promotional events are gaining popularity in marketing, but I believe they are still a relatively unexplored territory in terms of the powerful contribution they can make to a social branding strategy. Events are a great way to showcase brands in a festive, emotionally charged atmosphere—particularly to experience Gen Yers. Krystal, a sandwich chain with about 365 stores, has done some wonderfully appropriate work in this category. Its events are simple—college burger-eating competitions. Students who can scarf the most burgers in sixty seconds win prizes while their peers cheer them on. These events supplement traditional TV and radio campaigns and have the particular advantage of directly reaching their core audience. During the competitions, Krystal employees distribute coupons and other promotional items. Marketing that provides this all-encompassing brand experience may be the most novel, best way to reach these young consumers.

The biggest challenge with Gen Y will be to keep abreast of their fast-moving lifestyle and quickly evolving taste. Some publications describe this group as "prosumers"

The biggest challenge with Generation Y will be to keep abreast of their fast-moving lifestyle and quickly evolving taste.

because of their power and willingness to dictate what they will and won't buy. As the Internet brings more and more offerings to their doorstep from around the world and spreads trends at an unprecedented speed, businesses that once planned fashion aesthetics and purchasing plans six months in advance must learn to accommodate fashion evolution within a month. As demanding, optimistic, informed, and individualistic as this generation is, I must admit that all the clever branding schemas only succeed in providing a pale sketch of their character and vague hints of their future. The best advice I can give you is stand back and let them lead the way. They'll tell you what they want.

As they start to occupy the landscape left by the Boomers, Gen X and Gen Y will be the two groups that by embracing the same dreams and aspirations will bring a new form of thinking in life, culture, and business. This group called "xY" will underline the spirit of this book and its revolutionary spirit. Looking at those groups in the rigid confines of demographics will not give justice to their vast complexity and variance but will help open a major gap that will keep increasing between Boomers and the new, tech-savvy generations.

This segmentation has always helped me in my career while studying or designing the brands of the future. It gave me a framework and a funnel to go deeper into people's emotional states. I prefer to look at a deeper analysis of people's total lifestyle as individuals since it reveals so much more than just traditional data. A percentage of people using social media, for instance, is less intriguing to me than studying a few individuals. Seeing how some leaders use social media as a life transforming experience and use it as a benchmark to their lives or a platform for their philosophy can show a great deal about where this medium will take us.

This group called "xY" will underline the spirit of this book and its revolutionary spirit.

In the character of people live the seeds that make the leaders of the future and at the same time offer a glimpse of our world to come.

Welcome to social branding and the "xY" generation.

BABY BOOMERS

APPROX. 30% POP. BORN 1946–64
81 MILLION PEOPLE
SPEND OVER 900 BILLION ANNUALLY

Generation as Icon

"US"

DEFINING GENERATION

EXPERIENCED:
Rock and Roll
Television
Protests / Riots
Space Exploration
Vietnam War / Hippies / Protests
Racial Divides
Sexual Revolution
Yuppies
New Definition of 50

RESPOND TO:
Cues of Achievement / Status / Heroes
Iconic Authority
Heroes / Trailblazers
The things that are earned
Comfort
"I've earned it" luxury
Perks
Antiaging

EVOLUTION OF ATTITUDES △

ICONS-ROCK & ROLL, MOVIE, SPORT & POLITICAL, BUSINESS FIGURES
MARKETING INFLUENCED
RACE DIVIDED
REALISTIC
TECHNOLOGY FEARFUL
RELIGION
FORTUNE / PROSPERITY
ESCAPE / FANTASY
ASPIRATION
WARM NOSTALGIA
SEX
ANTIAGING / LONGEVITY / MENTAL HEALTH
MALE / FEMALE

GEN-X *or 13ers*

APPROX. 17% POP. BORN 1964–80
46 MILLION PEOPLE
SPEND 125 BILLION ANNUALLY

Generation as Individual

"I"

REBELS / INFLUENCERS

EXPERIENCED:
Disappointed Children of Divorce
Driven To Independence
AIDS Era Maturity
Crack / Gangs / Violence
Downsized Parents
Pop Culture
Information Explosion

TODAY:
Defy Traditional Structures
Entrepreneurial
Highly Educated / Money Driven
Taking Charge to Show the Power of Their Voice

RESPOND TO:
Themselves Reflected in Images / Messages
Fierce Sarcasm / Imagination, Creativity
Stupid / Smart Messages
Deconstructed Paradigms
Style
Luxury Goods and Mass-Market

EVOLUTION OF ATTITUDES △

ALTERNATIVE MUSIC / FASHION IDOLS / CELEBRITY
ANTI-MARKETING INFLUENCED
MULTIETHNIC
PESSIMISTIC
TECHNOLOGY PROFICIENT
SPIRITUALITY / CONSCIOUSNESS
FAME AND FORTUNE
EXPERIENCE / REALITY
INSPIRATION
HIP NOSTALGIA
SEXINESS
PHYSICAL HEALTH / WELL-BEING
UNISEX

GEN-Y *or millennials, echo boomers, baby busters*

APPROX. 28% POP. BORN 1981–89
75 MILLION PEOPLE
SPEND 35–100 BILLION ANNUALLY

Generation as Philosophy

"ALL"

CONSCIENCE

EXPERIENCE:
Integration
Understand Multilayered Info.
Brought up in the Era of Brands
Unity
Optimistic
Reared in the Era of Psychology
Birth of the Future
Recycling

RESPOND TO:
New Ideas
Companies with a Philosophy
"Multisensory" Experiences
Multigenerational Messages
Messages That Acknowledge They are Smart
Fun / Learning
Parents as Their Heroes
Interesting People
Sense of Community

EVOLUTION OF ATTITUDES △

BREAKTHROUGH VOICES / TALENT WITH MESSAGES
MARKETING SAVVY
GLOBAL CULTURE
OPTIMISTIC
TECHNOLOGY INDOCTRINATED
MYSTICISM
FUN / INTERACTIVITY
SOCIAL RESPONSIBILITY
FUN NOSTALGIA
SEXUALITY
HEALTHY ATTITUDE
EXTREME SPORTS
PEOPLE

The information contained in this document was gathered from research books, articles, interviews, focus groups, and Web sites. © 2000 dig¹ Consulting

2

Disconnection Alert: The U.S. Melting Pot Is Hot!

A surprising lack of awareness and some major communication gaps still exist today between U.S. corporations and the consumer market. We are on the verge of major demographic changes that are already affecting the country, and much of corporate America still seems to be, in many respects, dozing. Latino-American, Asian-American, and African-American populations are becoming highly influential groups with new sets of aspirations. Statistically, it is projected that the buying power of these three groups will triple in the next twelve years.

These groups contribute cultures and values that are very different from those of white European immigrants who have dominated the political and sociological landscape in the United States for the last two hundred years. Although we are already seeing the contrasts inherent in today's rich mosaic of population in the marketplace, most businesses don't yet have a management that reflects this diverse population. In most cases, companies are still run by a very homogeneous Caucasian male leadership. This has created serious problems for companies in terms of a complete disconnection from the market and, in some cases, the fostering of corporate environments where racism can exist, as in the deplorable case of

That is, people want to deal with corporations that are responsive and sensitive to their unique needs.

Texaco in which African-American employees were discriminated against by top management that made racist jokes behind closed doors. In today's corporate cultural landscape, this is viewed as inexcusable and highly dangerous; in the future it will be, quite simply, a company's death knell.

There is a new expectation out there, and it has everything to do with Emotional Branding. That is, people want to deal with corporations that are responsive and sensitive to their unique needs. They want a relationship with brands that understand them. Consumers of the future will discriminate between the companies that reflect their values and those that do not.

African-American Consumers

The disparity between the popular media's portrayal of African-Americans and their actual state, coupled with affluent isolation and misunderstanding within the corporate world, has unfortunately led some corporations to overlook opportunities with African-American consumers, perpetuating stereotypes instead of the kind of understanding that leads to real emotional contact with a brand.

Understanding the African-American culture means tapping into a market that will represent 15.8 percent of the population, half of which belongs to the middle class. This demographic is gradually becoming more affluent and educated, with buying power to exceed $1.1 trillion in 2012, which is indeed quite a sizable force.[16] This group's financial clout is considerable and seems to be only beginning to truly flex its muscle. From a social media perspective, 43 percent of African-Americans who use the Internet have social networking profiles, versus 31 percent of online white adults.

Despite the fact that most African-Americans have only known life in America, and parity with whites is creeping their way, they retain a sense of identity that separates them from whites and other minority groups, as well as independent and identifiable value systems. Both formal and anecdotal evidence indicates that African-Americans are proud of their culture and history. Nearly 70 percent of African-Americans feel the need to sustain ethnic traditions and symbols, as opposed to 46 percent of all other Americans. 78 percent of African-Americans believe that "parents should pass on ethnic traditions," versus 62 percent of all other groups, and 90 percent of African-Americans agree with the statement "I am proud of my ethnic heritage."[17] African-Americans spend more time at church and do less housework and more child care compared to their white counterparts with comparable education and wealth. The African-American population is also younger and more likely to have families than European-Americans. Approximately three-quarters of African-Americans reside in urban areas; however, as they grow more affluent, many more African-Americans migrate to the suburbs. Although there is a slow but sure rise to greater affluence in this population, the African-American population remains highly sensitized to the economic disparities in America. According to a *New York Times* poll of 1,003 adults spread out across America conducted in March 2000, 69 percent of African-Americans felt that the growing income gap in America is morally wrong, and still feel the same way.[18] African-American businesses have been growing at a rate exceeding those of whites, approximately 7 percent annually, as opposed to 5 percent for all other groups, and American society is witnessing the emergence of African-American enterprises in many skill-intensive areas of business and professional services. African-Americans have also been showing greater increases in college attendance and completion than Caucasians, Hispanics, and Asians.

African-Americans have consumption patterns which distinguish them from other groups, and brands should be aware of these patterns, even as they apply to industries which have no direct bearing on their own. For example, African-Americans have shown an increasing propensity in recent years to travel to places that have a history of their roots, such as the Caribbean, Africa, and South America. For that reason, an ad campaign that intended to appeal to the aspirations of African-Americans, even if it touted the advantages of a particular investment plan, might be more successful depicting an African-American family visiting the Virgin Isles than Prague. That said, some other trends worth noting include:

- **Cars:** the growth rate of African-Americans purchasing new cars is twelve times that of non-African-American auto purchasers over the last decade.[19]

- **Health and Beauty:** 10 percent of all dollars spent by African-Americans are spent on health and beauty aids (African-Americans spend 31 percent more on health and beauty aids than whites). Most cosmetic companies in both prestige and mass distribution categories do not market their products in a specific way to African-American women, and there are surprisingly few product lines created specifically for African-American women (or other women of color). This is an opportunity begging to be developed, since the ethnic HBC category for this group has risen by a total of approximately 12 percent, or $825 million, during 2004-2008.[20] African-Americans account for 30 percent of all hair-care products sold. In particular, the U.S. Census has noted that the African-American woman represents the greatest segment growth in consumption in this category. This demographic has very specific hair-care product needs and tends to be less straitjacketed by typical Western conceptions of beauty than other American women.

- **Food**: Big purchasers in a whole array of food categories, female, teenage African-Americans accounted for 60.3 percent of sodas in 2007, as well as large portions of candy bars, corn, sausage, coffee, canned meat, and tomato sauce. Particularly fond of sweets, African-American households spend, on average, 54 percent more on sugar than the average white household, and African-Americans account for a whopping 50 percent of the brandy market![21]

- **Retail:** African-American teens often spend a high amount of their income on retail, particularly clothing. Still, their fashion spending, estimated at $258 million, pales in comparison to the $260 million worth of video games and $123 million in PC software they spend. African-Americans also spend more per capita on children's apparel than whites.[22] This also holds true in footwear. African-Americans also spend 75 percent more on boys' clothes than their white counterparts.[23]

Many African-Americans report that shopping is their favorite activity, although few are loyal to any one retailer. In the past they have exhibited brand loyalty, although they are becoming increasingly sensitive to health issues. This group has become more critical of brands, marketing, and advertising, and less willing to blindly embrace irresponsible advertising promises. However, they will offer brand loyalty in return if brands remain attentive and respectful to these consumers. Over 60 percent cite "respect" as the reason they choose one retailer over another.[24]

Although African-Americans see much of the same advertising and promotional campaigns as other Americans, they often interpret these campaigns differently. Many commercials may come across as irrelevant, particularly those directed at white suburban families. However, it is to the credit of many brands and advertising firms that minority representation in advertising is more and more frequently prominent. There are specific means and methods that African-American consumers are particularly responsive to.

For example, African-American consumers strongly favor personal contact, as opposed to direct mail.[25] Churches, shopping centers, and sporting events are all excellent venues for approaching them. The advantage of face-to-face marketing is that it attaches a real person to a brand and establishes greater credibility. When companies are active and involved in the African-American community, demonstrating their investment and authentic interest, African-American communities clearly respond to this kind of commitment. Partnerships that raise money for local schools or support community events are also an excellent means for a company to illustrate its interest. Of course, marketing will likely be more relevant to these communities when it is managed by agencies that either are African-American-run or else have a great deal of experience with African-American communications. Volvo, which has received criticism in the past for neglecting minorities, formed a "minority diversity business council" in 2000 that consults with African-American and Hispanic business and community leaders in order to place future marketing and advertising. Also, advertising aimed at African-Americans must establish long-term relationships with African-American media, such as newspapers and radio, rather than present a sudden burst campaign that quickly fades. Because marketing to African-Americans is most often about creating resonance in smaller communities, grassroots work through small local newspapers should not be underestimated, and often offers some of the best-priced media buys available.

Marketing will be more relevant to these communities when it is managed by agencies that either are African-American-run or else have a great deal of experience with African-American communications.

One of the dangers of marketing schemas and demographic sketches is that they often reduce complex, multifaceted audiences to stereotypical simplifications that lack the original groups' rich diversity. Most crucial is an approach that is based on respect and emotional relevance. Ploys to sweep up a generic African-American consumer with a burgeoning income may very well fail, because they seem (and are!) insincere. However, *carefully crafted campaigns that articulate a brand's interest in serving and empowering individuals and their surrounding community will succeed, regardless of race and ethnicity.*

Hispanic Consumers

If there's one thing marketers, advertisers, and the media in general love, it's hype, and in the past year and a half there's been absolutely no shortage of hype about the growing power of Hispanic culture in the United States. "Latin U.S.A.," proclaimed one cover of *Newsweek* in 1999, while Ricky Martin graced the face of *Time.* However, while the subjects of media hype will come and go with whatever frequency is necessary to keep the public stimulated, the phenomenal growth and impact of this burgeoning Hispanic affluence, matched by increased political and cultural clout and sustained by a population explosion that will soon make them the major "minority" in the United States and, in time, enable them to reach population parity with Caucasians, make the importance of this population impossible to dismiss.

According to the 2000 U.S. Census Bureau, Hispanics composed 11.4 percent of the U.S. population, putting them only 8 percent behind African-Americans, the largest minority group in the United States. With immigration and high birth rates, in 2009, Hispanics numbered approximately forty-six million, putting their numbers just over those of non-Hispanic African-Americans. In the last fifty years, Hispanics have accounted for almost a quarter of population expansion in the United States, and today one out of every nine Americans is Hispanic. Currently, the United States is the fifth-largest Spanish-speaking country in the world; by 2020, half of American youth will be Hispanic, and by 2050, nearly one quarter of the population will be Latino.[26]

Brands that want to serve this expansive community will have to work hard to meet its needs and earn its loyalty. Businesses that start today will have an advantage over later entrants, but still must realize that Hispanics are not a new phenomenon in the States, nor is their consumer muscle. They are behind groups like Procter & Gamble, Sears, Philip Morris, and Toyota, which have been aggressively courting these consumers for years now. Fortunately for marketers and advertisers, particularly those that use the Spanish language, the Hispanic population is heavily concentrated in just six states: California, Texas, New York, Florida, Illinois, and New Jersey, and more than 60 percent live in just ten cities.[27] In all, 90 percent of Hispanics live in major metropolitan areas, and a full two-thirds of Latinos in the United States live above the poverty line.

Hispanics have accounted for almost a quarter of population expansion in the United States, and today one out of every nine Americans is Hispanic.

Although they share a common language and may appear to many uninitiated Caucasians to be relatively homogeneous, Hispanics are a complex composite that varies by nationality, age, and economic class, to name a few factors. Estimates have identified seventeen Hispanic subcultures based largely on approximately twenty-two different countries as places of origin. The resulting kaleidoscope of individual Hispanic communities across the United States includes every hybrid possible. These major communities are: Californians (primarily immigrant Mexicans and middle-class Mexicans), Tejanos (Mexicans and Guatemalans who have created a cowboy culture primarily in Texas), Chicago Latinos (primarily Mexicans and Puerto Ricans;

this group comprises 27 percent of Chicago's population), Miamians (primarily Cubans, Nicaraguans, and South Americans), New Yorkers (3.6 million Latinos in total, comprised mostly of Puerto Ricans, Dominicans, Colombians, and Cubans).

Of equal or greater import in understanding Hispanic subcultures, however, are degrees of acculturation among Hispanics. Over a quarter of the Hispanic population in America remains unacculturated (28 percent). A determined and hardworking immigrant population, these individuals remain Spanish-dependent. Largely impoverished or working-class, these Hispanics are working their way up from the bottom of American society. Although some conservative movements in the '80s and early '90s directly and indirectly disparaged these men and women (and sometimes their children, as well), their tenacity is admirable and their commitment to "making it" deserves the recognition and respect of brands which may now, or in the future, have the fortune of providing products and services for them.

The majority of the U.S. Hispanic population (59 percent), however, is partially acculturated, having been born in the United States or spent more than eleven years here. Largely middle-income and bilingual, these are the Hispanics who have successfully carved a niche in American society and cruise between American and Hispanic culture, watching Telemundo at home and telling jokes in English to their friends at work. Their children will, in turn, compose and enlarge the slice of Hispanics in the United States described as highly acculturated (13 percent). Generally United States–born and raised, this group is primarily reliant on English and tends to be upper-income. They are the most well-educated and affluent Hispanic group, and their numbers will swell dramatically as Hispanics become more fully acculturated.[28] *If integration and advancement proceed at current rates, Hispanics can expect to occupy almost four million positions in professional and managerial roles by 2020,* dramatically increasing their power to influence and determine national directions and agendas, as well as national identity.[29] It is highly likely that future Hispanics will play a definitive role in rendering constructions such as "ethnic majority/minority" and "race" irrelevant in the public mind. In order to speak to this audience, marketers must recognize the varying degrees of acculturation and English language usage.

It's also crucial that marketers remember that the Hispanic market is very young, with its median age merely 25.9, versus 33.2, the national median. Many of these young Latinos, called "Generation Ñ" by *Newsweek*,[30] in part because of the prominence of stars like Jennifer Lopez, Salma Hayek, and Ricky Martin, are trendsetters and widely emulated by segments of white suburban youth. Their rich cultural heritage, which may extend from Long Island to El Salvador, encompassing many gradations of Anglo- and Hispanic-American culture, puts them in a unique position to influence American society and appropriate trends and fashions from different cultures.

In 2000, I estimated that Hispanic buying power was around $300 billion and that by 2015 it would balloon to $450 billion. According to The Selig Center, Hispanic buying power is projected to grow to $1.1 trillion by 2009 and $12.4 trillion by 2011, making this group one of the most coveted in the U.S. With conservative values and a very disciplined borrowing approach, this group will better weather the economic crisis and become a great potential market for brands, as they will start spending sooner than other groups.

From a social media perspective, I found an interesting 2009 report by the Florida State University Center for Hispanic Marketing Communication (with the support of DMS Research). From a sample of nearly 2,500 people online, this study makes the observation that "ethnic minorities visit social networking sites more frequently that non-Hispanic whites." Of respondents that visit social networking sites at least two or three times a month, English preferring Hispanics lead the way with 36 percent, compared to 34 percent for Asians. 27 percent of Spanish prefer Hispanics, 26 percent African-Americans, and only 18 percent non-Hispanic whites.

The younger age demographics of ethnic minorities in general has something to do with these results, but a need to enhance one's sense of identity might be the emotional driver for minorities to connect online. The sooner brands recognize this potential and the cultural trends surrounding this growth, the better they can position themselves to cater to this market's current and future needs.

Although nearly all industries can and should tap into Hispanic consumers' needs, there are eight key areas in which Hispanics spend as much as or more than their non-Hispanic counterparts.

- Food consumed at home
- Apparel
- Telephone services

- Rental housing
- TV/radio and other equipment
- Personal-care products
- Public transportation
- Cleaning supplies

Among the spending patterns that distinguish Hispanic consumers is their high spending on personal-care products. They consume greater amounts of shampoo and conditioner than Caucasians, and Hispanic girls spend 60 percent more on makeup than all female teens.[31] There are also higher rates of spending for food eaten at home. Even breakfast patterns are distinguished by ethnic demographics. According to Strategic Research Corporation's survey in 1998, Hispanics were less likely to have eaten cold cereal and more likely to have eaten hot cereal than African-Americans or whites. Cultural influences act in their expectations of services, as well. According to Insight Research Company, for 53 percent of Hispanics and Asians, as well as 44 percent of African-Americans, customer service is the most important factor in choosing a phone company.[32] For whites, customer service is a priority for a mere 36 percent of customers.

Because brands play a role in how consumers construct their identity, brand managers must understand what aspects of identity are most salient and influential among Hispanics in order to better serve their aspirational interests. Relative to fashion, Hispanics consider celebrities important trendsetters, and 18 percent of Hispanic-American woman turn to stars for clothing ideas, versus a mere 10 percent among non-Hispanic women. Hispanics generally hold family, religion, and tradition in high regard. The women tend to have more traditional aspirations regarding family and child rearing. Children are seen as precious, and elderly parents are given particular respect and honor. Multigenerational households are common, and Hispanics emphasize their desire to retain traditions from their countries of origin. As is frequently the case, the best way to avoid making an offensive mistake is to constantly monitor lifestyle and inspirational cues from these groups and make diversity a priority in selecting men and women to shape a brand.

Hispanics are buying cars at four times the rate of the rest of the population, according to the AOL study in 2004, and half of online Hispanics have used the Internet to find cars and dealerships. Buick began seriously marketing to Hispanics for the first time in 1999 and, despite its inexperience, has shown acuity and sensitivity. It unveiled its first dedicated Spanish-language commercials on Telemundo and Univision. Buick had previously aired Spanish-dubbed versions of English commercials that improved brand awareness in Latino communities but lacked genuine resonance. Viewers knew it was a second-rate appeal to their culture and language. In contrast, the original Spanish ads that were managed by a Hispanic ad agency and taped in Mexico with local talent and crew have boosted sales of the featured vehicle, a Buick Century. Hispanic customers previously accounted for 1 percent of the Century's annual sales, even though they account for 5 percent of national auto sales. Although many businesses have used a low rate of Hispanic patronage as a reason for writing off that demographic, Buick had the insight to recognize that this demographic could become a very important customer for their brand. Research showed that Hispanics seek comfort and amenities in a family car at a reasonable price—exactly the same positioning as the Buick Century. Finally, Buick planned a miniature version of the Hispanic-dominated Florida Carnival that GM currently sponsors. Buick's version would tie into the vehicle, feature Hispanic celebrities, and visit twenty to twenty-five markets. Buick failed to deliver on its promise, but detailed and far-reaching plans like this are the key to any serious attempt at attracting the Hispanic markets.

Asian-American Consumers

Although slight in their population numbers, Asian-Americans are the fastest-growing ethnic group in the United States and, considering that these 10.5 million people have the highest per capita income of any American ethnic group, including the white majority, they are a force to be reckoned with and a market to crave. Asian-Americans outspend other ethnic groups in important categories like computers, insurance, and international long-distance telephone calls. Many marketers remain confounded by the diversity of Asian-Americans and the absence of detailed research, but this is all the more reason for companies to jump into this market now, thereby gaining an advantage over their competitors. Precisely because so few companies advertise to Asian-Americans, those that do are able to build incredible brand loyalty.

According to Admerasia, Focus USA,[33] out of today's Asian-Americans:

- 93 percent live in metropolitan areas
- 60 percent have an income of $50,000+
- 50 percent hold professional positions

- 37 percent of Asian-American adults have a bachelor's degree or higher
- 63 percent have credit cards

It is important from the outset to be aware of crucial cultural faux pas in terms of marketing to Asian-Americans such as the fact that most Asian-Americans follow numerology, and combinations of numbers in marketing messages may have undesired meanings for Asians. For example, six and eight are lucky in several Asian cultures, but four rhymes with the Japanese word meaning "good-bye forever" and is associated with death (a good reason why one airline's toll-free telephone number, 1-800-FLY-4444 did not go over well with this market segment!). The same goes for colors: white in many Asian cultures connotes death.

Although there exist at least seventeen different ethnic and linguistic groups in Asia, 90 percent of Asian-Americans belong to one of six groups.

Chinese-Americans are often broken down on the basis of whether they are foreign or native-born. Although the latter are usually more integrated into American society and wealthier, all Chinese-Americans tend to place family and education as high priorities. Particularly among foreign-born Chinese-Americans, advertisers must recognize the distinct meanings associated with symbols and colors otherwise innocuous within American culture. Chinese-Americans generally shop for the best price on goods, but will not sacrifice quality.

Japanese-Americans have been broken down into the less acculturated first- and second-generation residents and the more acculturated third-generation residents. Of particular interest: the seventeen-year-old female is the fundamental image of advertising within Japan. Plastered on everything from toothbrushes to computers, she embodies the future.

Filipino-Americans are diverse, culturally and linguistically, and because many of their names are of Spanish descent, they are difficult to identify. However, they are largely concentrated in five urban areas: Los Angeles/San Diego, San Francisco/Sacramento, Honolulu, New York, and Chicago.

Korean-Americans are a very aggressive minority, recognized for their business savvy and commitment. A full 80 percent of Koreans in the United States are business owners. Half of Korean-Americans are Protestant churchgoers, and findings indicate that 90 percent are active in ethnic, business, and church-based social organizations. Traditionally, Korean-Americans have shown a higher regard for brand-name recognition than for price.

Vietnamese-Americans are generally recent immigrants who have little familiarity with American culture. The traditions of their native culture are especially strong because they have so little distance from them. These values include a disfavor for public displays of affection, high regard for family and elders, and although women are regarded as the stewards of household budgets, men tend to make the decisions regarding very expensive items.

Indian-Americans are usually very well educated and fluent in English, the mother tongue of their former British colonizers. However, India hosts an array of subcultures, among which Hindi is the dominant second language.

California, New York, Hawaii, Texas, and Illinois are home to over two-thirds of all Asians in America. California alone hosts 40 percent.[34] The *DMA Insider* magazine classified Asian immigrants based on three factors:

- Ethnic Identification
- Degree of Assimilation
- Language Dependency

Although these factors can create a complicated number of categories and eventually illustrate the disunity in supposed "Asian-American" demographic, there remain values that generally unite Asian-Americans. Family and community are of powerful import, much more so than in Anglo-American culture, and most Asian-American households tend to be multigenerational as well as multifamily. Whereas American ads focus on personal choices, Asian-targeted ads may want to put options in the framework of family and community. Ads that flaunt personal status or undermine traditional hierarchies within these families will be ineffective. Ads should also recognize and respect Asian-Americans' desire to retain traditional values yet prosper in the American environment. By some estimates, a full two-thirds of Asian-Americans prefer to speak their own language at home, and studies have indicated that Asian-Americans see it as a sign of respect for companies to market to them in their own language.[35] AT&T concentrates on marketing in seven languages to

Ads that flaunt personal status or undermine traditional hierarchies within these families will be ineffective.

Asian-Americans from six countries. Advertising that emphasizes this love of traditional cultural values yet avoids stereotypes is effective. The importance of service is also pretty consistent across the various Asian market segments. This means a more polite, formal tone with customers (AT&T, for example, bluntly tells Caucasian Americans "We want you back," but informs Japanese customers, "We are waiting for your call") and a perspective which shows an understanding of the post-sales experience.

As commercial interests recognize the affluence of this group, there has been an increased presence of Asians in commercial advertising, as evidenced by the campaigns of Merrill Lynch, L'Oréal, Sprint, and Goldman Sachs. As research on this group grows, so will advertising budgets. Already, blue-chip companies such as Sears, Apple, Hallmark, MCI, and Charles Schwab are jumping into the waters. A Selig Center For Economic Growth (University of Georgia) report from 2004 predicted a jump in spending from the Asian-American community from 2004 to 2009 that would increase 45 percent, from $363 billion to $528 billion. In California, Asian-Americans are responsible for more than $1 billion in total buying power. As the second most frequent visitors of social networking sites, Asian-Americans will challenge brands and demand the highest level of transparency. This group will spur many more big investments from major categories in this market. Greater efforts than ever before have been made on several different fronts to stimulate participation. Thirteen percent of the Census Bureau's $165-million marketing budget for creating awareness was spent on the Asian-American population, and for the first time, the questionnaire came in four Asian languages in addition to English and Spanish. There were also efforts organized around getting an accurate count within the community itself.

The San Francisco Asian TV station KTSF has made some advances by funding research on their viewers' consumption habits. These recently published findings indicate that certain brands have been successful in reaching these customers. The brands that topped their consumer-preference survey had either made strong investments in uniquely "Asian" marketing and media, such as AT&T, or they were brands that enjoyed a strong presence in the Asian market and were carried over from the "homeland," such as Coca-Cola, Pantene, and Tylenol.[36] This survey is reminiscent of similar ones conducted by the Hispanic networks Telemundo and Univision in the '80s that were largely responsible for igniting widespread commercial interest in the Hispanic-American community. As research on Asians grows, it is likely that marketing and commercial investments will also flourish. However, this is no reason to delay investing in these communities. By tapping into the expertise of organizations like the Association of Asian-American Advertising Agencies, based in New York, successful Asian-American forays are fully possible now.

Although I have found few large-scale, well-executed, cohesive campaigns directed at the Asian-American population, I am impressed by the sensitive and thoughtful efforts made by the *New York Times* to attract Chinese-Americans. They started in February of 1999, when the *Times* distributed Chinese folk-art calendars during celebrations for the Lunar New Year. Subsequently, the *Times* pushed for an increase in dealers selling the *Times* within Chinatown. Although all of the *Times*'s vending machines had been blue until that point, the Chinatown machines were changed to red because blue is considered a color of mourning among many Chinese, but red indicates happiness. Finally, ads were aimed at Chinese via print, commercial, and direct mail. The commercials aired on local Chinese-language channels, and the direct mail was printed in English and Chinese and featured toll-free numbers for Mandarin and Cantonese, the two dominant dialects of Chinese. The *Times* is an ideal product for this market because it is well-established and positioned as the most respected and authoritative source for well-informed news. Alyse Myers, vice president of promotions and marketing at the *Times*, said of the campaign: "Culturally there is an emphasis on education as the road to success."[37] Chinese-Americans hold education in great esteem and aspire to success for themselves and their children. Consequently, the campaign specifically targeted professionals and the parents of precollege children, who would most appreciate the *Times*'s content, and advertisements emphasized the theme of parents' pride in watching their children excel scholastically. The campaign, designed by Asian-American marketing specialists Kang & Lee, New York, has been so successful that it has been expanded to San Francisco, Oakland, and the Silicon Valley. Other campaigns directed at New York residents of South Asian and Korean descent are also under way. It clearly pays to pay attention to the needs of the growing Asian-American market.

3

Women: The New "Shoppers-in-Chief"

The consumer is not an idiot, she's your wife.
–David Ogilvy

I heard another one: She's not an idiot, she's your boss!
–David Lubars, BBDO West

On the gender front, for some time now, women have been increasingly influential consumers. It makes me think of the line in the Woody Allen movie *Mighty Aphrodite* when Woody's son asks him who the boss is at home, "you or Mommy?" Woody's now-famous, very telling answer is: "I am the boss, your mom is just the decision maker." Women have long been a powerful but little recognized economic force; they represent 50.7 percent of the U.S. population and they influence or buy 80 percent of products sold,[38] spending close to $3.5 trillion each year in America and potentially above $20 trillion globally in the next five years.[39] Today they not only have more and more buying power, but there is a whole shift in what they are buying and why. For starters, they are buying more products and services traditionally sold to men, like cars, computers, games, hardware, liquor, and cigars.[40] According to the Consumer Electronics Marketing Association, women are great influencers in 50 percent of all consumer electronics purchase decisions, and for the past several years computers have topped the holiday gift wish list for women.[41] For some time now, these changes have been recognized by many of the smarter corporations, but it is still a whole new way of thinking to some!

Home Depot is built around the premise of making a friendly, attractive, "non-macho" hardware store women would love, and it works. Sears's highly successful campaign, "The softer side of Sears," was an insightful recognition years ago of the fact that most of the in-store purchases–including automotive products–were made by women!

In light of the auto industry debacle of 2008–2009, I was interested in figuring out how this could happen. My answer: women. I'm not saying that they wrecked this industry on purpose, but that the automotive industry did as much as they could to keep this powerful group away from their brands.

In 2000, I overemphasized that women were the shoppers-in-chief and encouraged corporations to bet their brands on that influential group. The American car industry is a particular good case to study as it shows what happens when brands try to market the wrong product with the wrong motives. The car industry is one of those old-world, male-dominated domains that exemplify the lack of understanding marketers have in making an emotional connection with women. When you know that there are few female executives in the auto industry and that only 8 percent of dealerships are owned by women, you can understand how this industry went askew.

Toyota did quite well and will continue to survive and strive again given its cultural attachment to women. In a 2005 article for Edmonds.com, "What are Automakers Doing for Women? Part II," Carol Traeger already expressed what made Toyota so special for this group.

Many brands kept on communicating to a male audience, even when it was understood that decisions were mostly made by women. For the future, it is always good to remind ourselves that, as the article well states, "Toyota may hail from a country where men make most of the decisions, but its success in the U.S depends on the attention it pays to the tastes and concerns of women buyers." The writer explains in her article that women purchase 55 percent of all Toyota vehicles and 60 percent of all Toyota passenger cars sold in the U.S. In this article, Sandi Kayse, Toyota's national advertising manager, confirms, "Women are extremely important to us from a product and marketing standpoint. Toyota was one of the first to offer wanted side-impact and head-protecting curtain airbags."

Features like power door locks, LATCH child-seat anchors, restraint systems, and child-safe window buttons are also found in Toyota models.

Most importantly, women just don't look at cars in the same way as men. "Women were all over the interior of the car, whereas the men looked at the exterior and talked about the sleek styling and the horsepower of the great engine," Kayse said.

A little piece of information that must have escaped the guys in Detroit is the fact that 65 percent of the customers that are taking their cars to be serviced are women.[42] In addition, women spend some $200 billion each year on new cars and servicing, women buy 45 percent of all light trucks, and women make their decisions influenced first by friends and family.

Which leads me to social media and word of mouth. Women are fighting back online with sites like Women-drivers.com, a great place to find real information on how women think about cars.

I truly encourage the new owners of the automotive industry, the U.S. government, to use the same advance research they did for their campaign to the White House to help them connect the dying auto industry to this buyer.

A great way to reach women is through social media. It is now common knowledge that women are a majority in the social media sphere. According to new research provided by Harvard Business Publishing, more women (55 percent) are on Twitter than men (45 percent). One interesting observation from this survey is that men and women have different criteria on who they are following and how they want to be followed, but again, as stated in this research, "an average man is almost twice [as] likely to follow another man than a woman," distancing himself even further from understanding the powerful, complex, and different approach women have to this medium.[43] Of the 42 million women engaged in some form of blogging activity, 75 percent participate in social media networks such as Facebook or MySpace, and 20 percent use Twitter. As a result of this increased activity, a 2009 study found that women online are now more than ever before spending less time engaging in traditional media activities like watching TV (30 percent), listening to the radio (31 percent), and reading magazines (36 percent) or newspapers (39 percent).[44]

The trend toward female dominance of MySpace and Facebook shows again that women want a dialogue and a connection with others and bond with brands. It is something we often forget with social networks: the fact that it is a leadership game where the most followed people are elected by others for their advice, observations, or thinking. Still, despite these examples, a surprisingly large number of companies continue to ignore female consumers, or when they do pay attention to them, it is often still through one-dimensional, stereotypical approaches with little understanding of their true desires and needs.

The truth is that no company today can afford to ignore women. The rising influence of women in our world extends far beyond their consumer power and evolving buying habits. Women are a veritable force to be reckoned with in the new economic landscape, and they do and will continue to shape this landscape in ways we can only imagine.

Although as recently as 2007, women still only earned 77.8 percent of every dollar men earned in full-time jobs, and as of 2009 only thirteen women hold CEO positions in Fortune 500 companies,[45] it is predicted that they will control some $13 trillion in global earnings, or more than half of the American wealth, by the year 2010.[46] In their article "The Female Economy," Michael J. Silverstein and Kate Sayre assert that "as a market, women represent a bigger opportunity than China and India combined." *The new economy has engendered a business atmosphere that requires problem solving, communication, and the manipulation of information, skills in which women are highly developed.* Not to mention the growing importance of creativity, flexibility, and humanism in business today. Women have long been in entrepreneur mode—the

No company today can afford to ignore women.

key business model of our time—often working outside of the system as a way of avoiding the glass ceiling. In 2006, there were an estimated 10.4 million firms privately held by women. This accounted for two in five (40.2 percent) of all businesses in the country and employed 12.8 million people nationwide. These firms generated $1.9 trillion in annual sales.[47]

The Internet revolution is opening more doors than ever before to women because it is an unstructured format with no "old-boy network" to be dealt with, making it easier for women to either strike out on their own or reach higher levels more quickly in companies. The Internet has created an enormous demand for seasoned marketers and media experts, many of whom are women. Also, as a communications medium in the business environment (i.e., virtual conferences, and so on), the Internet does not make gender differences immediately apparent; the focus is instead on content. In 1999, women were chief executives in 6 percent of Internet companies and held top management posts in 45 percent of start-ups. As women rise up through the corporate ranks, their influence on the business world is increasing enormously. Through different approaches to management and business strategy and by stressing the need for more quality time for the management of one's personal life, women are quite simply changing the way business is conducted and organizations operate.

We are seeing companies, such as the software company SAS Institute, that offer a myriad of family-friendly flexible benefits to employees, ranging from onsite daycare and medical care facilities to a family cafeteria. There are unlimited sick days and a thirty-five-hour workweek. They are doing this because they want to be competitive in attracting valuable female employees.[48] At Pepsi-Cola North America, CEO Brenda Barnes surprised the corporate world in 1999 by leaving her high position to spend more time with her family after years of having to miss important family events, such as her children's birthdays, due to her intense itinerary. In the early '90s, Deloitte & Touche noticed the retention of women slipping in the company, instituted many widespread changes, and now says that over seven hundred employees use flexible work arrangements.

Eventually, these trends begun by women will have a very strong influence on the whole of the population. In light of women's growing power and influence in the new economy, these companies are certainly smart to invest in their female employees. They are ahead of the game. But we are still at the tip of the women's empowerment trend. *Women are not yet included in the top echelons of many corporations, and diversity is often a concept that reads well in mission statements but is not put into practice in any kind of meaningful way on a regular basis.* In the coming years, we must recognize how truly formidable a force women are in our society and adjust our organizations to reflect their importance. After all, if women are buying most of America's products, why wouldn't companies want to have women at their helms?

Women are not yet included in the top echelons of many corporations, and diversity is often a concept that reads well in mission statements but is not put into practice.

The new media-convergence maven Gerry Laybourne, previously of Nickelodeon and now, of course, having launched the Oxygen cable/Web-based network for women, is a more recent example of the difference an uncompromisingly feminine approach to business can bring. Laybourne, who has been described as "a nurturing Earth Mother, but a powerful infighter too,"[49] brings to her network concept a unique focus on high-quality content programming that is nonviolent, nonexploitative, and emotionally vibrant, with a predilection for shows about "real" women with "real" problems. She is motivated not only by a desire for business success, but also by a passionate belief in her mission to improve the lives of women and humanity at large. She has described Oxygen as "a grassroots movement."[50]

The old idea of developing products or brand identities around the concept of something for men that women, too, could have, such as the old "Strong enough for a man, but made for a woman . . ." deodorant ad for Secret, seems ancient today! *Women want products, ads, and businesses that are without comparisons to a man's world. They are creating their own world! Companies will do well to tune into this mentality.*

I predict that women will become increasingly valued in the emotional economy and social branding because they value and are highly sensitive to . . . emotions! Market research has proven time and again that the primary thing that women want, as people and as consumers, is relationships. Women prefer personal, one-on-one networking as a way of finding solutions to business problems, and this is often how they discover products as consumers (i.e., through talking to friends or reliable sources). Women are also largely holistic in their approach to relationships, meaning that they are less likely than men to compartmentalize a brand or company solely according to what it has to offer them in a specific situation. They want to understand the big picture: what the brand stands for on the whole, if the brand's image, philosophy, and/or ethics are in sync with their own . . . They want to feel a deeper, more layered connection . . . Sounds familiar? It's what Emotional Branding is all about!

What Women Want as Consumers

As consumers, what do women really want? The five most important elements of an Emotional Branding program for women are:

Respect: Women are well informed. They research products well before buying. They read ingredients much more closely than men to make sure there are no harmful elements, and they are very careful about their decisions.[51] Acknowledge that they are intelligent and informed, and they will respect your brand.

Individuality: Women play multiple roles today and do not want to be talked to from only one, narrow perspective. They are feminine, powerful, nurturing moms or caregivers, independent, sexy, smart, and so on. Recognize their diversity as much as possible, and resist any and all temptation to stereotype!

Stress relief: In numerous studies stress has been shown to be women's number-one enemy. Women today feel overwhelmed by taking an equal role as breadwinner and primary nurturer to the family. In a survey conducted by *Redbook* and Women.com, 43 percent of women said they felt frustrated in trying to balance their work life with parenting.[52] Offer solutions, or at least understanding, of the tensions that prey on them daily.

Connection: Women base most of their decision-making on emotions as opposed to rational elements. Studies have shown that they don't like reading lists of numbers, specs, and stats. They want to know what the product will do for them, personally.[53] Find out what makes "your" woman tick!

Relationship: Women want dialogue, not just a transaction. Women are looking for brands to trust and will often remain extremely loyal to a brand that has built on their trust consistently—even beyond price. Part of the relationship a woman has with a brand has to do with that brand representing something important to her in her life. Brands that take a sincere stand for something and demonstrate it in real, concrete terms will do well with women.

Let's take a look at these five key elements of women as consumers–*Respect, Individuality, Stress Relief, Connection*, and *Relationship*–via several recent branding programs and ad campaigns. Although, as in the case of any successful Emotional Branding program, several or even all of these points are sometimes touched on in one example, I have for the sake of argument placed them in the categories that they seem to best embody.

- **Respect:** *Women know an awful lot more about carburetors and electric saws than you might think . . . Talk to them with respect!*
In addition to Toyota, Home Depot, and Sears, some other companies in traditionally "male" industries have begun to talk to women in interesting ways. Michelin targeted women in a clever way in their very successful 1999 ad campaign that showed women presenting tires to a friend at her baby shower. The ad plays with stereotypical images of women at a baby shower with the surprise element of a tire as a gift, and is meant to reinforce the brand's equity as a safe tire, giving a nod and a wink to the fact that they know women are buying more and more of these unconventional items.

A 2000 American Express ad is one example of what *not* to do in trying to show respect in marketing to women. The ad shows a woman in her fifties traveling in a foreign country. She has just left her wallet with a thousand dollars in cash–all her cash–in a cab. She appears hysterical and helpless. The solution would have been, of course, to have purchased American Express Traveler's Checks, but it is woefully too late. . . . Will women really be able to identify with the bumbling, fearful woman in this ad who exhibits very little foresight, resourcefulness, or street smarts? And even if they did, why do large companies like American Express tend to position themselves as the paternalistic "Big Company" with all the answers? Far better for it to attempt to create a relationship of equality with the consumer based on esteem. Why don't they show a woman celebrating with an expensive dinner after having lost her wallet because she was intelligent and organized enough to have bought American Express Traveler's Checks?

Although we are starting to see a lot of finance branding aimed at women, many financial firms are not doing much yet to market to women in an emotionally sensitive manner. This is baffling since, according to the National Association of Securities Dealers, women now represent 47 percent of all investors, and they are savvy investors, too. In a study of more than thirty-five thousand brokerage customers, the University of California at Davis found that women's portfolios earned 1.4 percentage points more than men's, with single women earning 2.3 percentage points more. The reasons behind their success with investments provides interesting insight into women. Just as with other consumer decisions, women research their investment decisions thoroughly and are more consistent and patient with their choices. Men are risk-takers and move around a lot in their investments, the cost of their numerous transactions bringing down their return rate. According to Brooke Harrington at Brown University, who studies the performance of male and female investors, women also ask themselves more personal questions before making an investment, such as whether their own personal firsthand experience with the company suggests that it is a quality product or service and if they would feel comfortable with the company on ethical grounds. Harrington also says that while men tend to base their investment decisions around the industry they work in or on outside information from the Internet or TV, women get investment ideas from their own direct consumer experiences.[54]

- **Individuality:** *Boss, mama, woman, worker, nurturer, girlfriend, biker, wife, business owner, seductress, friend, cook, volunteer, industry leader, activist, artist, sports fan, etc.*

The luxury watchmaker Patek Philippe has captured the essence of women's multifaceted lives today in their new branding program. Patek Philippe recently introduced its first line of watches for women called Twenty-4. The watches are targeted to women in the twenty-eight-to-thirty-five-year-old age group with emphasis on modern styling to fit in with every moment of the lives of busy women. Its ad campaign, which asks women "Who will you be in the next twenty-four hours?" reinforces an understanding of the many varied roles women play in the course of a day in a simple, intriguing, and eloquent manner.

In the cognac industry, which has traditionally vied for an older, often male consumer, Hennessy in its latest ads has been appealing to a more modern, aesthetic audience–young women, in particular. The Hennessy ads attempt to capture an urban, hip young woman in all of her complexities.

A recent Corningware cookware commercial with the tagline "Find your inner chef" is a welcome relief from cookware advertising campaigns that show women in a state of Betty Crockerish kitchen perfection. This commercial shows a relaxed young woman in a sexy, elegant cocktail dress having fun putting the finishing touches on dinner and laughing at her own "wonderful little blunders that only make her appreciate her final masterpiece that much more." By her dress and the lit candles, we know she's expecting company, and there is a sense of excitement and enjoyment. But instead of the focus being on the pleasure her cooking will bring to others (which is such a cliché in this category), it is on the great time she is having in the process of cooking itself.

The following Women.com ad with its word play around "doll" is a very ingenious, direct-line approach to the problem of stereotyping and a humorous, tongue-in-cheek look at just how varied women's interests are.

- **Stress Relief:** *A woman's job is never done!*
Obviously, the main reason stress is women's number-one pain today is because women have continued to be the primary family caretakers at the same time that they have vastly expanded their roles and levels of responsibility in the business world. Studies have shown that while it is true that men are doing more to help out around the house, women still shoulder the majority of the responsibility.[55] This is an incredibly important point for marketers to understand and respond to with sensitivity. *Since Emotional Branding is about solutions, what can be done to help women find and feel more work/life balance and relief from stress in the brands in their lives?* A practical approach is never a bad idea. In response to women's busy schedules, some supermarkets, for example, are beginning to group products in their stores around solutions, such as beauty sections, allergy, and cough and cold sections. Foods are beginning to

appear grouped according to menu ideas–all this to make a woman's errands quick, easy, and fun. Grocery stores could and should do more to develop a relationship with women by adding more creative solutions to the mix, such as having health or beauty professionals onsite to offer tips, seminars or local speakers on important neighborhood issues that affect their daily lives in which they may wish to participate more actively but have trouble finding the time . . . or play areas for children. . . .[56] The possibilities are endless. If the supermarket, or any retail space, could become a dynamic public and social space where women could see themselves reflected and their needs responded to–I don't think it would feel much of a threat from the Internet at all!

An Eckerd ad, which emphasizes the ease of its return policy, lets women know that it is well aware that they are pressed for time and would rather spend it with their loved ones than in returning makeup products that aren't quite right. A MasterCard commercial from the McCann-Erickson "Priceless" series shows with humor how its debit card helps a modern Cinderella complete all her errands in time to meet her handsome prince for dinner. An L. L. Bean ad takes a different tack, responding to the fact of stress in women's lives by

A website for dolls. Also: women who played with dolls growing up; women who ripped the heads off dolls growing up; sugardolls; honeydolls; women who get dolled up; doll collectors; anyone who can hum Hello Dolly; women who wear babydoll pajamas; anyone who's seen the Dalai Lama; and every woman who's tired of hearing "hey doll" when walking by construction sites.

portraying a blissful moment of peace and relaxation. What woman would not love to be lying in that hammock?!

• **Connection**: *Give me an F-E-E-L-I-N-G (not stats or lists of numbers!)*
Philips has understood this principle and is using it wisely in the way it markets its home cinema collection to women. Instead of giving tons of specs for the system or zeroing in on performance, the campaign focuses on the pleasures (particularly social pleasures) of its home cinema. The print campaign features a young woman with the headline, "None of my friends go to the movies anymore. They come over to my place instead." This is a key element of the connection approach to marketing to women: tapping into a communal bonding, often between women, and often through humor surrounding women's issues.

What can be done to help women find more work/life balance and relief from stress in the brands in their lives?

Even makers of female-oriented products are also realizing they can update and improve their dialogue with women in some interesting ways. Always

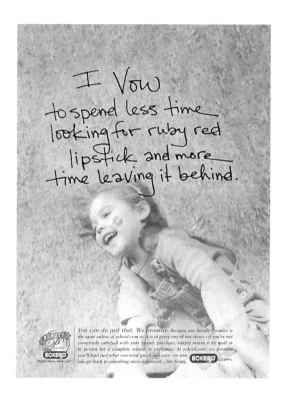

sanitary napkins recently launched a campaign to introduce their Always Ultra Quilted Maxipads that was very different from previous campaigns (absolutely no demos surrounding the efficacy of the product, for starters!). One of the humorous spots shows a group of handsome men in kilts dancing to funky techno music as the female voice-over says: "Hey, guys. Guys. Stop! It's the new *quilted* pad from Always. *Quilted*, not kilted." The guys' expressions turn quizzical as they try to stop a gust of wind from lifting up their kilts. The tagline is: "Being a girl just got better." Another spot shows apparently naked men marching in tall grass, wearing helmets and guns to emphasize Always Ultra's superior protection. In surprising women with an unusual approach to a mundane product and giving them a chance to laugh at men in silly situations, these quirky ads succeed in emotionalizing a "serious" and highly practical product for the consumer. Andy Abraham, North American marketing director for Always, says, "Consumers were tired of seeing women on sailboats out in the deep blue sea wearing white pants. . . ."

Also an amusing departure from the usual in branding a well-known "women's" product is a playful campaign in France for Mr. Clean, which seeks to connect

TO DO: *Throw out to do list.*

L.L.Bean
start here
GO ANYWHERE

FOR YOUR
FREE CATALOG
CALL US AT
1.800.588.1328

with women on new ground, eschewing the traditional presentation of scientific data about germs. The ad shows the ubiquitous bald, muscled icon Mr. Clean bare-chested, without the usual white T-shirt, with the tagline, "There's nothing like a man who offers you his body." This is in the direction of Emotional Branding simply because in a clever, humorous way, it recognizes that women are sexually empowered and may be amused by such a "come-on" from their friendly old housecleaning buddy who's been around since the invention of the television!

• **Relationship:** *It is a two-way street!*
Women will give their trust and long-term loyalty to brands that enter into a meaningful dialogue with them as opposed to merely focusing on the transaction at hand. Women want brands that reflect the values that are important to them. One of the major issues that top women's concerns today are mental, physical, and spiritual health for themselves and their families. Middle-aged women are responsible for making 80 percent of all health-care decisions in America,[57] and in a recent study it was found that younger, twentysomething women also consider health issues to be of major (and growing) importance for

themselves and their loved ones. Their concerns surrounding safety and health cause women to view many products through a very different lens than men. Interestingly, in auto ads, for example, Langer & Associates found in a study that the word "power" conveyed excitement to men, while to women it was seen as a safety factor in maneuvering in tight situations.[58] Women are and like to see themselves as caretakers and nurturers of themselves and others. And by others, they often include a wide scope of humanity as well as their "near and dear." It's important to talk to women from an understanding of this emotional perspective. Avon's long-term commitment to breast cancer, Target's work in education for children, and Liz Claiborne's fight against domestic violence are good examples of getting this right, among many others. What is most important is that women feel they are dealing with a real brand personality that stands for something meaningful on some level, not an amorphous corporate entity.

While women *are* nurturers and caretakers, this is certainly not to the exclusion of their own needs. Of course, one of the most meaningful causes for women is the one that has to do with themselves! In this era of feminine empowerment, women see themselves very differently today than in the past, yet much of our marketing still plays to the "old woman." An *Advertising Age* article says, for example, that in commercials, "women like to see other women who are diverse, confident, and naturally beautiful. Women respond to emotional truth and real-life experience."[59] This, along with the fact of the aging Baby Boomer population, is surely the reason behind the trend of older and/or more natural (i.e., what was previously considered "flawed").[60] In an informal poll of the women in our New York office, we found that across the board, the number-one offense in advertising for women was one-dimensional, unrealistic ads that objectify women.

This, of course, does not mean that women don't wish to see and be inspired by images of beauty. The Maidenform communications program of several years ago, with the tagline "Because inner beauty only goes so far," provided an interesting angle on this issue. This ad uses a humorous tone to point out that while women want to be recognized above all for the strength of their inner qualities, it is also important for women to feel attractive, so why not aim for both? Brands that avoid sexist imagery and build on positive, inspirational messages that recognize the multifaceted nature of women and the key challenges women face today will go far in building a relationship with women. And in today's age, this really goes for all brands given the fact that the stereotypical division of the sexes is really and truly going, going, gone. Consider, for

example, the audience for the Super Bowl. According to Nielsen, it was 42 percent female.[61] How many brands recognized this fact in their advertising?

As we progress farther and farther into an era of female empowerment, brands will need to learn to speak to women in new, inventive ways. Finding out how to create a loyal female consumer is probably the best investment a brand can ever make!

Today's Girls, Tomorrow's Women

Furthering that last thought, focusing now on the Gen Y female consumer and where she will lead us in the future is an even smarter investment. Today's brand of feminism is rampant in popular culture, wed to the concept of a new kind of feminine empowerment that embodies the attitude of younger Gen Y women. "Girl power" is everywhere, as evidenced by a slew of celebrities, books, movies, and media (and brand!) images that portray sassy, sexy, extremely confident and successful women in a woman's world. These are girls who aren't afraid to take a stand for what they want (think Spice Girls lyrics: "Yo,

I'll tell you what I want, what I really, really want . . .") and go their own way. They do not feel compelled to compete against men–they may, however, wish to seduce them! Then again, maybe not . . . sGirl power is, above all, about women being empowered without suppressing–or conversely, being compelled to prove–their femininity or sexuality. They are playing by their own rules, able to wear a miniskirt and, like the Disney heroine in the 1998 movie *Mulan,* defeat an all-male military at their own game. Gen Y girls have begun to carve out a strong new definition of beauty that has more to do with personal style and health than size. This is probably due in part to the fact that Gen Y has had a very dramatic increase in involvement in sports over the past several years.[62]

As this generation of women matures, one thing is certain: they will bring their very distinct influences to the world of commerce, both from a business management and a consumer standpoint. As we saw in the Gen Y section in chapter 1, this generation equals the Baby Boomer generation in size and will surely exert the same kind of social muscle. We already know that these girls and women are and will continue to be much more likely to step outside of traditional stereotypes of all kinds, including buying products traditionally purchased by men. Studies have shown that this generation is more likely than their Boomer counterparts to part with any and all tradition and make purchase decisions for cars, computers, and electronics.[63] This, of course, also means that they will be much less likely to tolerate stereotypes in branding programs for all types of products.

Brands mired in stereotypes, such as Barbie, have had to undergo some dramatic changes to keep up with Gen Y girls. It was not long ago that Mattel was lambasted for the talking Barbie whose comments included the insight "Math is hard," but Barbie has learned a lot since then. As showcased in the *Generation Girl* series, nowadays, Barbie spends her time cruising the subways of New York City, studying to be an actress, and serving as the contributing film and lifestyle editor at *Generation Beat,* the school newspaper. While hanging out with her multicultural friends, she's apt to shout out her favorite (and empowering) phrase "Go for it!" This new Barbie is intended to appeal to girls nine through twelve, who have been outgrowing Barbie earlier than their Gen X and Boomer predecessors. Mattel has also added more sports-oriented Barbies, such as NCAA Barbie. Yesterday's blonde bimbo Barbie is definitely a thing of the past. Her more intelligent and active counterparts have taken the stage.[64]

Maybe it's finally time to give up a good chunk of the blatantly sexist images in branding programs in favor of a more holistic view of women. Expecting nothing less than respect for their multidimensional selves, Gen Y may very well be the ones to bring about this revolution as they grow and evolve in our society!

Women and the Web: An Incredible Force

Women are arriving online with incredible force. They currently make up 55 percent of the online population, a far cry from their 48 percent of the online population in 2000. Because they handle or influence 80 percent of all purchase decisions, they will obviously quickly surpass male online spending as well. "The number of moms who use social media regularly (e.g. Facebook, MySpace, community.babycenter.com) has significantly increased from 11 percent to 63 percent since 2006, a change of 462 percent. 44 percent of women now use social media for word-of-mouth recommendations on brands, and 73 percent of them feel they find more trustworthy information about products and services through online communities." (MarketingCharts.com)

Women's primary online activities are:

• Gathering information (business/career/family/shopping/health/travel/ computer)
• Sending and receiving e-mail and instant messages
• Chatting and sending photos
• Looking for coupons or savings

While a large number of women do go online for entertainment and pleasure, women are increasingly dependent on the Internet to save time.[65] Netsmart found that 88 percent of women say that the Internet simplifies their lives.

A significant difference between men and women online is that women tend to go online for a specific purpose and men are more likely to be surfers or browsers. This means that user-friendly, intuitive design is key, as is tailoring sites toward convenience. Contests or helpful tips are more valuable to women than games.

What we already know about women as consumers translates well to the Web:

Respect: Women use the Web to conduct thorough research of products, services, and companies in order to make highly informed decisions. An interactive survey by Northstar Interactive demonstrates that for women, the Web has surpassed newspaper, television, radio, and even their friends as a source of buying information: 67 percent use the Internet, 55 percent friends, 44 percent newspapers, 27 percent television, and 20 percent radio.[66]

Individuality: Women use the Web to reinforce their sense of themselves as multidimensional people. They enjoy the power the Web gives them to expand their horizons in all the roles they play. They use the Web to do business and personal research and to explore current events, fashions, travel, and entertaining escape sites.

Stress relief: The major reason women shop online is convenience. Twenty-four-hour availability means that midnight shopping after the busy day is over is a real, viable alternative. Women also find the Web to be a great resource for a little relaxation and self-gratification. 96 percent of the women in the Netsmart survey found the Web to be entertaining and pleasurable.

Connection: Sites such as Oxygen, Women.com, and iVillage are increasingly popular with women. These sites have become successful by offering free, easy-to-navigate information and content that is highly relevant to women in a way that fosters a sense of community. They also offer resources such as free e-mail, weather, and stock quotes.

Relationship: Women use the Web to help themselves and their families. 83 percent of the women interviewed in an online study by Netsmart said that the Web helped them to help their children (69 percent said they use it to help their children with homework).

4

Gay and Lesbian Consumers: Sincerity Is the Best Policy!

IBM, Subaru, Anheuser-Busch, American Express, AT&T, British Airways, Allstate, Starbucks, Levi Strauss, Waterford, Philip Morris—these companies all share at least one thing: each has had the sensibility and intelligence to identify that gays and lesbians compose an important segment of its market *and* that they merit the kind of individualized attention that meets their cultural specifics. No longer is targeting homosexuals reserved for daring companies with specialized or marginal goods. As the preceding list attests, American society is at long last recognizing homosexuals' claim to legitimacy, and even the most mainstream companies are now courting these consumers with sizable disposable incomes. These companies have perhaps even begun to realize the enormous importance of the gay and lesbian population as key cultural influencers of our times.

Companies that ignore this audience not only lose valuable business, but also reveal themselves to be unfortunately ignorant, and our society—most notably the soon-to-be monetarily empowered, highly discrimination-averse Gen Y—is becoming less and less tolerant of this kind of ignorance. In keeping with their overall widespread policy of tolerance for ethnic and sexual diversity, today's youth provides a glimpse into the future for gays and lesbians in America: in a 2007 *USA Today* article, Marilyn Elias observed, "Teens are coming out in an era when more Americans than ever consider homosexuality acceptable." In 2006, 54 percent found homosexuality acceptable, compared with 38 percent in 1992, a Gallup poll shows. Today's youth also swims in a cultural sea that's far more pro-gay than ever, says Ritch Savin-Williams, a psychologist at Cornell University and author of *The New*

> Companies that ignore this audience not only lose valuable business, but also reveal themselves to be unfortunately ignorant.

Gay Teenager. From MTV's *The Real World* to *Will & Grace* to Ellen DeGeneres hosting the Oscars, "kids can see gays in a positive light," he says.

I anticipate this trend will continue, and as more teens accept the gay and lesbian population, and these teens become adults, yesterday's archaic taboo against homosexuality will largely evanesce. And as this happens, more and more brands will make attempts to attract these consumers. In the sea of brands newly fighting for gay and lesbian dollars, those that have demonstrated a long-term and unwavering commitment to this community will stand out, and that, in turn, will engender a genuine emotional connection with the brand and, ultimately, loyalty–branding at its best.

Largely due to the prejudice and intimidation which confront many of the men and women of this demographic, statistics about the group's size and influence vary considerably.

The concentration of gay/lesbian/bisexual persons is somewhere around 8.8 million based on the 2005-2006 American Community Survey, an extension of the U.S. census.[67] A 2003 survey by Forrester Research estimates that "the average household income for gay people is $61,300, compared with $56,900 for heterosexuals. The income gap for men is negligible, but gay women earn $6,600 a year more than straight women do. Nineteen percent of both gay men and women have postgraduate degrees, compared with 14 percent of heterosexual men and 12 percent of heterosexual women.[68] On one hand, the urban concentration of many gays and lesbians, and their lower likelihood of raising children, increases disposable income for many. On the other hand, discrimination in the workplace poses an obstacle to many gays and lesbians, and those who live in more rural areas where income is lower are less likely to reveal their sexual orientation for fear of persecution. Fortunately, with the rise of the Internet and the proliferation of gay communities, it seems likely that better and more reliable statistics will become available concerning the size, affluence, and lifestyle needs that distinguish this population of consumers. Such data will empower gay activists and marketers alike, as they are better able to identify the wants and needs of these consumers.

What is certain is that gay and lesbian consumers are among the consumers most responsive to companies' positioning in their community, be it a positive or negative presence. This demographic is definitely paying attention to how they are being treated by corporate America and avidly searching for companies

A new version of the famous Grant Wood *American Gothic* portrait of Middle America.

that know how to talk to them with respect. According to a tracking survey by Greenfield Online and Spare Parts, 77 percent of gays and lesbians have changed brands based on a company's positive stance regarding their group. Of that 77 percent, 76 percent stayed with the brand for a year or more. The response to companies which took a negative stance was even stronger: 87 percent of gay respondents had changed brands based on a negative stance, and 79 percent of that number never purchased that product again![69] This, the power to piss off consumers, I consider to be one of the most striking illustrations of Emotional Branding!

To realize their full potential, brands must recognize from the outset that their emotional identity is not only a result of ads and products, but also corporate policy and stances. The Coors family has in the past contributed to antigay organizations, and this, combined with allegations of the mistreatment of gay employees, has cast a dark shadow over that brand within segments of the gay community, resulting in boycott actions since 1977. Coors is clearly trying to rectify its image within the gay community, and the brand has made positive steps by advertising in gay media with gay-specific ads that are increasingly daring, incisive, and amusing. Coors has now clearly made a commitment to speak to gays in a targeted manner "on their own turf." Coors would be wise to follow up its marketing efforts with a more consistent, message-cohesive corporate policy.

An unfortunate and unnecessary result of Exxon's merger with Mobil in 1999 was that Exxon revoked health-care coverage it had previously provided to gay employees' domestic partners. Although Mobil had previously received little or no attention for denying these benefits, Exxon Mobil attracted outrage and condemnation throughout the gay community for revoking them. Such a reversal, gay activists accurately stated, flies in the face of public and private trends. Today, about 15 percent of major corporations offer domestic partner benefits,[70] and that number is slowly but surely growing. Exxon Mobil's decision generated bad publicity within a small but sensitive minority without winning much applause or benefit in the way of PR or savings. Furthermore, in an industry such as oil, outraged consumers can easily switch to a competitor. Finally, the change in policy undermines company morale and illustrates ambivalence about supporting its workers. Worst of all, if Exxon Mobil reversed itself again and returned the benefits, its waffling would draw the criticism of the right, which would accuse it of buckling beneath the pressure of gay-rights organizations, while homosexuals would probably remain uncertain about the authenticity of its returned support. It would have been far better for Mobil to have quietly adopted Exxon's policies, thereby showing its unwavering support for its employees, and it probably would have escaped unscathed by controversy.

To realize their full potential, brands must recognize from the outset that their emotional identity is not only a result of ads and products, but also corporate policy and stances.

Think of the consumer activism generated around American Airlines's openly supportive and nondiscriminatory policies toward the homosexual population. The fact that American Airlines has been criticized by right-wing contingencies for its humanistic, inclusive policies has only served to mobilize large numbers of people (far beyond the gay population) in support of the airline, creating a very positive grassroots PR campaign!

Additionally, because so many large companies have begun advertising in gay media with gay-specific ads, corporate policy plays a more important role in distinguishing a company's loyalty and interest. Howard Buford, president of PrimeAccess New York, specializes in gay and other minority media. As he told *Advertising Age*, "We're looking at a lot more companies coming into the gay marketplace. It's not so pioneering anymore; now they're just covering their bases."[71] The companies that have already started talking to this community have rapidly developed sophisticated and subtle ways of addressing them without condescension or pandering. Gone (or fading fast, at least) are the days when heterosexual ads were pasted into the pages of *Out* magazine with their opposite-sex couples intact.

IBM has been lauded for its gay-directed ad in 1999 which showed a male couple in Irvine, California, who run a photo-processing business, with the headline, "We're not your typical mom & pop operation . . . We're not even your ordinary pop & pop operation." IBM received thousands of e-mails, phone calls, and letters from gay consumers praising the campaign. Maureen McGuire, vice president of worldwide integrated communications at IBM, says, "Our research found that the gay audience feels advertisers often talk down to them."[72]

Still, many companies seeking to win over the gay and lesbian market but who are afraid of controversy are trying to play it safe with ambiguous ads which leave consumers guessing in terms of the real sexual orientation of the portrayed models in the ad, such as a Chase Manhattan Bank ad which showed two handsome young men shaking hands with the tagline promoting bank services for "unique individuals." This "safety zone" approach has had mixed results, leaving some in the homosexual community feeling sought after for their wallets, but not truly accepted. In addition to homosexual-friendly corporate policy and unambiguous ads, another important sign of commitment can be running ads in the mainstream media. Paul Roux, who runs a gay-oriented marketing firm in New York, says, "People in focus groups repeatedly tell me they want companies to show they are truly committed to the gay market by running a gay ad in *Time* magazine, not just in the *Advocate* or *Out*."[73]

Subaru has been one of the first companies to take this step. Since 1994, Subaru has been relying on niche markets to drive sales of its vehicles, and its success within the gay community is noteworthy. Research indicated that their all-wheel drive vehicles were popular with a number of unique markets that, in addition to health-care professionals and educators, included lesbians. Subaru turned to the agency Mulrayn/Nash, which had experience in advertising to gay and lesbian populations, in order to design Subaru's homosexual-directed media. Before releasing four or five ads featuring same-sex couples, Subaru prepared press releases and retained PR consultants to handle the anticipated public backlash. However, other than several dozen phone calls and a box of petitions from one church down South, the controversy was minimal. Since then, increasingly clever gay-directed ads have been released by Subaru, including some that are found on public billboards and buses. Featuring the text "Different Drivers. Different roads. One car," the ad was unwavering in its direct message to the gay and lesbian community and yet sophisticated enough that it was unlikely to raise the eyebrows of many heterosexuals. The ad cleverly speaks to gay and lesbians through encrypted "insider" symbols that are highly recognizable to gays. One of the vehicles had a bumper sticker with a yellow and blue equal sign, the symbol of a gay activist organization. The other two cars boasted the cryptic vanity plates "XENA LVR" and "P-TOWNIE," the first referring to the program *Xena: Warrior Princess*, which is renowned for its popularity among lesbians, the second referring to the popular and almost exclusively gay and lesbian Cape Cod vacation spot Provincetown. Subaru's decision to place these subtle, clever ads in mainstream media sent a powerful message to homosexuals and proved Subaru's true commitment to serving that community.

Subtlety can, in many cases, be much more effective than an all-out embrace. It is important to really spend the time to get to know this highly perceptive, intelligent, and complex demographic and attempt to form a genuine relationship. Grant Lukenbill, president of New York–based G. L. Communications, a consumer relations and advisory company, and author of *Untold Millions: Marketing to Gay and Lesbian Consumers*, says that "The message can be sent in subtle ways that a company is supportive of the gay community. The key components are inclusivity, sophistication, and subtlety; you don't want to toot your own horn too much."[74]

In creating a campaign for Gay Financial Network (*www.gfn.com*), a gay-friendly financial news and information site, Mad Dogs & Englishmen supplemented the usual focus groups with their own creative internal research. The agency wanted to better understand what it feels like to be gay and the perspective of a gay person within the context of a traditional business environment, so they did some role-playing. One art director had a fake "coming out" and told her mother she was gay. Two men at the agency posed as boyfriends applying for a joint loan at a Staten Island, New York, bank. Says account planner Spencer

Baim, "We explained that we wanted to set up a home together, used the same last name, and touched each other's arms a bit. We felt the embarrassment and discomfort of the woman behind the desk, as well as our own anxiety."[75] This effort to literally step into the shoes of the consumer is a terrific example of the Emotional Branding approach. The resulting groundbreaking campaign, which will run in major mainstream American media, is funny and sensitive, taking a gentle swipe at homophobia in the business world. Each ad shows a businessman who appears uncomfortable or unknowledgeable about gays. In one ad, a balding, cigar-chomping man says, "You're GAY!!! . . . Well, I'm feeling quite happy myself." In another, a silver-haired man reacts to a same-sex couple by saying, "You're partners? Oh! . . . Then this must be a business loan!" In a third ad, a man jokes, "Two ladies living together? Look out, fellas!"

Naturally, the sooner companies venture wholeheartedly into the relationship realm with gay and lesbian consumers, the greater their capacity to show their cultural relevance, distinguish themselves from competitors, and, in the process, win the valuable loyalty of these markets.

section II:
sensorial experiences

the uncharted territory
of branding

A Sense of Strategy

Think about a bad experience you've had at the DMV licensing center or some other unpleasant governmental office. Surely the frustration of waiting was coupled with a stifling, if not downright oppressive, environment. Now reimagine that experience inside a bright and spacious foyer. The large glass windows lining the walls allow soft sunlight to flood the room, flattering the attractive and stylish interior. In the spaces between the windows, where faded three-tone "Buckle-up" posters once drooped, now hang colorful reproductions by famous modern artists. After completing your licensing forms, you hand them to a pleasant, engaging agent whose disposition puts you at ease. At her suggestion, you stroll across the temperature-controlled room and help yourself to a glass of fresh orange juice. Subsequently, you retire to a comfortable–nay, *inviting*–lounge sofa and glance through a recent edition of your favorite magazine while serenaded by soft, soothing music. How might this change the DMV experience?

While this may be a very utopian vision as far as the DMV is concerned (!), questions such as this are invaluable considerations both for products and retail environments in the Emotional Economy. The nuance of an image, the delight of an unfamiliar taste, the memory of a familiar sound, the gentle caress of a soft fabric, the associations of an ancient smell–these are the cues which form indelible imprints on our emotional memories. Although we all have direct experiences with the powerful effects of sensory input, and their importance has been well documented, it has been given short shrift in terms of branding issues. Sensory experiences are immediate, powerful, and capable of changing our lives profoundly, but they are not used to their full extent in branding initiatives at the store level, in product development, packaging design, and advertising. This, despite the well-documented evidence illustrating the effect of the five senses on consumer behavior.

Given the competition among today's corporations, it is my feeling that no business can afford to neglect the five senses. Carefully crafted sensory appeals can create that consumer preference which distinguishes a brand amidst a sea of competing commodities. As commercial offerings of increasingly similar goods proliferate, sensory elements can be the key factors distinguishing one brand experience from another. As the authors of the article "The Experiential Aspects of Consumption" propose, "many products project important nonverbal cues that must be seen, heard, tasted, felt, or smelled to be appreciated properly. . . . In the experiential view, the consequences of consumption appear in the fun that a consumer derives from a product–the enjoyment that it offers and the resulting pleasure that it evokes."[76]

Although consumers generally do value products' tangible qualities, the lifestyle and image of a product should never be neglected. Every product–from Kleenex tissues to opera at Lincoln Center–has symbolic qualities, many of which are conveyed through sensory associations rather than verbal description. But how does one interpret and apply abstract experiential elements such as "smell" through branding? The translation of sensory language is difficult, but Michael Pham from the Columbia Graduate School of Business has uncovered some of the keys in his own work, which states that "To select appropriate symbols, marketers must be aware of the current trends and fads of their target markets. This suggests that marketers who attempt to use mood-related strategies–especially at the point of purchase–must maintain intense, informal contact with their consumers."[77] In essence, know your customers, find out what they like, what they want–and give it to them. Through the senses!

Sensory elements can provide a fertile and imaginative shopping experience for consumers–one that inspires what Charles Osgood describes as "associative hierarchies." In this view, *"although product satisfaction certainly constitutes one important experiential component–the stream of associations that occur during consumption (imagery, daydreams, emotions) are equally important aspects of consumer behavior."* Most consumers are not even conscious of the effects these stimuli have on them, and will *claim* independent reasons for their choices,[78] but it is essential that the seller is fully conscious of the effects. Successful sensory appeals only occur through intelligent strategy. This raises a whole series of questions in brand design, such as:

- What music can be played on a Web site or in a store to convey the emotional identity of a certain brand?
- How can color set the appropriate emotional mood of my brand?

- What images on packaging, in a store or within advertising, enable customers to identify with a product?
- Can serving food affect the behavior of my customers?
- Can scent create desirable associations with a brand?
- How much is too much? Is there a point when customers are overstimulated?

It is my aim to answer these and many more questions about sensory branding, but above all, these chapters can only hint at the wealth of material and powerful branding solutions to be found in the realm of the senses. One starting point for further inquiry is the beautifully written book by Diane Ackerman, *A Natural History of the Senses,* which offers a plethora of social, scientific, anecdotal, and artistic inspiration for exploring the uncharted territory of the senses from a totally fresh perspective. Ultimately, however, it is up to all of us to do our own "sensory sleuthing," since sensory data must, above all, be experienced firsthand to be understood!

5

Sounds that Transport

I will never forget one particular Saturday I passed with my parents at a golf club in Paris. We were casually sipping cocktails on the terrace, wrapped up in a world seemingly insulated from the dilemmas and difficulties of daily life. Then, without warning, my parents became very tense, and a look of dread overtook their faces. Confused and disturbed, I could not understand what had shaken my parents' equanimity. It wasn't until later that they understood themselves and were able to tell me what had caused this reaction—*golf shoes on stone.* Or, rather, the memories this conjured. The clacking shoes on the patio reminded them of the German soldiers' boots marching down French streets during World War II. This sound evoked memories of terror nights when the Gestapo took people from their beds and no one ever knew who would disappear next.

This anecdote, albeit a dramatic one, reveals what numerous studies have confirmed—sound has an immediate and, to a large extent, cognitively unmediated effect on recall and emotions. A friend's voice, a song from the prom, waves lapping on a beach—these are only a few examples of the sounds that can set off an uncontrolled hierarchy of associations within the brain. In fact, studies indicate that activities such as listening to music encourage the release of endorphins in the body, activating the very powerful pleasure centers of the brain. Although we have an intuitive awareness of this, most branding programs do not take advantage of sound (that is, beyond poorly chosen Muzak used to placate callers and numb shoppers). But with well-planned application, sound is not simply a means of occupying consumers but also of engaging their emotions. And there are many, many ways to do this. I am fascinated, for example, by the way the Japanese brand Nagusakiya Mera Chan sells chocolates to kids with a musical instrument integrated into the packaging,

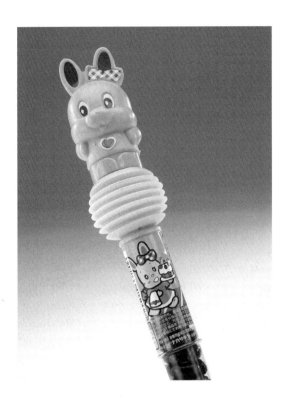

inviting children to explore the product through the senses of touch and sound before or alongside that of taste.

Let's start out by reviewing some theoretical aspects of sound, and then examine some of the cutting-edge applications of sound in branding.

Sounds Like Good Marketing

Generally, when consumers are exposed to products and their advertisements, they don't perceive a personal "need" for the product, nor do they intend to buy it. Because so many individuals are not actively seeking information about products, stimulating emotion and affect is a better way to distinguish a product and draw interest. Music is a particularly effective approach because it circumvents the rational mind and petitions directly to the emotional mind in which desire-driven shoppers revel.

Gerald Gorn demonstrates this in his study *The Effects of Music in Advertising on Choice Behavior*. By playing music while previewing products, Gorn found that subjects overwhelmingly (80 percent) chose products accompanied by the music they liked. Interestingly, subjects attributed their product preference to the qualities of the product (in this case, pen color) rather than the music. After documenting and observing this effect, Gorn concluded that "an audience may be largely comprised of uninvolved potential consumers rather than cognitively active problem-solvers. Reaching them through emotionally arousing background features [such as music] may make the difference between their choosing and not choosing a brand."[79] There are very real examples of the power of sound and music, such as a musical optic promotion created for Southern Comfort that increased sales by 112 percent![80]

The Canal Jeans Co. in Manhattan successfully puts this idea into practice. It has hired DJs to spin hip and trendy record mixes while customers shop. These DJs are elevated on the store floor, near the entrance, so that customers pass by them as they shop. This provides the edgy and exciting feeling of a club for the young shoppers. The in-store music at Abercrombie & Fitch also does this, although in a less theatrical manner. Abercrombie carefully selects music that appeals to its shoppers. Because its clientele is relatively particular in its tastes, Abercrombie & Fitch has the advantage of being able to tailor its music to their particular preferences. The sound is fast and lively, brimming with youthful energy. This is consistent with the personality of Abercrombie & Fitch's aggressive, attitude-laden brand. Hence, the music not only stimulates customers, but also enables them to identify with the store. This is continued on the Abercrombie & Fitch Web site, where these songs and many others are available as "A&F-Approved Tunes."

Particularly with Generation X and Generation Y shoppers, music is a device used for constructing an identity.

This brings us to a second valuable application of sound—identification. Particularly with Generation X and Generation Y shoppers, music is a device used for constructing an identity. By associating a brand with a particular genre of music, a firm can contribute to the distinction of its identity, which is vital for attracting consumers. A growing number of retailers such as Gap, Toys "R" Us, and Eddie Bauer are investing in customized music programs with AEI Music Network, a company that crafts music collections specifically tailored to a company's brand image from its library of over seven million songs. American Eagle Outfitters includes music reviews within the catalogs that it mails to customers, as well as profiles of select musicians. The selections range from rock to hip-hop, assuring that most visitors will find something suited to their own taste. Staples of hip youth culture, such as the Beastie Boys, are featured, as well as little-known emerging acts, thereby catering to shoppers' current pleasures but also providing means to develop new interests via the inside filter of their favorite brand. All music featured in the catalog is also available for purchase on the AE Web site. For those shoppers who discover a new favorite band in the catalog, the band, as well as its image and sound, is permanently associated with AE. Such thorough and personalized service enables AE to transcend remedial product-oriented marketing and reach into the much more sophisticated and satisfying realm of supplementing and enabling entire lifestyles for its clients.

The Discovery Channel has intelligently incorporated sound into its stores in such a way as to tailor an engaging and personalized encounter as well as enhance its own brand identity with consistency. For example, certain sections within the stores are demarcated not by partitions, but rather by amorphous sound zones. Customers drift from one section of the store to the next, and the product changes are accompanied by corresponding changes in sound and music. This makes the experience of wandering through the stores a fun adventure. Shoppers don't know what kind of sounds or music will surprise them next, which encourages them to explore the entire store as opposed to one area of interest. This exciting sound experience, as well as tons of interactive devices, also entertains the kids, keeping the little ones occupied while mom and dad shop and explore. Kids and adults have a better shopping experience. The Santa Monica store has an attraction for children that features representations of various animals that emit the corresponding sounds, as well as weight scales that indicate your weight on different planets in the solar system.

The media in the Discovery Channel stores is designed to be a function of the space; some areas have sound, some none, and some areas have sounds, music, and video all together, depending on what works best. All the music and sounds are available for sale, which adds to the pleasure of the trip, since a part of the fun can be brought home, and this will contribute to the recall of the store and overall brand experience at a later date.

The Museum of Modern Art (MoMA) in New York City is another innovator in the use of sound and technology for creating stimulating, personalized service. For a $4.50 rental fee, visitors to the museum can rent Acoustiguide, a digital player and headset that provides a personal tour of the museum. Works and genres throughout the museum are labeled by numbers that correspond to tracks on the Acoustiguide. Visitors can pick and choose among these tracks, tailoring their own, personal tour. With this technology, MoMA (and certain other museums) are providing service that price considerations previously precluded from being available to the masses.

In addition, MoMA has turned the Acoustiguide into an independent marketing device. In MoMA's exhibition *ModernStarts* (Fall 1999–Spring 2000), the Acoustiguide tour was set to music from the late nineteenth and early twentieth centuries, which it encompassed. Other tracks were freestanding, only there to embellish the viewing experience. And as the Acoustiguide informed listeners, the songs on the digital tour were sold as *ModernStarts*, a $14.98 CD compilation in the museum gift shop. In this way, MoMA has created in its digitally recorded tour individualized service, enjoyable atmosphere, *and* a vehicle for (subtly) advertising one of its product offerings. Incentive for attending the museum, learning about art history, and buying museum merchandise are cleverly wrapped up in one considerate, economical service.

Megastores should consider emulating the MoMA Acoustiguides with headsets of their own.

Megastores should consider emulating the MoMA Acoustiguides with headsets of their own. The potential of such devices is immense. Headsets could offer shoppers musically-oriented guided tours or simply be a way of relaxing and "tuning the world out" while they shop to the music of their choice.

The research on sound, as well as its applications in branding, is so extensive that to provide a comprehensive illustration of its potential uses is impossible. Research has shown us that music most definitely affects the speed of shopping, the amount of time spent in the store, the amount of time people will spend waiting for things, and the amount of money people will spend. But in terms of the type of music, it is necessary to experiment.

SOME SUGGESTIONS

In addition, I suggest incorporating aural considerations into the store design. Should the structure accommodate "sound zones," such as the Discovery Channel's stores? What about the product itself–if it makes sounds, can the customers hear those sounds inside the store? Any item that makes noises, from a blender to Tickle Me Elmo, needs to let customers hear those sounds in advance. Additionally, build a library of music around your clients' preferences. By selling that music in the store, you can keep track of customers' tastes and capitalize on the promotion provided by the in-store music. As with all branding, the methods and devices are only limited by one's creativity, and each firm must determine the applications that best suit its needs. Lastly, as with all branding, be creative! You must determine the applications that are most appropriate. In time, your brand will reap the benefits of this "sound advice."

Although it's difficult to distinguish instinctual perceptions from cultural ones, scientific research has confirmed the broad generalized responses that music can cause and the connections between particular sounds and music and certain emotional states. Scherer and Oshinsky (1977), for example, tested different sounds on subjects who reported the following connotations:

TEMPO	slow	sadness, boredom, disgust
	fast	activity, surprise, happiness, pleasantness, potency, fear, anger
PITCH LEVEL	low	boredom, pleasantness, sadness
	high	surprise, potency, anger, fear, activity
AMPLITUDE MODULATION	small	disgust, anger, fear, boredom
	large	happiness, pleasantness, activity, surprise

SOURCE: *Sound, Music, and Emotions: An Introduction to Experimental Research* by David Huron, featured in Meryl Paula Gardner, "Mood States and Consumer Behavior: A Critical Review," *Journal of Consumer Research*, 12 (December 1985).

In another study by Fried and Berkowitz (1979), subjects reported the following states associated with these particular songs:

SONG	CONDITION REPORTED BY SUBJECTS
Mendelssohn's "Song without Words"	Peaceful feelings
Duke Ellington's "One O'clock Jump"	Joyful feelings
John Coltrane's "Meditations"	Irritated Feelings

Interestingly, subjects who heard Mendelssohn's "Song without Words" were more likely to be helpful immediately afterwards than those who heard the other songs or no music at all.

SOURCE: Meryl Paula Gardner, "Mood States and Consumer Behavior: A Critical Review," *Journal of Consumer Research*, 12 (December 1985).

6

Colors that Mesmerize/ Symbols that Captivate

From the age of ten on, sight is the predominant sense for humans' exploration and understanding of the world. Personally, as a designer, I have always held the sense of vision in great esteem. It is incorporated into everything I create. This is why I am often amazed by the optical neglect to which certain brands are subjected. (I suppose this is why I decided to enter design–I am on a sort of evangelistic brand "rescue mission"!) I would like to show such brands the alternative to dull and mundane design–*vision.*

Visionary Branding

Consider the following: red, white, and blue. Golden Arches. A red can of cola. Your favorite sports team. In each instance, the associations of color enable identification and prompt particular images and emotions. Every Emotional Branding strategy must consider the effect colors (or their absence) will have on the brand. When making such considerations, I suggest a need for something more than beauty, continuity, and vividness as components of brand experience. Color, among other elements, is a crucial vehicle of this experience.

COLOR THEORY

As I just implied, color branding is *not* about being pretty or aesthetic. Color *is* about conveying crucial information to your consumers (which may, in turn, relate to being pretty or aesthetically pleasing). Colors trigger very specific responses in the central nervous system and the cerebral cortex. Once they affect the cerebral cortex, colors can activate thoughts, memories, and particular modes of perception. This arousal prompts an increase in consumers' ability to process information. Properly chosen colors define your brand logo, products, window displays, and so on, and encourage better recall of your brand, as well as a more accurate understanding of what your brand represents. Poor color selection will confuse your message, confuse your customers, and, in extreme situations, contribute to the failure of a brand. The most effective color-branding strategies will come from designers who are able to make use of the color palette and its meanings for consumers.

The effect of colors arises both from acculturation and physiology, and these influences are enforced by one another. For example, colors with long wavelengths are arousing (e.g., red is the most stimulating color that will attract the eye faster than any other) and colors with short wavelengths are soothing (e.g., blue, which actually lowers blood pressure, pulse, and respiration rates). This physiological quality of color lends itself to the development of cultural associations that reenforce this effect. Consider, for example, red lipstick. Although it draws on lips' natural color as well as the evocative qualities of red as a color, the social meanings of "lipstick" (sex and seduction) have acculturated us to consider red even more provocative. Similar determinants operate in other colors: yellow is in the middle of wavelengths detectable by the human eye–it is therefore the brightest and easily attracts attention. Hence, yellow is in objects that demand attention, such as road-safety signs and police scene-markers. This creates associations of caution around yellow that train us to pay even more attention to its presence. This is also the original reason for making the Yellow Pages yellow: to heighten the attention level of bored or sleepy telephone operators. However, the entire array of color associations is much more complex, and the subtle variations are endless. A few other color generalizations: true orange is friendly, pastel tints are gentle, yellow orange is welcoming, pale blue connotes calm, navy blue symbolizes dependability. Gray is generally perceived as a professional color, and often implies qualities of seriousness and anonymity. For this reason it is very popular in offices and with office supplies and hardware, although I personally do not think those qualities should always dominate in the workplace. Why not be daring and spice up offices with the energy of a bright red-violet to energize employees, or ease stress with refreshing aqua that has connotations of the ocean and relaxation for many.[81] No one can fully explain why colors affect us in these ways, but awareness of this effect enables designers to convey information and, more importantly, moods. A friend of mine told me a very interesting story about her experience working at one of the most prestigious art galleries in the world, a place that had been selling Old Master and Impressionist paintings worth millions of dollars for centuries. She was fascinated by what was called the "red room," a room that was literally red everywhere—carpet, walls, velvet curtains, even the ceiling—and once asked the owner why the paintings were always shown to potential buyers specifically in this room. His answer was that it was because red caused people to become emotional and that he needed to create this kind of intense emotion to make a sale!

Creative use of color can also be quite unobtrusive, and yet remain just as effective. I recently went to a private screening of a French movie (at the MoMA in New York) called *Hometown Blues* (or *Le Bleu des Villes* in French) by Stéphane Brizé, and in the question-and-answer session that followed the screening someone asked him why in a particular scene he chose to film the heroine next to a red teapot. He surprisingly answered that if you watch his film carefully you will notice that every time the main character is happy in a scene, she is either wearing red or the color appears nearby as a part of the set, and otherwise, there is an abundance of blue throughout the movie's sets, the color of her uniform for her mundane and stifling job as a traffic cop. This is a brilliant artistic use of color!

COLOR AND BRAND IDENTITY

Color often sets the mood of a brand through logos and packaging. Generally, it is desirable to select a color that is easily associated with your product: John Deere uses green for its tractors. Green implies nature. IBM has a solid blue that communicates stability and reliability. The short wavelengths of its blue have a reassuring impact upon the mind. However, as Al and Laura Ries note in *The 22 Immutable Laws of Branding*,[82] "it's more important to create a separate brand identity than it is to use the right symbolic color. Hertz, the first car-rental brand, picked yellow. So Avis, the second brand, picked red. National went with green." The salmon color of the paper on which the *New York Observer* and the *London Financial Times* newspapers are printed is unmistakable and is a successful use of color branding in that it visually sets these newspapers apart from all the others, indicating perhaps that they offer a decidedly different perspective. FedEx chose the colors orange and purple for their logo, two of the colors in the spectrum that clash the most, precisely in order to grab the visual attention of consumers, hoping that the packages would be immediately noticed by everyone in an office every time a FedEx delivery arrived. The role color choice can play in brand identity is not to be underestimated.

PRODUCT COLORATION

Henry Ford invented modern manufacturing. His brilliant implementation of mass production created quality products at pricing and in quantities that made them available to all. The secret to his success: standardization. When asked what colors the autos would be produced in, Ford quipped, "You can have *my* car in any color you want–as long as it's black." This epitomizes the manufacturing mentality: brilliant in its time, but certainly very limiting in terms of a consumer-driven model.

People, not machines, determine what will be produced and how. The secret to success: customization and individuality. Today modern manufacturing precepts have, of course, given way to postmodern consumer realities. People, not machines, determine what will be produced and how. The secret to success: customization and individuality. However, many would-be brands implicitly sustain the Henry Ford mentality when it is actually design-conscious thinkers like Andre Leon Talley, the current editor-at-large for *Vogue*, whom they should be listening to. Talley says, "There's a demand for color across the board. These are good times and people want to feel good. I'd like to see public transportation in hot colors. Trains, buses, subways in Peter Max colors: pink, yellow, aqua, chartreuse, and peach. Children ride to school on yellow buses, why can't adults?"[85]

Pink subways? Aqua buses? These seemingly outlandish suggestions are the types of considerations occupying the minds of the best designers because *bored consumers need bold options*. Colors can demand attention and incite responses. An orange, translucent, curvaceous iMac screams "fun" and "different." Contrast that with your typical gray, rectangular desktop that communicates a "utilitarian" and "standard" (boring) identity. Neither computer is necessarily functionally superior, but the iMac is distinguished–the iMac is a brand (which does, however, make the iMac FUNctionally superior). This is a major reason why Apple's unit growth for the last quarter of 1999 was 2.5 times the industry average.

Why did it take nearly twenty years for a personal computer to make this relatively simple innovation? The less important reason: today's euphoric economic situation in the U.S. influences a consumer market particularly accommodating to color and fun. The more important reason: the prevalence of uninspired assumptions about what a computer is and how a computer looks.

It took Apple, an underdog with the need for a big success and the *willingness to be daring*, to reveal what a computer can be–fun.

Actually, I don't think all dull coloration can wholly be attributed to unimaginative producers. In fairness, retailers must share a portion of the blame. According to Nada Rutka, the president of the color-consulting firm Nada Associates, "Many manufacturers who sell primarily to the Big Box retailers may have a colorfully diverse product line but are limited to what the store buyers will put on their shelves, which is really very basic, mass market." Consequently, manufacturers who rely on these mass retailers for their sales must conform to certain color choices and the consumer has no say. In the words of Nada, "With the significant amount of business that is done via these majors, we find the retail buyers are the arbiters of America's color taste, not the consumer." Retailers cannot continue to pursue this narrow direction–today's consumers want dynamic colors and excitement, and the Internet provides means for them to get it if their local stores refuse. Moreover, there's no reason for the terms "retail" and "diminished choice" to be linked, and in the Emotional Economy they are a fatal pairing.

COLOR AND DEMOGRAPHICS

Selecting colors is complex, and the interpretation of color independently of its product or without the guidance of a color designer is ill-advised. Pat Brillo, a consultant for Color Services & Associates in Huntley, Illinois, stresses that "Selecting the right color is about audience. Who's your audience? What's the message? Just picking a trendy color is not the answer. Different consumers are affected different ways by that color, and trends are constantly changing."[84] Well-intended coloring can easily have unintended consequences. For example, Americans, especially younger Americans, associate green

To choose colors without the consultation of a professional designer is like hiking the Andes without a guide.

with environmentalism: in fact, according to Cooper Marketing Group in Illinois, people aged eighteen to thirty-four are especially likely to link green to images of health, ecology, and nature. So, adding some green to your environmentally sound product for this demographic may increase sales. However, in Egypt, green is the national color, and its use on throwaway packaging could be very offensive. Similarly, white represents purity in the United States, but as we saw in chapter 2, in certain Asian countries it is the color of mourning. Just as there are national trends in color perception, there are color perceptions associated with age, social class, gender, and religion. To choose colors without the consultation of a professional designer is like hiking the Andes without a guide. Maybe you'll get lucky, but don't stake anything too important on it.

VISUAL IDEAS FOR INTERIOR BRANDING

The Johnnie Walker in-store clothing shop relies on nonverbal visual elements to convey the elements of the brand identity appealing to the sophisticated world traveler. For example, a backlit screen displays seasonal travel destinations and a series of clocks read different times around the world. Such nonverbal symbols carry multiple advantages. Particularly in the instance of photographs, images allow fantasy to carry customers away in a wave of pleasant associations mixing the brand identity and the lifestyle which they, as individuals, aspire toward. Furthermore, although words can often work wonders, pictures can cut to the chase with an immediacy yet breadth often more useful than words. Finally, large images can remain alluring even from a significant distance, whereas words are confined by the need to be legible. It is vital that store displays work from all directions and distances.

Lighting is also a crucial element of designing interiors. Generally, products simply look better with attractive lighting. Furthermore, with the mere change of a bulb and flip of a switch, lighting can transform any interior. When Victoria's Secret held a fashion show at the Plaza Hotel in New York City, the entire exterior of the building was illuminated—in pink. The sight for passersby was unforgettable. Although it's not often considered fully and creatively, lighting is a potentially inexpensive means of transforming any space, and an easy way for a store's color scheme to evolve from season to season and one product line to the next. However, lighting shouldn't and needn't be limited to mundane single colors or static displays. Recently, I attended a party that had a small disc with patterns cut into it rotate over the lighting fixture, causing moving shapes to project upon the wall. The Appliance Design Studio, a part of the Royal College of Art, has conceived of a light called "DataLamp" that uses computer technology to project ambient, floating imagery with multiple colors onto the walls. Particularly when combined with the appropriate music, these methods can create a positively magical and mystical atmosphere that can easily be installed and manipulated at a moment's notice to create different effects.

This chapter can only provide the most cursory sketch of the interesting properties of color and vision, illustrating certain applications that will, hopefully, act

as stepping-stones toward creative and imaginative new uses. A professional guide is certainly eventually important, but first of all, the most important thing is that companies themselves begin to think about and see with new eyes the visual aspects of the brand. The best starting place for a new perspective on the possibilities of color is to get a copy of the *Color Harmony Workbook: A Workbook and Guide to Creative Color Combinations*.[85] This book is easy to use and beautiful, laid out in a series of highly descriptive color categories, such as powerful, fresh, friendly, vital, magical, and so on with a color wheel, themed color schemes, and tear-out swatches of color that encourage experimentation and allow for 1,400 color combinations.

Entering into the wonderful world of visual identity is also sometimes only a question of attention. Just a little bit of increased consciousness can, I promise you, dramatically inspire anyone's sensibility. Whether in New York City, the Sahara desert, or the Louisiana bayou, stunning visuals confront us every day, and we can become numbed to them in the course of our daily exposures. Where does a shadow fall? What patterns characterize a particular tree's bark? In how many shapes do windows come? Simple observations of this type feed into great branding, believe it or not. These observations and awareness are vital and worthwhile–they provide a new sense of the world. Every time we walk out the door, there is a myriad of opportunities to discover and rediscover the subtlety and detail that characterize every day of our lives.

7

Tastes that Tantalize

One of my colleagues recently related to me the story of his psychology teacher's eccentric test-taking methodology. Before each exam, candy would always be distributed to all the students in the class. Why? Well, the teacher, well-versed in the theories of I. P. Pavlov and B. F. Skinner, intended to reduce the stress of test-taking by attaching this positive stimulus to each exam. Hopefully, instead of associating exams with stress and worry, students would begin to associate the exams with tasty treats. More importantly, speculated my colleague, the candy illustrated the genial and kind nature of the teacher, which transcended psychological theory and instead relied on friendliness. Students appreciated the mere effort and thoughtfulness of their teacher.

How Customers Are Starved for Affection

Proffering food indicates kinship, makes us feel at ease, and even provides pleasure. If guests in our homes receive this basic courtesy, why do so few customers? Shoppers are looking for a place to escape from the demands of work and the responsibilities of home, a place where they can relax and interact pleasurably. In-store cafés and restaurants allow patrons to feel relaxed and enjoy tasty pleasures while accomplishing a few small errands. However, even a cup of coffee, a glass of wine, or some candies can make a difference. For many shoppers, these services are far more valuable than the price tag that accompanies them, both for their tangible benefit and for the symbolic value of the gesture. Furthermore, there is no cyber-substitute for relaxing with friends and having a bite to eat after a good shopping excursion. Despite all of these positives, although some businesses have caught on to the branding value of food, most have left their customers starved for affection.

Barnes & Noble is one of the first national retailers to exhibit true culinary savvy. Rather than throwing a hot-dog stand in the store corner (which more than a few retailers have done), Barnes & Noble assessed the meaning of its brand—the meaning of books. Some literature aficionado (I suspect) recognized the long-standing affinity between literature and coffee shops. Capitalizing on this association, as well as on the desire to sit down and enjoy a cup of joe and a pastry while leafing through a *New York Times* bestseller, the cafés have become inviting and profitable components of the Barnes & Noble brand experience.

Nordstrom, whose hallmark has always been high-quality customer service, also realizes that customers want and deserve food. Nordstrom has four different restaurant concepts, and at least one is present in most of its stores. The Espresso Bar, which is usually located outside Nordstrom entrances, offers a selection of gourmet coffees, Italian sodas, and pastries to customers and passersby. Café Nordstrom proffers a selection of salads, sandwiches, soups, pastries, and beverages in a cafeteria-style eatery. The Pub is an English-style bar serving breakfast in the morning, as well as food, stouts, ales, and cocktails the rest of the day, while broadcasting televised sporting events. Barbara Erikson, former vice president of store design, explains that "When customers are spending the amount of time they do in our stores, you need a place for them to sit down and relax, have a meal, have some coffee."[86] For a long time coffee was provided for only twenty-five cents a cup because, as cochairman Jim Nordstrom said in 1992, he doesn't like restaurants "that charge a dollar for a cup of coffee when it cost only a few cents."[87] (Unfortunately—and unwisely, in my opinion—this has since changed, and now coffee is regular price.) Lastly, and I think most impressively, if there is a wait to be seated in a Nordstrom restaurant, customers are given a beeper. They can continue shopping, and when their table is ready, the beeper alerts them. This consideration for customers coupled with acute business intelligence accounts for Nordstrom's tremendous reputation for service over the years.

"When customers are spending the amount of time they do in our stores, you need a place for them to sit down and relax, have a meal, have some coffee."

Then there is the mecca of sensual marketing: Central Market, probably one of the most innovative and exciting supermarkets in the United States. Its vice president John Campbell says that at Central Market, despite its enormous size and huge array of products, "It's about the shopping experience, not about selection.

We want people to feel uplifted when they walk out of here."[88] One of the most popular tourist attractions in Austin, Texas, Central Market demonstrates that vivid sensual experiences make for great success. Central Market has hired a team of "foodies," comprised largely of ex-chefs, nutritionists, and so on, who wander throughout the store, talking to customers about cooking and eating. Besides engaging customers on a relevant and pertinent subject, the foodies help shoppers plan meals and special events, often developing personal relationships with certain customers who regularly turn to them for advice. The foodies are also authorized to open any package in the whole store, and they constantly do so in order for customers to be able to explore new products and product combinations and to taste the foods before buying them. Delectable delights are available for the kids, too. Inside the store's entrance is the children's fruit counter where girls and boys can pick the piece of fruit they want for twenty-five cents. On the weekends, Central Market hosts children's birthday parties at which children bake their own pizzas and participate in printmaking using cut-up vegetables. Central Market provides classes on cooking and shopping and hosts cultural events, such as concerts, in the lovely parklike landscape outside the store. This area also attracts locals who picnic and socialize out front after buying their goods inside Central Market. Seeing the Central Market phenomenon, Ron Lieber of *Fast Company* was compelled to write: "Central Market lives in the experience economy–a place where stores offer experiences so vivid that retailers could probably charge admission for them."[89]

Most stores (even food stores!) are still neglecting food, however. Although Kmart, Costco, and other national chains are increasingly providing in-store restaurants, more often than not they appear to be a mere afterthought–a sort of watered-down version of fast food that merely enables longer bouts of shopping rather than the pleasurable and slightly indulgent experience of dining and discovering. Shopping should be an event, and brands–well, brands should be a celebration. And what celebration would be complete without food? Some opportunities that I think are being neglected:

- Having just noted Central Market, here are some other ideas for supermar-kets: supermarkets have become far too sterile. Cellophane and Styrofoam are pleasant assurances of any food's freshness, but it is still vital to make shoppers realize that they are in a food market. A symphony of smells should fill the air, and a sundry supply of samples should always be at the shopper's disposal. This is particularly true for those expensive specialty goods that consumers often need to discover firsthand before incorporating them into their regular shopping repertoire.

- Stores that specialize in home goods, particularly culinary implements (such as Kitchen, etc.) could have in-store chefs demonstrating how to cook gourmet foods (Orlots, for example, has implemented such a program). After watching the demonstration, shoppers could sample the food, speak with the chef, receive recipes, and purchase the corresponding kitchenware and cookbooks. Perhaps shoppers could even try cooking meals themselves with the kitchenware and the aid of an in-store chef. Not only would this increase sales of the kitchenware, it would help build a communal and personal environment, which is essential to branding.

- Although commonly overlooked, I think men enjoy shopping together if the right occasion presents itself. Hardware stores, particularly of the Home Depot variety, should hold pre– and post–Fourth of July barbecues. Painters, carpenters, and other professionals could provide instruction on home improvement similar to the popular TV program *This Old House*–only with hot burgers and cold beers, as well as the necessary building supplies available and on sale!

- No customers like idly waiting on lines. Certain establishments have begun providing finger foods to their waiting customers. When a wait threatens to stretch past three or four minutes, why not bring out chips and salsa? I think most customers would be so pleasantly surprised by the gesture they'd all but forget about the line wait.

These are just a few ideas among millions of others. Even simple, relatively inexpensive gestures like complimentary coffee, soda, or a glass of wine will make a big difference and may be the final factor in drawing certain passersby inside, as well as in sustaining tired shoppers who may want to continue shopping but need a moment of refreshment first.

In Santa Fe, some of the many wonderful galleries that line up one after another on Canyon Road serve sherry, coffee, or hot mulled wine in the winter months and cool drinks in the summer. This is a very inviting reason to visit one (as opposed to another!) of these galleries and could certainly help put people in the mood to buy a beautiful work of art. It is also certain to become part of the associative memory of the pleasurable time spent there.

Perle de Lait
Rallonge Le Plaisir
Et Fait Pétiller Le Regard.

Perle de Lait

Une femme qui se fait plaisir est toujours belle.

Through well-done ad campaigns, even products not necessarily related to taste can evoke a delicious sensory association all the same!

It's a known fact that if men are able to sit in a store, the women they are with will shop longer (and, of course, it's also a known fact that the longer consumers spend in a store, the more they buy).[90] How much more time and money would a woman spend in a store if her "shopped-out" husband was not only able to sit in a comfy chair, but if he was also given a cold drink? Besides, if nothing else, it's basic courtesy. The Australian fashion brand Country Road is one of the few retailers to extend this courtesy gratis. When customers walk into their New York store, they are offered a cold glass of water or coffee that is also prominently displayed on a self-service table near two inviting armchairs.

> "Food is a form of social exchange, and is imbued with special meanings in many cultures."

Each Thursday afternoon through the evening, the customers are also offered a choice of red or white wine (Australian, of course!). When asked if there is an issue of spillage on the clothing or in the store, the charming saleswoman told me, "Oh no! We are very attentive to our customers and are always aware if they need assistance to find a place to set their drink down or someone to hold it for them while they handle a garment."

It seems that Country Road has carefully thought through the important details of the execution of this gesture of serving drinks and, most importantly, decided to ensure that its salespeople see that it is smoothly managed as a potential basis for social interaction between the customers and themselves. Psychologist Paul Rozin writes that "For humans, where the search and preparation of food and its ingestion at meals are social occasions, food is a very social entity. Ingestion of food means taking something of the world into the body, and that something typically has a social history: it was procured, prepared, and presented by other humans. Food is a form of social exchange and is imbued with special meanings in many cultures."[91] Brands that recognize this and respond accordingly will never leave customers with a bad taste in their mouths.

8

Shapes that Touch

In my research for this book, I encountered a puzzling problem: there is a remarkable absence of literature exploring consumers' tactile sense. Why is this? It is the most essential of the five senses, and also the most immediate–consider the impact of a lover's gentle touch. How about the differences between linen, cotton, and silk? While most of the senses inform us of the world, it is most often touch that enables us to ultimately possess the world, to wrap our consciousness around it. Perhaps it is because the sense of touch is so integral that it is so frequently neglected in marketing.

I suspect that modern and particularly Western society has also suppressed our awareness and attention to touch. Public objects are usually considered dirty and bad to touch. But when we encounter one of those little signs saying "Please do not touch," what do we want to do? We want to touch it! Holding, feeling, caressing–these are all basic and pleasant ways of exploring and experiencing in the world. Additionally, studies have found that as brand recognition declines, customers are more likely to touch a product in the process of evaluating it. Presumably, this is because shoppers compensate for an absence of information by using their senses to gain more knowledge. Touch, whether it's the product itself, the store fixture, the room temperature, or even the floors or the front door's handle, is a dimension of brand experience. Particularly in this tactile-deprived world, which is becoming even further limited by the advent of the Internet, I think businesses that cater to touch will be rewarded by their customers.

> **When we encounter one of those little signs saying "Please do not touch," what do we want to do? We want to touch!**

Tactile Tactics: Branding that Feels Good

Although the proliferation of shrink-wrap, cardboard, and paper wrapping has made leaps and bounds in protecting merchandise, it has robbed us of the opportunity to touch and discover too many products. Within the limits of reason, just about everything in a store needs to be accessible to touch. We want to feel our clothing, pens, strollers, fiber paper, leather briefcases, shovels, towels, lotions before we buy. This is not just for the most practical, obvious reasons, such as to test the shade of a lipstick, but for deeper, more primal reasons that have to do with the sheer pleasure of holding and playing with something and imagining it belonging to us before we take (or buy) it. If a woman is going to wear a lipstick, she wants to know the texture of the product: how it will feel against her skin, as well as how the actual tube will feel in her hand and how the top will feel to open and close! If there is secondary packaging, it should be designed so that we can touch the product. If an object absolutely needs to be wrapped, an example of the object should be on display. Sephora has built their retail success story on the touch, try, and play principle for cosmetics. Their stores are a fabulous example of what can happen when you give people the power to explore beauty products for themselves. Sherry Baker, Sephora's former head of marketing for the United States and Asia, says of their "free to roam, free to try" policy, "Frankly, we get longer shopping time when people are left alone."[92]

I hate going to stores and finding that everything has been torn open because people wanted to see what the object felt like and someone wrapped it in plastic. Nobody wants to buy something that's been torn into and strewn all about. Consequently, packaging as well as unsold product both go to waste. If the product is unpleasant to touch, then something is wrong with the design. Even a cactus can have a lovely flower that is smooth to the hands no matter how prickly the plant itself is. Unfortunately, many brands don't even consider touch.

However, some businesses do undertake inspiring designs with the express aim of making their brands pleasant to touch. We designed the Victoria's Secret Dream Angels line in smooth, arching, curvaceous shapes, specifically to be pleasant to touch and be held in the hand in a way that would convey the sensuousness of the brand identity.

Glass Coca-Cola bottles are another brilliant example of appealing to the tactile senses through a curvaceous bottle that is a pleasure to touch and hold. Obviously, the soda is not better when touched, unless it is being swallowed.

But through the original design of the Coca-Cola bottle, Coke translates the identity of the brand to handheld touch. So well designed is the Coke bottle that it embellishes the identity of the whole brand–touch, vision, and taste all come together beautifully.

Since touch is a way of quite literally taking possession of an object, stores can really provide customers with an exciting emotional connection to products through an instant gratification of the desire to touch. Have you ever bought a new pair of shoes and worn them out of the store? A wonderful feeling, isn't it? As a child, I remember putting those new shoes on my feet–they felt so comfortable, they looked so good, I simply couldn't wait to put them on. Give your customers that tactile pleasure! Encourage it! That's what they're paying for.

A store is a product playground! Objects and interiors should be designed and laid out to be experienced, felt, and unfolded.

A store is a product playground! Objects and interiors should be designed and laid out to be experienced, felt, and unfolded. Remember the scene in *Big* when Tom Hanks and his boss play "Chopsticks" on the piano in FAO Schwarz? Well, go to FAO Schwarz any day of the week, and I promise you'll see that scene reenacted over and over all day long by a stream of customers. Is it because people love Tom Hanks? Well, yes, partly. *But* the rest of the reason is that it's fun and involving. The store becomes a playground meant to be touched, hit, and jumped on. That is vivid, and vivid is good. Additionally, anytime a product combines two senses in a dynamic way (in this case, touch and sound), it becomes twice as pleasurable.

Although some brand managers have considered touch solely a matter of the hands, sometimes it's a matter of, well, the sole. Our shoes more directly come into contact with the store than any other part of the body and, as a result, so do our feet. Some stores need to put more thought into their floors and what they say about the store. Crappy tile floors are bad. True, they're easy to clean, but somehow those floors always look the dirtiest, anyway. However, that doesn't mean lush carpeting is the answer, either. The Kitchens Etc. near my home has large ceramic tiles on its floors, just like a kitchen. *That* is brand identity. Other stores could do this. For example, why not have a gym floor at Sports Authority? Maybe even a small gym court for people to try out basketballs and try on sneakers, as the Nike store offers in its Chicago location? Maybe green turf could be laid throughout the golf section. These are the types of questions retail designers should ask themselves.

But sometimes integrating a tactile sensory experience into a retail environment or product design can be incredibly simple (and inexpensive). Take Banana Republic's 1998 Stretch campaign, for example. To emphasize the elasticity of the fabrics used in their new clothing collection, Banana Republic placed large bowls of rubber bands in their stores for customers to take and play with–a fun, sensory, inspired way for them to get their message across!

Ergonomics: Designing Products and Retail Environments for the Human Race (Not the Rat Race)

We are moving into a world where people matter more than technology, and ergonomics has taken on an increasingly important role as a solutions methodology that connects emotionally to consumers. It not only says that we care, but *proves* that a brand is listening (after all, actions speak louder than words!). Designing products and retail spaces for humanity is beginning to come to the forefront of many companies' visions, but many important strides have not yet been made. How many products are too high or too low on shelves for an average person to access? Paco Underhill's retail research firm, Environsell, which has amassed fascinating data on retail behavior that can be found in his wonderful book *Why We Buy*,[93] has observed, among many other "ergonomically incorrect" retailing moves, that very often drugstores stock cosmetics that older women are most likely to use, such as concealer cream, at the very bottom of a wall display, forcing the customer who least appreciates it to bend down to reach the product![94] Think about that, then consider handicapped persons who every day must face retail environments that do not cater to their needs. With an increasingly aging population, how important is it to use large enough copy on products to make information readable for that market segment? Have you ever tried to drive a car with so many blind spots that it is almost unsafe? Have you noticed older people in the cars where you can barely see their heads behind that big steering wheel? This uncomfortable situation occurs because very few cars have an "up/down" function for the seats in addition to the "forward/backward." Contrast that with lawn-mower manufacturers who have realized that the natural way for people to push is with vertical handles, not the traditional horizontal ones, since it is more efficient and better uses our body strength.

Because of my background as a designer and my personal interest in the way people experience their shopping environment, I spend hours watching people shop and have observed the difficulty they sometimes have in their buying rituals. One very obvious problem is that shopping carts are either too small or too large. Carts are difficult to maneuver in tight or crowded aisles, and baskets quickly become too heavy for everyone, but especially for older customers. Shouldn't we invent a modular shopping cart, upright on wheels, to which you can add the size of basket you need for that particular day? I think this is just the kind of thing that would make shopping more comfortable and would increase the amount of products people bought. In the same vein, shouldn't we have modular shelves that could be lowered or raised for convenience when a product is too low or high on the shelf? Sometimes I wonder what size of hand the manufacturers use as a standard to define packaging and bottle proportions. I look for the shelves surrounded by products that have been dropped on the floor—and for the ones that look messy. The problem is always caused by product, retail, or packaging design that does not take ergonomics into account. This makes customers uncomfortable and unhappy, and sometimes even embarrassed. It gives them one more reason to shop on the Internet, instead.

Sometimes I wonder what size of hand the manufacturers use as a standard to define packaging and bottle proportions.

Sometimes intelligent ergonomic design is a cultural issue. Because ergonomics requires an understanding of how products can be easier to use, it requires a knowledge of how products *are* used, which varies from one culture to the next. For example, many European companies have discovered that in order to succeed in the American market, you need to think big. The president of IKEA said that until they realized that Americans put lots of ice in their glasses and therefore need bigger containers, they had a hard time selling their smaller European glasses. They also realized that Americans sleep in bigger beds, need larger bookshelves, and like to curl up on their sofas rather than sit on them! These are certainly sufficient differences that made their now-booming U.S. business difficult at the start. In today's global economy, companies must take into consideration these sorts of cultural considerations.

Which cuts to the heart of tactilely minded design—how does an individual use and experience any product? What constitutes added value and an enhanced experience for that individual? The question for designers should not be how do we make this product work? That's a given—the only question is how do we make this product worth working with? More often than not, intelligent tactile design can contribute significantly to answering this question and subsequently become a constituent of brand personality. For a great inspirational source regarding ergonomics—products and information—see *www.ergoweb.com*.

9

Scents that Seduce

We have all known individuals who could be identified by a particular smell—
hopefully a good cologne or perfume—or felt our emotions stirred by the faint
smell on an article of clothing left behind by a loved one (the individuality of
which was probably determined, in part, by a particular brand of detergent).
But have you ever thought about the smell of Scotch tape? A new car? Or even
the Galleria Malls? Each smell is unlike anything else and provides clues about
subtle ways odor can be used to manage brand identity.

Better Branding Is Right Under Your Nose

Smell is arguably the strongest of the senses, yet scent is an oft-neglected tool
for providing consumers with engaging and emotional experiences. A whole
array of studies reveal that odor has the potential to evoke our emotions with
more potency than any of the other senses.[95] This is probably because there are
more connections between the olfactory region of the brain to the amygdala-
hippocampal complex (where emotional memories are processed) than any
of the other senses have. Scent is not filtered out by the brain; it is instinctive
and involuntary. Hence, your customer's nose is actually a direct link to their
memories and emotions awaiting your stimulation. *Where do you want your
customers to be?* A romantic bedroom? A zoological garden? Or, perhaps, mom's
kitchen? Regardless of the location, the richer the environmental stimuli, the
better, and scent should be a vital part of your branding plan.

In a fascinating study by Susan Fournier exploring the relationships consumers
develop with their brands,[96] it is shown that scents are used by some consumers
to manage their own identity and, in turn, identify with particular brands. Viki,
one subject of the study, says that "I am very, I wanna say, wholesome, pure,

whatever, but I mean, to me, that's what's important. My hair, my scents, my clothes. Everything is very feminine and wholesome." Viki has been compelled to buy many products based on their smell and its appeal to her sense of identity, and clearly connects scent to the construction of her identity, saying to the researcher, "Like, right now I can tell you used Aveda Elixir [shampoo]. I can smell the tree bark. I smell Aveda a mile away. Trying to be all earthy and responsible, are you?" Is Viki alone in her penchant for scents?

"Everybody tells you they hate scented products. They lie." This, according to Gail Vance Civille from Sensory Spectrum in Chatham, New Jersey. Her firm manages and designs product stimuli which appeal to the five senses. According to Civille, "people love scented products and will choose them over other products. People will give scented products other positive attributes based solely on their smell. You can give someone two identical paper towels, the only difference being one is scented, and he or she will tell you the scented one is softer."[97] In recent years, businesses have become increasingly adept at deriving these benefits.

With the rise of aromatherapy (the use of smells to heal and relieve stress and illness and evoke spiritual well-being), many products incorporating scent have taken off. Robert B. Goergen, president of Blyth Industries, a company that owns Colonial Candle and is one of the largest candle manufacturers in the United States, said to me that "The rapid expansion of the candle business has been based on the possibility of creating scented candles." The expansion of scented products today is indeed incredible. In recent years, sales for aromatherapy products have increased approximately 30 percent annually, and scented candles have posted 10–15 percent yearly growth since the early '90s.[98] Scented clothing, hosiery, and even tires are sold in Japan, and the British company Contour Mobel has sold "aroma" sofas that emit rose, lavender, and vanilla scents when their cushions are plumped. A spokesman for the company selling the sofas, which start at $3,300, said that "the potential for scented products is enormous. Scents are very evocative and appeal to our emotions, and we think there is definitely a market out there."[99] David Easton, a New York interior designer, has an interesting point of view about why we are so enamored of scented products today. He says that "Artificial environments have developed our primal cravings for the natural,"[100] going on to point out the sealed windows in offices, hotels, and fully air-conditioned houses, saying that these aromas of nature can summon up worlds we've fallen out of touch with.

Scent need not be limited to the product itself and should be considered the way other, more typical dimensions of product presentation are. Well-planned smells encourage sales, just like excellent color and lighting design. Susan C. Knasko, senior research associate at the Monell Chemical Senses Center, found through research that "customers stayed longer in two sections of a store when the areas were scented with pleasant scents, compared to when the areas were not scented."[101] Recognizing this, many companies have designed fragrances specifically for their stores.

Robert A. Baron of Rensselaer Polytechnic Institute elaborates on the effects of odor, writing that "pleasant fragrances in the air influence human behavior by enhancing individuals' current moods. In other words, as informal experience would suggest, pleasant fragrances are one aspect of the physical environment that can make people feel somewhat happier—just as pleasant temperatures, attractive lighting, and the absence of distracting noise can produce similar effects."[102] In this same study, he finds that shoppers exposed to pleasant odors such as perfume, coffee, and cookies are not only in better moods, they also are more likely to engage in amiable and even altruistic behavior!

Well-planned smells encourage sales, just like excellent color and lighting design.

Fragrances may be one of the oldest marketing techniques around. Since ancient times, open-air vendors have used burning incense to lure passing traffic over to their wares. Today many commercial spaces have jumped on the scent bandwagon, experimenting with the possibilities for branded scent, such as the London-based shirtmaker, Thomas Pink, that scents its stores with the smell of "line-dried linen," the Rainforest Café that pumps fresh-flower extracts into its retail sections, and Jordan's Furniture stores in Massachusetts that uses scents such as bubble gum in the children's section and the smell of pine in the country-style section. Jan Hedrick, design director at Jordan's, says that sales have increased substantially since scent was brought into their marketing plan five years ago. Also, there are now systems available that can restrict a smell to within eighteen inches of the point of sale![103]

Alan R. Hirsch, neurologist, psychiatrist, and founder of the Smell & Taste Treatment and Research Foundation, Ltd., in Chicago, is a specialist in developing scents for commercial use. Hirsch says that "If you're looking to increase sales, the best approach is an appeal based on the emotions, and the quickest way to reach the emotions is through smells."[104] Hirsch also says that his clients have seen their profits jump as much as 40 percent after going through his "odorizing process" that has designed scents for everything from jeans to Galleria Malls.[105] Another great source for scents designed for commercial usage is the International Fragrance Foundation in New York that has designed scents for places like the American Museum of Natural History, where the smell of African grasslands was replicated, and specific smells to lend authenticity to amusement parks, such as the odor of a cave.

Gail Civille says, "I actually get upset over how often scents are chosen arbitrarily. Someone, usually the executive, will say 'I think our store smells like this,' and that's it." Good research, says Civille, should be used in choosing a brand fragrance. "Give your customers a product to taste, smell, feel, and then give them pictures, words, or logos. Ask them how much this scent goes with that image. Find the particular sensory stimulus that matches your brand."

The possible effects of well-designed scents should not be underestimated. In another study conducted by Knasko, it was found that among visitors exposed to various scents while visiting a museum exhibition, "A more positive mood was reported by visitors in the bubble-gum [odor] condition compared with those in the leather or no-odor condition. Visitors exposed to incense odor reported that they had learned more from the exhibit than visitors exposed to no odor. Visitors in the incense condition also reported that the odor of the room had a more positive influence on their enjoyment of the exhibit compared with visitors in the other odor conditions. Odor condition interacted in complex ways with a number of variables to influence lingering time." Other findings indicate that individuals born before 1930 more frequently associate natural odors, such as pine, with childhood, while younger individuals associate chemical smells, like Pez and Play-Doh, with their youth—an important fact for the designer targeting consumer's emotions because odors associated with youth possess the most emotive power.[106]

Just think—Web surfers could log on to the Starbucks Web site and immediately be enveloped by the smell of freshly brewed coffee.

Fragrance choices take into consideration not only age but also gender and cultural differences. For example, researchers at Duke have found that fragrances, regardless of whether they're liked or disliked, improve the mood, specifically of middle-aged women. Therefore, stores targeting that clientele certainly want to make a point of having smells distilled in the air. According to Hirsch, women have a better sense of smell than men, and Korean-Americans have the most acute sense of smell. Japanese have a relatively poor sense of smell, and American Caucasians and African-Americans tend to fall into the middle range. However, any brand that plans on using smell should *not* rely solely on this data to make choices. Rather, this complicated array of findings demonstrates the need for brands to experiment for themselves and develop an understanding of clients' specific tastes and qualities.

In the very near future, technology may improve the ability to tap into these emotionally laden smells with unprecedented precision and even across great distances. DigiScents, a company based in Oakland, California, is currently creating a digital language which accesses a scent cartridge to recreate smells. Each cartridge can instantly create about one hundred different scents, and DigiScents hopes this technology will find application in Web sites, movies, and video games, for starters. I think one great application would be on the Starbucks Web site. Just think—Web surfers could log on to the Starbucks Web site and immediately be enveloped by the smell of freshly brewed coffee. Consumers could then buy different coffees online and use the varying smells to aid their selection.

Organizations interested in sharpening their brand identity or simply improving their stores or showrooms should capitalize on the advantages provided by smells. Perhaps an in-store aroma system is the answer. Alternatively, fresh baked cookies might contribute to a gift shop's "homey" atmosphere while appealing to taste and smell simultaneously. The only limit is a creative one. Civille goes so far as to say, "What about refrigerators, televisions, furniture? Almost anything can be scented." In other words, scents make sense.

Soothe the Senses:
Some Peace, Please!

Having noted the importance of sensory appeal, it's also important not to overdo it. Think of it this way: what's more seductive? A whisper or a shout? Generally, a whisper. A whisper carries a soft and subtle message to another. A shout is jarring and attention-getting. Throughout this book, I speak about ways to get attention and surprise consumers pleasantly. However, in the Emotional Economy, sometimes the best way to get someone's attention is *not* to shout, but to whisper. In our wired age, it seems that many people believe strongly that everything should be action, motion, excitement, and saturation, while countless consumers want nothing more than a seductive oasis. It is a known fact, for example, that when we are bombarded by visual stimuli, the ability to assimilate the information is restricted to seven different messages at a time. We do not know very precisely what this number of messages would be for the other four senses or what the combined effects of messages playing to too many different senses at once are. Hence, brands should be sensitive to our need for peace and relative quietness at times. Brands should know when to whisper. Consumers may not hear them the first time, but once they do, I believe they will listen.

In the retail world, Nordstrom recognizes that sometimes shoppers just want to relax, and it provides for shoppers' peace of mind with consideration and class. First, there is a wealth of seating within the store for shoppers as well as shoppers' companions for those all-important momentary breaks. "So what?" you may say, but Nordstrom is no ordinary store. On the contrary, Nordstrom puts the customer first in all its considerations, and does not implement any changes without thinking about their valued customers. Nordstrom has selectively redesigned much of its seating, raising the chairs' height and thereby making it easier for weary shoppers to sit down and stand up. It is these most basic considerations like "Can we make our chairs better for the customers?" that are the mark of conscious brands–and these are brands with optimistic futures. Another wonderful aspect of the Nordstrom experience is its Spa Nordstrom. Located within the store, Spa Nordstrom provides facials, manicures, and massages to Nordstrom customers for a certain charge. Customers can just walk in or make appointments in advance to assure availability and certify that they are treated by their favorite masseuse or beautician. What better escape from the harries of life than an hour-long massage after several hours of shopping? Spa Nordstrom illustrates that shaping a brand identity is not about providing clothing and shoes. Rather, Emotional Branding is about crafting an intimate and reassuring experience for each customer.

Another wonderful example of commercial architecture tailored to meet our need for tranquility is the Ian Schrager hotel in London, The Sanderson, which has been called a "chic chill-out zone."[107] This beautiful hotel beckons to peace-craving travelers as a unique urban spa. Says Anda Andrei, one of the hotel's designers, "We want to create a feeling of being enveloped in calm comfort the moment you step through the door. It's a sanctuary."[108] Building-wide semi-sheer curtains, the postworkout "quiet zone," and the paintings of country scenes that hang above beds help achieve just that. Embodying the Emotional Branding principles of dialogue and personal relationships, another one of the hotel's designers, Philippe Starck, says that "There is no style. Our job is to make people blossom, not to show *our* talent. It's giving them the minimum so they can find out about themselves as individuals."[109] However, design is carried into every corner of the building–even in the workout dumbbells designed by Starck himself. But in place of dictated environments that dazzle the visitors, beautiful but open-ended architecture and interior design aim to soothe and empower the hotel's visitors' introspection.

Another recent response to people's current level of overstimulation can be found in a current advertising trend. Some advertisers are realizing that in a media-saturated environment, advertisements that use lush, relaxing visuals with music (or even sometimes silence) and a minimum of words either spoken or in typeface, can be a much more effective way to get consumers' attention than traditional booming voice-overs with jingles and lengthy product explanations. While these ads may require that consumers pay extra attention to discern the brand message (or sometimes even what is being sold!), if done in an aesthetically pleasing, soothing way that speaks to people's emotions, they can intrigue consumers and build a stronger bond with the brands than more intrusive commercials. These ads prove that less can indeed be more.

As marketers and technology conspire to further infiltrate, accelerate, and complicate our daily routine, demand will grow for these soothing sources of stimuli. They will emerge in increasingly unexpected places. Meditation rooms in the rear of your favorite stores, art galleries within the office, ambient and abstract cable channels which feature flowing imagery and gentle sounds–all of these are possible, if not probable. Let's not forget Jean-Paul Sartre's famous line, "If I eat a pink cake, the taste of it is pink."

section III:
imagination

innovation is a brand's best friend!

Thinking Outside of the Box

After looking into the fascinating shifts taking place in the current demographic landscape and delving into the untapped realm of the senses, we are more fully prepared to immerse ourselves in the dynamic world of Emotional Branding. The following chapters are the true backbone of this book because they explore the real everyday challenges of bringing a brand to life as a multidimensional, emotionalized entity that people will fall in love with and continue to love.

Convincing people to buy a product or service in a very saturated, competitive environment is obviously fraught with difficulty. The key to success is to begin to understand the formidable and undefined emotional power that ultimately sways everybody's decision-making. As with all worthwhile endeavors, there are no pat answers about the best way to do this. Creativity just doesn't work that way! It demands an ongoing commitment to building an open-ended, relationship-oriented culture that encourages emotional sensitivity and understanding and the questioning of the status quo, which, in turn, will inevitably lead to the most thrilling expressions of creativity.

The kind of inspiration that leads to innovative brand-design programs in product development, packaging, retail, brand presence, and advertising cannot simply be bottled or bought–but it can be sought . . . and eventually sold!

108

10

Sensory Design: The New Branding Power Tool

People need an escape and an experience that is different from their day-to-day lives. I often use that analogy with our car designers: we're not creating great automobiles, we're trying to create great experiences.
–J Mays, creator of the Volkswagen Beetle,
interviewed by Jim Blair for *Artbyte*

What if manufacturers and retailers took this statement by Mays seriously in terms of viewing their products and store environments as, above all, creation of an intense and wonderful experience? Imagine what could be done if corporations had this kind of commitment to design from the standpoint of creating an emotional relationship with consumers. As we progress toward an economy that thrives on personal relationship, the value of designing consumer products and retail environments as sensory experiences will require, more than ever before, emotion, imagination, and vision.

From Function to Feel: Welcome to the Twenty-first Sensory!

I believe that design is the most potent expression of a brand and that ultimately bringing powerful ideas to life through design is the best way to create a lasting link between a manufacturer or retailer and the consumer. The Volkswagen Beetle, the Gillette series, Issey Miyake's couture, and the Sephora and Godiva stores are among a long list of examples of product or retail designs that work. They are proof that at the end of the day, design creates emotions, sensory experiences, and, ultimately, sales.

I always believed that design would eventually belong to the twenty-first century–the emotional age–and this prediction is now starting to become reality. *Time* magazine's March 20, 2000, cover hailed the "Rebirth of Design"

a little over fifty years after Raymond Loewy, the much-celebrated French-born designer of his generation, made the cover. Such a mass-media tribute to a designer was unprecedented at the time and signaled design's golden age in the '50s. *Time* magazine now tells us that, once again, "Function is out. Form is in. From radios to cars to toothbrushes, America is bowled over by style." The *New York Times* responded to this trend with a full issue of the spring 2000 edition of the *New York Times Magazine* devoted to home design with "Larger than Life" designer George Hansen, inventor of the swing-arm wall lamp, on the cover. We have seen major, important design exhibits such as the Triennial Design Retrospective at the Cooper Hewitt Museum in New York. Catherine McDermott, the famed author and consultant curator at the London Design Museum, has published a book called *20th Century Design,* which presents "a collection of the most important and influential pieces of design produced in the modern age."[110]

Today's broad media coverage of design has elevated the status and recognition of designers—such as Philippe Starck, the French "enfant terrible" of furnishing design; J Mays, the mastermind behind the Volkswagen Beetle; Jonathan Ives, the genius behind Apple; and Tom Ford, the multifaceted Renaissance designer for Gucci–to the heights of stardom in both the business world and with the general public in a way never seen before. Companies like GM are hiring star European designers like Anne Asenisio, who helped transform Renault into one of the top automotive brands in the industry.

It is encouraging to see that design is once again taking the driver's seat in defining the aesthetic of products that we buy on a mass level. Loewy, whose product designs became some of the most successful marketing tools of his time, and who once said "There is no curve as beautiful as a rising sales graph," would be proud of this crop of new designers with their finger so firmly on the pulse of the emotional and practical needs of consumers

These are primarily needs for individualistic expression within the confines of a budget; the need for objects to have an approachable, humanistic feel in a cold, high-tech world . . .

in a new economy. These are primarily needs for individualistic expression within the confines of a budget–the need for objects to have an approachable, humanistic feel in a cold, high-tech world . . . These needs are being answered with finesse and a ferocious creativity.

But what happened from the '50s until the beginning of this century? There was a gap of time between the '60s and '90s when design faded quietly into the background and a bland industrial production controlled the aesthetics of mass products. What prompted this return to the popularity of design after such a long crossing of the desert for designers? What exactly are the changes in the world and in our economies that have encouraged such a renewed focus on design? These are interesting questions to ponder because they tell us a great deal about the Emotional Economy and why consumers desire great design today.

Obviously, design was not dead during this gap, but it did not have the same impact and visibility as it has today. So what is it about the atmosphere of both the '50s and today that fosters a love of design? For starters, there is great similarity between the '50s, a period of booming economy following World War II, and the beginning of this century, which is witnessing the longest prosperity period in the history of this country. Today's new economy, fueled by the advent of breakthrough ideas inspired by technology as a new business model, is not at all dissimilar from half a century ago, when the industrial economy and the advent of consumerism had an incredible impact on the prosperity people enjoyed. Good

Even a dish scrubber can be personified and convey humor.

economies encourage growth through imagination, risk, and rewards in business. Good economies, of course, thrive on people's seeking a better standard of living. The difference is that the '50s offered people the opportunity to get better jobs, and the possibility of acquiring new homes, new cars, and new appliances did not even exist before, whereas *in the twenty-first century, the accumulation of goods is not as critical as the need to reach out for a better quality of life.* Yes, we are spoiled today . . . but that is not the only reason we are becoming so choosy about the way things look. Overall, this shift represents an evolution from the material to the spiritual.

Veronique Vienne, author of *The Art of Doing Nothing*, a book I will talk more about later, and one of the most respected journalists writing articles on design, told me that she felt that this design explosion can be attributed to "the nostalgia for times when things happened more slowly, and [to] our quest for the art of living a quality life."[111] In this new world where speed and computer screens are moving our life more and more out of touch with physical reality, the direct experience we have with the products we interact with on a daily basis can impact our moods and our feelings in the most profound way. The products in our immediate proximity, whether they include a portable phone, a palm anything, or the most banal objects from a dish scrubber down to the garbage can, need to bring with them a new sense of reassurance and pleasure. *In an out-of-control world, it is the most human instinct of all to want to be able to impact our immediate surroundings with things of beauty and originality. This gives us a new sense of control.* "People need to be engaged emotionally, and design is proof of the presence of the human dimension," explains Vienne. Finding an element of personal human touch reconnects us to what's real.

A truly talented designer can tap into our universal need for permanence and beauty. As we are leaving the old economy, its cold industrial ugliness might be leaving us . . . replaced by the warmth and beauty associated with a new art of living. Designers seem to have understood this emotional expectation from people.

THE RETRO-CHIC STYLE

By taking inspiration for their designs from previous decades, designers have foreseen our craving to anchor ourselves with known cultural values that are adapted to our time. The iMac computer looks like a TV set from the '50s, and the latest Jaguar aesthetics as well as the new Volkswagen Beetle design are a modern interpretation of past models. Philippe Starck recently redesigned Emeco's famous lightweight brushed-steel Navy chair from the '40s in another attempt to bring continuity to new generations by translating for today's tastes design successes of the past. Michael Graves's designs for Target take their inspiration from the Memphis postmodern design movement he helped create, and the list, quite literally, goes on and on!

A truly talented designer can tap into our universal need for permanence and beauty.

The main thing these designs have in common is that they are created to become irresistible, pleasurable sensory experiences that have both meaning and attractiveness. Design today has transcended the element of functionality so prevalent in the industrial economy to "embrace psychology and emotion," as Susan Yelavitch, the assistant director of the Cooper Hewitt National Design Museum, says.[112] Bulthaup, the home design systems company, expresses this idea well in its advertising copy: "When you furnish your home with Bulthaup, you have arrived in your own conscious and sensitive world of design," a

Gift Wish No. 1

Blender from Michael Graves Design®
For the artful kitchen, a stylish blender that's
wonderfully practical, too. 400 watts with
five speeds, pulse and 40-oz. glass jar.
Only at Target. $59.99

statement that design is a state of mind, which invites the consumer to enter into that state of mind.

And consumers are entering . . . in droves! *Design's past elitist association with high pricing and exclusivity has evolved to extend its definition of the profession to also be about design solutions for everyone.* The professional designer has been taking a more expansive and democratic route. Many design firms have recruited anthropologists and psychologists to help create designs that are people-friendly, and mass outlets have used well-known designers to create and promote their brands. Target stores' former VP Ron Johnson, who masterminded the Michael Graves's line of products that has had a double-digit sales growth since it was introduced last year, said that "Customers really respond to products that involve new thinking and connect with their souls."[115] In the past, this comment may have surprised a lot of manufacturers who did not even consider until now that the mass market had a soul to start with! Design is all about personalization and customization. *Because well-designed products have real personality, it helps us identify a real person behind what we buy, and puts some aspect of our lives into a slower motion in a faster and*

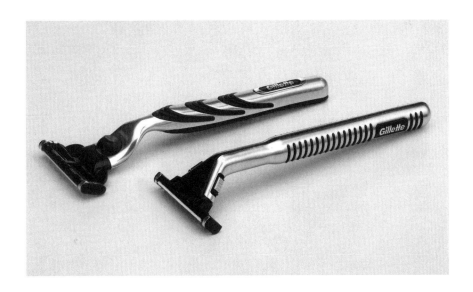

faster moving world. We can mentally imagine how long it takes a creator and a craftsman to offer us their artistic vision of the environment we live in, and we can appreciate the time and care it takes to render the most innovative and exquisite products. Design can deliver on the promise of emotional and sensory experiences. It takes the edge off of standardization and mass production, destroying the robotic concepts of homogeneity and bulk to bring a new sense of humanity to our lives. The eternal question of whether design is about art or commerce is clearly answered by today's designers. It is about people and our role in making people's lives more fulfilling though beauty. The title in French for Loewy's book, *Never Leave Well Enough Alone*, is *La Laideur Se Vend Mal*, or "ugliness does not sell," a much more appropriate title for today's business atmosphere!

The Gillette Sensor, the father of the Mach III and the brainchild of Gillette's Phyl Symons and Peter Hoffman, is a case in point for the powerful role design can play in business. What makes this packaging great is not that the shaving system, the handle, and the blades look pretty, but that the shaver's handle sends a strong message of the best technology any man or woman can get in the world of shaving. Blades are small and unconvincing unless their efficiency is explained to you in detail. Visuals communicate better than words, and in the case of the Gillette razor, the handle is the messenger for the blade. But it is the packaging here that really sets the stage–a most glorified stage–for this innovative product. After all, the blades can only speak for themselves when

you shave! It is no wonder that they are now clearly the worldwide leaders in the shaving category.

But there are still so many brands today that are missing out on this opportunity because they do not yet understand the difference design can make in their business and have yet to consider the meaning and power of design as a strategic tool. *Most talented designers are also challenging, and sometimes companies become frustrated by what they think is a designer's lack of pragmatism when, in fact, it is mostly a commitment to fresh, unusual solutions.* I will never forget the conclusion of the production department of Gillette when we presented our design for the Gillette Series, the grooming line that was launched following the success of the Sensor razor. It was a completely new way to package grooming products in this category. When we proposed very innovative designs with special finishes giving the effect of silver to build a feeling of freshness and technology in line with the core image of the Gillette brand, we were told point-blank by their production department that it could not be done. During an intense silence, I watched the look of disillusionment sweep over the faces of my team, and I realized not only their disappointment but also their conviction that it *would* work! Knowing for myself as well that only bold thinking could make this project a success, I replied, "Well, if you can't do this, you can't be a leader in your industry, challenge yourself." A bold and gutsy statement that certainly could have gotten us fired on the spot! However, fortunately for us, in the room that day there were two great marketers who supported my assumption. And Gillette, a company that considers design the lifeblood of its business, found a way to help us do this project on time, on budget, and with the silver design we recommended.

On the other hand, an example of a missed opportunity for both us and a client was a fragrance bottle design we did for Procter & Gamble, which recommended an off-centered opening. To our dismay, this design was turned down by the company for technical reasons. Later, we saw the very same concept successfully implemented by Estée Lauder for Tommy Hilfiger's Tommy Sport . . . guess who is one of the leaders in beauty products today?

We are now on the verge of a renewed partnership between corporations and designers. Corporations need innovative designs along with a strong understanding of trends in the marketplace to compete and reach a blasé consumer. This is something that connected designers can provide. *The smart companies have already understood that "trend-focused designers" can offer so much more than just "design!"* These are the companies that will succeed in the twenty-first century.

Global Design Sensibility and Taste

Inevitably, the next question for designers and corporations alike is: "What really constitutes 'good emotional design'?" Does it have anything to do with the equally ambiguous concept of "good taste"? This is a debate that encompasses everything from personal perceptions to gender differences to national origin! I would argue that design is first and foremost about cultural and sociological values. Design that works in Brazil might not work in France. Different cultures very often have different aesthetic sensibilities born of their distinct traditions of art, architecture, ways of dressing, and so on, which are reflected in their products and retail designs. In Japan, retail environments tend toward a sharp, clean minimalism; in France, an eloquent expressiveness is sought after. In Morocco, themes are more colorful and visceral, and in the United States, a kind of energetic abundance is often a basic rule of thumb.

In this new global culture full of diverse influences, our taste in design—just as our taste in food—has become much more varied and eclectic. As we travel—either by plane, TV, magazine, or computer—our expectation is that we will experience the exciting influences in our "travels" at home or abroad. This presents a great challenge and opportunity for corporations to expand their vocabulary to speak to consumers in these new ways, and for us designers, the world becomes a great source of inspiration.

In this new global culture full of diverse influences, our taste in design—just as our taste in food—has become much more varied and eclectic.

Besides speaking for a culture at large, culturally sensitive designs immediately talk to us in a highly intimate language all their own, creating a brand personality that is expandable far beyond the product or store.

GOOD DESIGN IS COURAGEOUS

The iMac started a revolution in the way desktops looked and created a new benchmark for the design of any computers to come. Urban Outfitters, the growing Gen X– and Y–oriented retail chain, is a thrilling, funky place to shop and feel connected to an "underground" New York fashion and furnishing sensibility. I sometimes wonder how the iMac could be used as an inspiration for a store, or what an Urban Outfitters computer would look like. Design is clearly more about inspiration and imagination than logic and analysis.

The late Bill Bernbach, renowned for his brilliant advertising for Volkswagen in the '60s, said, "Rules are what the artist breaks." The best design ideas are always immediate, and consumer-enchanting, and, very often, they do break all the rules.

Good design *is* courageous. But apart from its aesthetic value, let's not forget that it represents a long-term investment that can increase a company's value tenfold and over. Can anyone dispute that Gucci's or Apple's turnaround is design-driven? I am sometimes amazed by the financial risk CEOs take every day with acquisitions, industrial investments, and even advertising, while design is left by the wayside—not a clear priority, and generally not considered an investment in terms of potential return. Corporations will spend tens of millions of dollars on mediocre advertising year after year with sometimes poor results, forgetting about the single element that sells itself: design. In an article in *Advertising Age* about the outstanding campaign for the new VW Beetle,

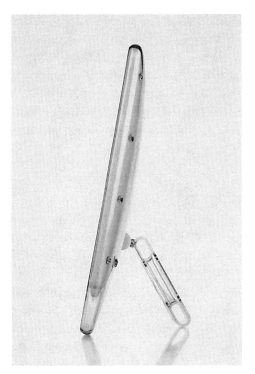

The twenty-two-inch Apple Cinema Display is one of many product designs that attest to the company's commitment to great design.

the author talks about the difficult challenge of creating the ads specifically because the car is, in his words, "a work of art on wheels, a 115-horsepower advertisement for itself."[114] The ads are remarkable because they show us the brand personality through emphasizing the product design itself in simple, clever ways.

Unless you have an innovative product, it will be very difficult to build brand emotion that will reach people and make a lasting connection. Take Apple's "Think Different" campaign as an example. While the advertising was arresting and original, I personally could not equate something so profound as the larger-than-life personalities of Martin Luther King and Gandhi with a commercial brand. It felt to me like desperation at its best (or worst), from an advertising perspective—no product news to communicate, nothing else to say. Then came the iMac, and suddenly, "Think Different" made sense. I could see just *how* Apple was thinking differently about technology! The motto was validated by the product—an innovative, well-designed, relevant one. The association between the advertising and the product was vivid, evident, and real. The communication concept and the product together made the message truly break through! Modern design could bring to the new millennium a whole new language for consumers to enjoy—a language of trust, elegance, and intimacy. Apple has continued this exciting design dialogue with consumers through other groundbreaking designs, such as the new Mac Cube that encases Apple's most powerful technology yet into a clear plastic case about the size of a toaster with an eight-inch screen!

DESIGNING PLACES AS MUSEUMS

Brand-driven architects could also impact society by bringing a renewed sense of beauty to all of the places we visit. People look for experiences of newness, excitement, and fun in stores, museums, restaurants, offices, or amusement parks . . . well, maybe *all* these places should be amusement parks!

Frank Gehry's design for the Bilbao Guggenheim museum changed the economy of the town of Bilbao as well as the entire region. The innovative architecture of the building is so unique, compelling, and dazzling that the place is in and of itself an attraction, regardless of what is presented in the museum. Out of the four million people from around the world who visit this incredible structure of luminescent curved metal plates (made of titanium) every year, at least 40 percent say they mostly come to experience the uniqueness of the architecture. The museum has largely transcended its role as an exhibition provider to become instead a destination, with the work presented in the building partnering in enhancing the visitor's experience. What is more important here? The concept, the place, or the content? They all work beautifully together. The content is on the level of some of the best museums in the world. The concept is indeed powerful. The difference here, the reason why it works, is that Frank Gehry, an incredibly talented architect and artist, was successful in his *emotional* objective of mesmerizing people in a world built around art through design.

Frank Gehry's design for the Bilbao Guggenheim museum changed the economy of the town of Bilbao as well as the entire region.

Stores—even discount stores—don't need to be designed in a cookie-cutter fashion with a fixture book in hand outlining what has worked in the past. Brands like Old Navy have caught on, providing hip fashions at cut-rate prices in a delightful, concept-oriented environment (i.e., a retro "grocery store for clothing") and leaving more traditional discount retailers in the dust. As we

move into a new age of globalization and cultural sharing, designers are really the interpreters, ambassadors, and visionaries of worldwide creative influences for consumers everywhere. Think about the most memorable store you ever visited. and analyze what made it so great.

I would bet that a really good design firm was involved. A very good friend of mine who is a professor at Columbia University once told me that for her, going to "Pottery Barn or Crate and Barrel was like visiting a museum except that one can afford and buy the art presented in the store!" She told me that she felt that art has transcended its perception as only paintings on a wall or sculptures on a pedestal. She feels that art today needs to be found in all the things we buy in our private lives. I couldn't agree with her more!

Designing products and stores is first and foremost about understanding consumers and respecting their needs and desires.

Designing products and stores is first and foremost about understanding consumers and respecting their needs and desires. For a very long time, mass-distribution stores looked very "mass," as if saying loudly, "this is for poor people, and the quality here is only what you can afford–style is not important." Well, a very smart designer has changed that at Kmart. Martha Stewart's wonderful home furnishings collection is a total success. Innovation and fair price associated with style is something any consumer appreciates, whatever the size of their wallet.

TOMORROW'S TECH-DESIGN MAGICIANS

The future of design is as vast as the possibilities that new technology is bringing us. The burgeoning world of high tech is design's new frontier and the realm of endless, exciting opportunities. All of these fast-becoming-necessary objects–high-tech devices such as cell phones–will increasingly be differentiated by sensory-oriented, exciting, and fashion-conscious designs. Design will be the element that adds the all-important human element to our wired world. Mitsubishi's portable convergence phone with Internet capabilities was specifically designed with a comfortable shape and a velvety texture to the silver exterior to give pleasure to the user. It was designed to stand out from the crowd. It is fascinating to imagine what the future of technology could be and how this future will be married to design as every day more and more ordinary, mundane objects become infused with technology, and entirely new, inventive tech products are created. Nike has now created a new division named Techlab to develop sports technology products, such as a digital audio player which plays MP3 files as well as Microsoft Windows Media audio files, high-tech walkie-talkies, and portable wrist monitors. The products come in shades like "fire warm," "green leaf," and "cool sparkle," and are most definitely designed to be fashionable.

In 2000, IDEO, the innovative California-based product design firm, launched a six-month Project 2010 to visualize products ten years in the future. Based on a continued evolution of our current technologies, they predicted a new generation of cool products, such as flexible computer LCD screens of all shapes and sizes that can be pulled out from a cell phone for larger visuals or used in a portable scroll format (instead of a book), eyewear equipped with earphones that screens out the stimuli of the world but has interior displays for information or entertainment, and workstations and homes with computing and communication technology embedded in the furniture and walls for 3-D holographic information and entertainment. Already, we have seen watches designed to double as cell phones, such as the great-looking ones by Swatch or Motorola. *Wallpaper,* the trendy design magazine, said of the Motorola watch, "A person could get tired of mobiles, but not when they're this cute."[115] And in fashion there was a hot new "cyber fiber" trend of fabric technology allowing designers to create clothing out of "intelligent" materials that can protect the wearer from UV exposure and bacteria, perfume the wearer all day, or monitor one's heart rate. Ten years later, most of these ideas have come to life. The iPhone has become the micro-laptop it is today, and designers have proven again their acute perception of what's next.

Conclusion

Designers have an uncanny ability to define the future with their vision, bringing the most remarkable concepts to life. They can be magicians, creators, and real think-tank and R&D resources for companies. *Design solutions will evolve toward design creations, which is a much more effective way of defining the profession.* Designers are transcending the realm of engineering and technology to embrace market-driven opportunities

Designers have an uncanny ability to define the future with their vision, bringing the most remarkable concepts to life.

through product stories that are always much more emotionally potent than either of the former; this is what will make a real difference in the marketplace. In the Emotional Economy, the role of designers as assets to corporations is growing, and they will not only create surprising and great-looking shapes, but also act as incubators for new ideas.

Raymond Loewy designed for speed and efficiency–industrial-production speed and efficiency–key values for the culture of his time. Streamlining, the modernistic, motion-inspired design style he created was meant to help manufacturers win in the marketplace with high functioning products that had an aesthetic edge over their competitors. Today, from the perspective of Emotional Branding, design must be responsive to people's emotional needs and desires for sensory pleasure. This demands passion, honesty, and, above all, commitment to a mission to improve the world we live in. Sound utopian and radical? Well, just ask those folks on the street.

11

Emotionally Charged Identities: Unforgettable Brand Personalities

There is a fundamental truthfulness and legitimacy in a brand that will never change, but its execution must always be defined by the market.
–Philip Shearer, CEO, Clarins

There are unemotional brands, such as Kmart and Compaq, and emotional brands, such as Wal-Mart and Apple. The difference between the two is the vision, visualization, and emotional connection the latter have been able to convey to the world.

From "Dictated" to "Emotionally Connected," corporate identity programs are the expression of a corporation's culture, personality, and products or services it has to offer–the very symbol and signature of the values that should inspire trust with consumers, employees, clients, suppliers, and the financial community. Logos and their colors–whether expressed as symbols (like Nike), logotypes (unique typographic treatment of the name, such as the FedEx identity of upright Roman letters designed by Landor), or a combination of both (as in the case of the AT&T logo)–have been an essential part of all major branding strategies since the middle of the last century. Coca-Cola, IBM, and Mercedes are examples of successful identity programs that have withstood the test of time. Coca-Cola's particular typographic script and powerful red color are unmistakable and memorable; the IBM logo–in its distinct blue–is recognizable worldwide; Mercedes's three-pointed, encircled star logo is not only seen as a guarantee of superior engineering, but acts as a signature of cachet value of the automobiles and translates easily to a sign of good taste and status for the cars' owners.

Powerful logo identities like these make advertising and public relations programs more effective by becoming a visual shorthand for the meanings attached to them and thereby influencing consumers to be receptive to a company's message. Products bearing the logo of a well-known, high-quality corporation benefit from the perception that they are also of superior quality. The products' appeal to the consumer is further enhanced by the comfort level that is evoked from a brand with which the consumer is already familiar.

Logos can be very memorable and can crystallize many different meanings. *A logo by itself is not necessarily a communication tool, but it can most definitely act as a symbol of what a company represents (or hopes to represent) and the resulting consumer perceptions.* As the flag of a company, a logo is its most important visual asset as well as a catalyst

A logo without "heart" is like a person without "heart": cold, uninteresting, a robot.

for good and bad feelings, and therefore needs to be managed with intelligent care. Today this intelligent care means becoming more flexible and far-reaching. Corporate identity programs in the new economy are far more vivid and effective if the identity has integrated elements such as *social sensitivity, cultural relevance,* and an attempt to find *a real connection point with people.* Creative solutions are necessary to help find this combined and crucial "human factor." A logo can be very visible, but without being humanized–that is, without "heart"–it is like a person without "heart": cold, uninteresting, a robot.

Designing Logos for the Heart

In order to reflect a changing business environment, corporate identity programs have evolved over time from an approach based purely on the concepts of visibility and impact (products of an "industrial economy" and in the language defined by corporations) to one based on the concept of *emotional contact* with consumers founded on interaction and dialogue (couched in a new language of a "people-driven economy"). As we have moved into this consumer-driven economy, corporate identities have begun to expand the expression of their character, becoming more flexible and dynamic in order to bring levels of added meaning and soul to consumers' perceptions of them. Corporate identities are transforming from the "dictated" visual identities of the past (corporate-centric identities that "tell" us what will be the unconditional values they represent) to the "personal" visual identities (those designed around an emotion and whose interpretation is often different from one consumer to the next) of the present and future.

To balance a corporate-identity message today, it is also important to consider the power of its emotional message within the context of the strength of the visual message. Just as the *emotional meaning* of a brand needs to evolve from dictated to personal, the *graphic expression* of the brand needs to evolve from "impact" to "contact." ("Personal" identities tend to be more illustrative and imagina- **The *emotional* meaning of a brand needs** tive, just as "dictated" ones tend to be more **to evolve from dictated to personal.** abstract in their graphic style.) Both aspects need to be managed to build the proper message. Clearly, the dictated and impact models connote a more passive consumer stance than the newer personal and contact models do, which implies a closer, even bilateral connection. Indeed, logos are now designed specifically to bridge the gap between corporations and people, and these "connected," branded logo designs can help to better define and communicate the desired personality of the company.

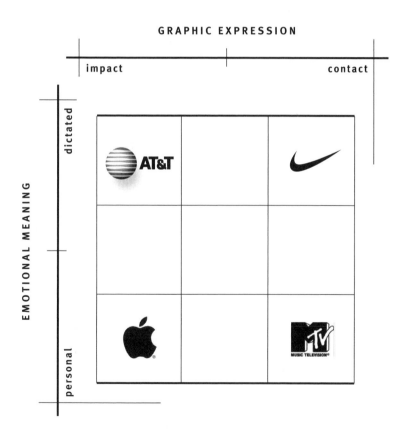

Before the process of building a strong corporate identity program from the perspective of Emotional Branding can be understood, it's important to examine the way the development of corporate symbols of leading corporations has changed over time toward the successful "connected" logos of today. Successive generations indeed define their approaches with their own language, cultural values, ethics, idols, myths, management principles, and corporate logos; and three clear eras evolve: what I call the Pragmatist Age (roughly 1940–67), the Evangelist Age (1968–89), and, most recently, the Sensualist Age (from 1990 to the present).

THE PRAGMATIST AGE

Americans in the '40s and '50s experienced an unprecedented economic boom based on the globalization of the American industry and new, more efficient distribution systems. Fueled by a strong postwar economy and America's newfound position as a superpower, this era saw the advent of single, large corporations producing multiple and multifaceted products and services, with an emphasis on function, reliability, and the pragmatic. As these corporations began to venture into the global market, corporate design began to be recognized for the first time as an important tool which could help address the need of presenting an unequivocal corporate voice through a cohesive visual identity to world markets. Corporations realized that their identity needed to be the very emblem of their business through a simple, powerful, easily recalled symbolic form of a logo or logotype–one that would be retained and remembered by millions of people.

At a time when there was a global desire to own a piece of the American dream (the United States was relatively prosperous compared to many of the devastated European nations), brand design strategies were created to help U.S. brands compete not only at home, but abroad as well. Corporate images created by such brand-design experts as Raymond Loewy, Walter Landor, and Paul Rand, and campaigns masterminded by American advertising agencies such as Young & Rubicam, McCann Erikson, and Leo Burnett were the voice of the entry of American products into the global market. These efforts left an indelible impact on the culture of our era, because these brand identities were themselves cultural symbols reflecting the corporate profile and pragmatic glory of this industrial age. Visibility, stability, and consistency were apparent in the visual expression of the corporate values of

Visibility, stability, and consistency were apparent in the visual expression of the corporate values of the time.

the time. Mass standardization and production were at the core of the business equation, and the typical corporate objective was nothing less than conquering what was truly now a global market.

The success of American brand icons such as Coca-Cola, McDonald's, IBM, Ford Motor Company, TWA, Marlboro, and Levi's, for instance, were largely due to communications tools that stood powerfully above their competitors'. The objective was to visually dominate markets with commercial messages supported by omnipresent advertising and unwavering corporate-identity programs.

THE EVANGELIST AGE

In the '70s and '80s, the Baby Boomers of the Western world went on to enjoy an even higher level of economic freedom and prosperity than their parents, and the United States was becoming the most active consumer market in the world. At the same time, the soon-to-be-called Baby Boomer generation did not share its parents' view of the American dream; the Boomers had a different perception of the ideal world than that portrayed in the '50s and '60s. The Vietnam War, the growing negative perception of the influence of international big business in local and foreign politics, and the realization that the same socioeconomic opportunities were not available to everyone led business entrepreneurs for the first time in history to speak about righting political and social wrongs through business practices—to literally evangelize about values they believed in. Apple, for instance, created a corporate culture based on the belief that technology will give power back to people. César Chávez—a Hispanic union leader—led an unprecedented boycott of California grapes to help negotiate better terms for Hispanic farmworkers. And the Vietnam War, with its dubious necessity, helped raise the social conscience of Americans and made people realize that they did indeed have power and could positively change the course of politics and the world around them. Corporations needed to appeal to this empowerment of the common man and woman on the street.

The most innovative and assertive entrepreneurs of this generation injected into their business practices new ideals representing philosophies of justice, equality, and sensitivity to the environment. For the first time, business practices and pragmatism were intertwined with a concern regarding the impact business had on people and the planet. Consequently, a new business language was formed. Benetton, for instance, started to preach to the world about injustice through its radical advertising campaigns that forced issues like violence, racism, and the AIDS epidemic into the forefront of social thinking. As I mentioned in chapter 3, The Body Shop, led by Anita Roddick, built its success by creating a business model that was extremely proactive regarding issues of the human condition, the environment, and animal rights. Patagonia, the clothing brand, was very strict in imposing the most stringent ecological standards on its suppliers. By implementing new management practices that were less rigid and more people-friendly, Apple computers spearheaded a new corporate lifestyle that influenced its time. Apple deliberately distanced itself from IBM by making IBM appear as an Orwellian Big Brother firm (in the famous "1984" television ad, quite literally so).

Nike broke all the rules by creating a counterculture marketing program that focused on people (in particular, women), motivating them to challenge themselves physically and spiritually. Virgin Atlantic caused an upheaval of the rules in the staid travel industry by promoting a more fun, friendly style and better responsiveness to consumers' needs. I still remember the innovative design of early Gap stores in San Francisco: they were places where you could find all the ⊕ jeans you wanted in stores that were decorated in bold, modern, colorful graphics–a completely revolutionary idea at the time, and one that should be considered again. Taking another tack, Ralph Lauren gave us a very clear perception of the "American look" and broke open the doors of exclusivity by giving permission for people to buy into the private lifestyle of the upper middle class. Lauren personally introduced a level of pride into American fashion that eventually wooed the world.

Brand-identity programs reflected new logos, packaging, and store designs that were hugely personal statements about the brand's philosophy.

Corporate symbols reflected these companies' innovative cultures. The Body Shop logo, with its open, curvaceous, freestyle design, used a typography that did not have the corporate, mechanical look inherent in the corporations of previous years. Benetton's green logo and round typography was unique in its graphic statement, while Apple's identity was a completely different attempt at connecting with people, with a graphic style clearly not expressed in the terms of the unemotional, corporate world. Virgin developed a logo that looked like a handwritten signature to evoke a personal and approachable feeling. The Ralph Lauren Polo logo helped us aspire more to "the good life" in its expression than did, let's say, Levi's jeans.

These new strategies meant that new branding agencies were beginning to

convey some of the day's new counterculture messages: Chiat/Day for Apple, and later Wieden & Kennedy for Nike, became the messengers and the voice of a new generation. Brand-identity programs reflected new logos, packaging, and store designs that were hugely personal statements about the brand's philosophy. This era was teaching "the world to sing," like Coca-Cola, to "just do it," with Nike, to share in spreading humanistic vision and responsibility with Benetton and The Body Shop, and to enjoy the "good life," as defined very precisely by Ralph Lauren. These lifestyle-oriented, "evangelistic" brands were true believers in their dual mission to build successful businesses and influence people's lives.

THE SENSUALIST AGE

The values of the '90s were geared more toward hedonism, glamour, fame, and individual expression. Through the social construct of Generation X, the emphasis began to shift toward the individual, toward seeking immediate, often sensual rewards, and toward a need for constant change. The Internet revolution is now introducing a new set of values (based on the premium of speed) and is whipping branding strategies into a frenzy, stirred up by the rush to take advantage of the enormous financial opportunities. The digital generation–among it the creators of Amazon.com, Yahoo!, AOL, and eBay–are immersed in a world of innovation and financial rewards that is unprecedented in the history of the planet. Never before have there been so many millionaires, and so young.

This same generation is creating its own language, culture, and symbols that are derived from the energy associated with this unbridled, digital playground. Naming conventions for portals such as Yahoo! and Excite, digital communications

firms such as Razorfish, and magazines such as *Red Herring, Fast Company,* or *Wired,* are a few examples of the new and very different corporate vocabulary this generation of entrepreneurs is creating. Speed and the willingness to change are of the essence. Branding strategies need to work in six months or less, and corporate identities are often created at a moment's notice or even sketched out on napkins over lunch. A logo's two-dimensional role as a signature of the business has been diminished in comparison to the bigger role logos can play on Web sites. Digital identities operate by different rules: the online world is one of instant buzz, where the merger of wireless modes of communication with the Internet will bring a new era of online business and where entertainment will add an entirely new dimension to commerce. This new economy is more like a *Star Wars* universe, where multidimensional battleships are always

moving, always reinventing themselves through technology. Corporate and brand identities will begin to reflect this new business attitude, transcending forever the role of the logo as a two-dimensional property.

THE SHAPE OF LOGOS TO COME

Forty years ago, as we've just seen, an identity was required to look great on smokestacks; it was designed to last forever and look appropriate in any context as a true reflection of the conservative values of the time. Today, corporate identities are changing to become consumer-driven, flexible, multisensorial expressions of not only what the company thinks it is, but also reflections of how a company wants to be perceived by people and how they want people to interact with it. When designing a corporate program today, designers manipulate not only graphics but also sounds and textures. One must animate the logo on a Web site and define its cultural connection to society. *An identity program in the twenty-first century is a multidimensional expression of a brand vision brought to life in the most imaginative way.* Identities need, therefore, to be more modular, continuing to innovate along the lines that MTV has done in the past with their varying and highly expressive logo presentations.

Companies are just now beginning to explore how a logo can become a living, breathing creature that can foster a great deal of awareness for a brand in a very positive way. *Logos can be a lot more than a minuscule corner portion of an ad! And considering the money corporations spend to develop a corporate identity, why not put them to work a little harder?* Target's use of their logo in so many creative ways in their advertising communicates the store's innovative approach and overall commitment to change. Target has created an entirely new story with its brand by leveraging the strength of their red bull's-eye

MTV was a pioneer in creating modular, interpretive logos that were flexible to the brand's expressive needs.

logo to send a message of fashion, modernity, and fun. Some Gen Y–oriented brands, such as Bonfire (a snowboard label owned by Adidas), are beginning to take this trend of flexible logos a step further by allowing consumers to pick from a selection of different logo designs available as stickers (Bonfire has a choice of seven) that are then displayed for them in a personalized way on the product. This is a concept that will continue to develop, particularly in the realm of mass customization.

Given the life span of some identities, in the marketplace there is currently a jumble of different visual languages reflective of different generations and economies, juxtaposed in magazines, on television, and on the Web. Today, the business of creating corporate identities faces the challenge of how to stay current. There is the danger of being pegged as irrelevant because the corporate identity you created ninety-five or even five years ago is outdated, or the new name you built your identity around is suddenly . . . not hip!

Not surprising, then, logo designs, the most important signature of a brand, have evolved to reflect the different philosophies of each generation of entrepreneurs.

Even though established identities have had to adapt in order to remain relevant, most are still stuck in the past. Three technology logos that clearly epitomize their times—IBM, Apple, and Yahoo!—exemplify how corporate expression has evolved over the years. The IBM logo designed by Paul Rand is a strong example of the corporate-driven business approach of the time: pragmatic, industrial, and conservative in typography. Apple, on the other hand, as a name and a symbol, is humanistic, a trait consistent with the "evangelistic" values of the Baby Boomer generation. Yahoo! mirrors the quirky spirit of the Internet generation. It is sensual, expressive, fun, and uses the hip retro-chic style of the '50s that appeals to members of Generations X and Y.

In our new virtual world where rules are reinvented every nanosecond, logos are not merely physical markers.

In our new virtual world, where rules are reinvented every nanosecond, logos are not merely physical markers, but serve as a cultural connection to people. In this unruly epoch in which change is a constant, the priorities are different. The amateurish look of the AOL logo would perhaps make Paul Rand or Saul Bass (the designer behind the AT&T logo) cringe.

Typography Is about Personality

A computer has yet to be made which can cross-reference knowledge and interpret novel situations with the complexity and originality of the human brain. Even from the perspective of today's electronic age, it's hard to imagine machinery ever matching this human ability in its full and dynamic complexity. One of the most fascinating aspects of human processing is that it's often unprompted and subconscious—it just happens. I offer the following examples:

Reaganomics

Reaganomics

𝕽eaganomics

What's the difference between these three messages? The word is the same in each case, but although the semantic definition is consistent, there is clearly a difference in the three representations. For me, the first message conveys seriousness and importance; the second indicates a comical repetition of the phrase, such as one might encounter in mocking satire; the third has a strange and ironic sophistication to it. Most of us, by the time we're fifteen years old, have been significantly acculturated by the world around us to interpret these relatively subtle typographical nuances of meaning. No classroom formally trains us in making these qualitative evaluations of lettering, but somehow the information is stored in our minds, anyway. The ability to immediately and creatively reference stimuli is inherent to the human brain, and on this fascinating quality rests the power of typography.

The way letters conveying a message are designed is an important visual element of branding that can utilize powerful emotional connotations. It is a kind of science that can be used for a real strategic advantage, and it is unfortunate that it is not always given the attention it deserves. Typographic styles speak volumes about another kind of style—the lifestyle, that is, the Époque or character of a brand.

The way letters conveying a message are designed is an important visual element of branding that can utilize powerful emotional connotations.

In our design for the Coca-Cola Olympic City logo, we used the typeface Confidential—a typeface with a gritty, urban feel—to communicate the "For the Fans" positioning. We rendered the type in the soda's proprietary red and white colors, yet far enough from Coke's classic scripted type that it gives the brand a contemporary edge—we expanded the brand meaning while not taking it too far from the original brand. People decode these kinds of typographic messages on a subliminal level, extracting subtle nuances of meaning that would otherwise demand lengthy and unwieldy explanations that defeat the message. (To see our work for the Coca-Cola Olympics, please take a look at Tool #3, Brand Presence® Management, in chapter 17.)

Many enduring corporate identities of monolithic brands have been built almost solely on typography. IBM uses typography that is modern, reflecting the bold character of the industrial world. The thick, solid, and calming blue letters convey the reliability and unwavering strength that the company aspires to project. Paul Rand developed the trademark logo in 1956 from an infrequently used '30s typeface called City Medium. This geometric slab-serif font was designed along lines similar to Futura. Rand's original logo was updated in the '70s with the stripes we see today. The positive association of these characters with the IBM brand identity, compounded by their consistency over the course of many years, contributes to the formation of "consistency" and "reliability" as associations with the company.

Magazine titles use typography to express something even more abstract: the values the publications represent to readers. *Vogue*, for example, connotes a classic elegance with its Bodoni serif type. *Wired* magazine has an audacious, innovative, and dynamic typographic look that suggests the speed, energy, and unpredictability of the world of technology it covers. The *New York Times* uses a Gothic typeface associated with Gutenberg—the inventor of the printing press—for its title to communicate the grounded heritage and authenticity of the newspaper. This typeface is a highly recognizable aspect of the *New York Times*'s identity and is immediately associated with the newspaper.

The look of the IBM typography design is highly recognizable even when the "IBM" is replaced by ".COM."

While it is true that typography is often taken for granted, some firms do understand the power of typography and even develop their own proprietary typefaces for a stronger corporate identity and message consistency. In the advertising and print world, typefaces have been created to differentiate one company's message from those of its competitors and sometimes even to differentiate its own new message from an old one.

The current electronically inspired revolution in typography reminds me of the revolution brought about by the playful and illustrative typography that blossomed in another period. Psychedelic posters, like the ones designed by Peter Max or the Pushpin Group in the '70s, made a strong statement that immediately signaled an epoch of mind-blowing change. I asked Seymour Chwast—one of the founders of the Pushpin Group—what gave them the inspiration to create this new look, and he mentioned that the music industry and record albums were a tremendous medium for them to express their creativity. Remember the 1967 Bob Dylan *Greatest Hits* album and poster designed by Milton Glaser?

People's deepest emotions, aspirations, and dreams always need a new language that crystallizes their mind-set and sends their message to the world.

A new, graffiti-inspired look is redefining the revolutionary language of this era's youth movement. Look at today's CD graphics for inspiration. The music industry is always ahead of its time in typographic trends and a true barometer of generational graphic expressions. But politics has taken this role with now-President Barack Obama's hiring of street artist Shepard Fairey to design his official campaign portrait.

Brilliant typography can not only seize the moment (e.g., Solidarsnok— the political movement led by Lech Walesa against the Communists in

Poland), but preserve its brilliance and vitality indefinitely. People's deepest emotions, aspirations, and dreams always need a new language that crystallizes their mind-set and sends their message to the world. Typography is an ideally suited tool for these times because it often delivers more powerful yet more subtle messages than images or lengthy explanations.

Nomenclature and Organizational Structure in the Emotional Economy

Connecting corporate ideas and the market in the simplest way is so much a part of the new consumer-driven economy that all corporate nomenclature systems–that is, the ways companies choose to name their divisions and products–should reflect an emotional model that has humanity at its core and allows for a free flow of ideas between corporations and people. In order to be relevant to our new economic order, corporate identity strategies must evolve to encompass a larger social and cultural context through a dialogue-based approach–internally and externally–that encourages contact. Most corporate programs are top-down and internally driven with minimal input from people and reflect organizational charts that, in most cases, fail to indicate this all-important human factor of the company.

Taking this system to an even more–to me–puzzling and extensive level is Ralph Lauren's brand architecture. It includes so many brands and sub-brands that it dilutes the power of the creator. From Polo to Chaps, to Polo Sport, Polo

THE OPERATIONAL BUSINESS MODEL [system based]

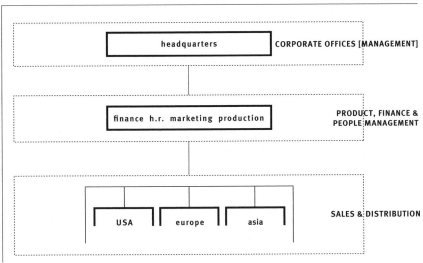

headquarters — CORPORATE OFFICES [MANAGEMENT]

finance h.r. marketing production — PRODUCT, FINANCE & PEOPLE MANAGEMENT

USA europe asia — SALES & DISTRIBUTION

THE CORPORATE-IDENTITY OPERATIONAL MODEL [system based]

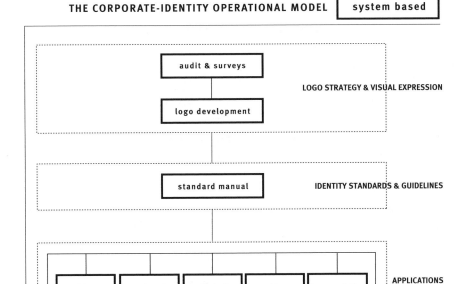

audit & surveys
logo development — LOGO STRATEGY & VISUAL EXPRESSION

standard manual — IDENTITY STANDARDS & GUIDELINES

uniforms printed materials digital applications outdoor signage transportation — APPLICATIONS

139

Jeans, Double RL, Ralph, Lauren, RLX, etc., the brand system is set up from a corporate and distribution point of view that could vastly benefit from being addressed from a market-driven perspective.

These identity programs are a pale reflection of the human dynamics found in the new economy that companies based on the relationship model that encourages communication. The much more organic, people-driven model allows for simplicity of consumer contact as well as internal-external dialogue.

For one of my former clients, a large, well-known Japanese corporation, we designed a new relationship-based model of nomenclature that captured their corporate organizational architecture. The objective was to unify the company behind a new business strategy and to simultaneously change perception of the company as an old-economy corporation in the eyes of the financial community, the public, and the employees. The company asked us to create a corporate identity that would communicate a new vision of it as a global entity. However, after months of auditing the company, interviewing employees, and analyzing the organization's brand equity, we realized that what was asked of us would have only been a short-term, cosmetic solution if the company did not fundamentally change its overall philosophy. We began helping the top management of the company rethink their business strategy and to approach it entirely from an emotionally branded perspective. And a new visualization of their organization chart proved to be very powerful in making the organization understand this new vision.

We felt that the company needed to evolve from a factory-based business to a "brand incubator." The idea was a very bold and challenging one, since the core culture of the business was totally driven by industrial capabilities and the feasibility of their equipment. It was a hierarchical and traditional model based on the strength of their operations.

The company's enormous success had come from smart industrial ideas that were on the level of genius forty years ago. Starting out as a small company manufacturing glue for bicycles, the founder searched for ways to expand his business by finding other tube-based products to develop around this industrial expertise. They found it in toothpaste and, as a result, almost overnight, this small operation became one of the biggest Japanese toothpaste manufacturers. The company went on to develop more than a hundred oral-care products for all population segments and distribution channels. They enjoyed tremendous

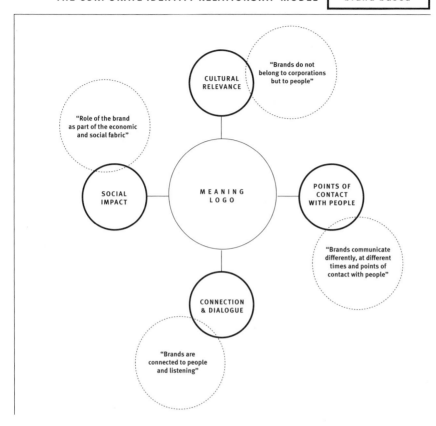

Inside the diagram:

- **CULTURAL RELEVANCE**
- "Brands do not belong to corporations but to people"
- "Role of the brand as part of the economic and social fabric"
- **SOCIAL IMPACT**
- **MEANING LOGO**
- **POINTS OF CONTACT WITH PEOPLE**
- "Brands communicate differently, at different times and points of contact with people"
- **CONNECTION & DIALOGUE**
- "Brands are connected to people and listening"

growth in the Asian market until Japanese protectionist policies softened and new megabrands from the West began to infiltrate the market. Suddenly, this strong, industrial-based business was threatened by brand-driven companies with the reputations and money to conquer them on their home turf.

The exercise went far beyond traditional identity charts, nomenclature systems, and good-looking logos—all of which would have been ineffective against the far stronger brands now challenging the company. Rather, our goal was to show our client the opportunities offered by a new brand strategy vision. We set out to help them leverage their strengths by using the power of their people to rebuild a dynamic, competitive global business. *We did this by focusing on moving from a culture of rationality (based on the functions and benefits of products) to one of desire (based on the emotional bond people have with a brand).* We

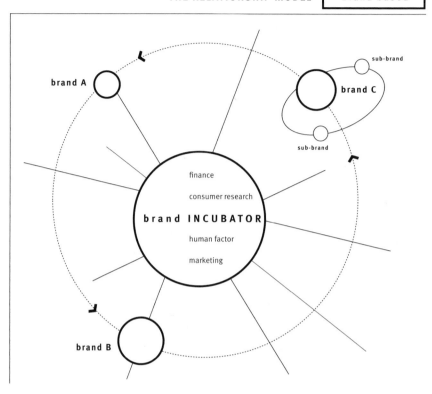

wanted to help take them from a culture of creating brands that people need to a culture of creating brands that people desire. Our recommendation was to emphasize the company's branded "intellectual properties" beyond the limitations of their existing factory capabilities—in short, to change the company from an industrial mentality to a market-driven one. To communicate this idea, we devised an organizational chart and brand architecture that emphasized a *relationship model* that helped clarify roles and responsibilities as well as facilitate communications between all divisions.

The difference between the relationship model we created for the company and their existing structure can be likened to the difference that exists between algebra and geometry, between 2-D and 3-D—between a flat earth and a round one! In trying to create a more dynamic model that would promote interaction—connection and synergy—we took our inspiration from the circling planets of the galaxy. We divided the roles and responsibilities of each group and defined the connections between the divisions and groups to headquarters, which was represented as the sun, a symbol of life and creation (the incubator). The brands and brand groups were seen as planets circling the sun that was seen as a provider and consultant, with financial, R&D, and marketing capabilities to assist the brands in evolving freely in their different markets so that they could consolidate their positions worldwide.

The language that we used made a difference in explaining the human and emotional dynamics needed to rally a corporation behind a new, powerful idea and vision. This model clarified the corporate message and struck an emotional chord with our clients, helping them better envision the possibilities of their brand.

The language that we used made a difference in explaining the human and emotional dynamics needed to rally a corporation behind a new, powerful idea and vision.

Corporate branding works when it is based on a total market-driven business vision. Emotional Branding enhances corporate branding with a powerful point of view that can integrate the human factor to provide a more cohesive vision consistent with the financial, business, and marketing objectives of a company. The first step toward a new vision is an emotionally driven identity program that involves people at all levels of the organization as well as influences from the outside. It is about simplifying and clarifying the possibilities and charting new, innovative paths.

Flexible Signatures

Abercrombie & Fitch in the United States and many fashion brands in Europe—such as Fendi and Gucci—have developed identities that help them carry their fashion signature further, in a wider variety of contexts, expanding the expression of the personality of the identity to be more flexible and less "dictated" on their clothing products and accessories. Chanel's interlocking Cs, the superimposed L and V for Louis Vuitton, the G for Gucci, and the famous Fendi double F designed by Karl Lagerfeld are powerful visual signals that connect in a personal and emotional way with people on all their products. Corporate identities such as Tommy Hilfiger's powerful flag-inspired logo, Ralph Lauren's polo player symbol, and the Victoria's Secret heart have developed intense brand meaning because those brands know how to manage the different expressions of their visual identity—whether it is a fragrance or an article of clothing—all in concert to bring a brand to life.

RUSTIC ACTIVE BRIGHTS

Heart-Stopping Brand Personalities

Corporate identity programs such as those for FedEx or AT&T are powerful, memorable, and dominant visually, thanks to extremely well-designed nomenclature systems that are engineered to create ubiquity for the brand. On the other hand, fashion, retail, and Web companies have steered away from that path, building strong, flexible emotional personalities around their businesses and designing brand identities that closely match the cultural and personal aspirations of their customers. The challenge of pleasing people day by day, season by season, in these sectors requires flexibility in brand expression to match the cultural appetite of the time. This is why fashion, retail, and Web brand identities are some of the most powerful examples to study for building corporate identities that conform with the philosophy of Emotional Branding. They are about personalities that easily cross all boundaries of media expression. These are "brand characters" that are less about rationality and order than they are about desire and cultural connection. They are personalities that show more than just a superficial façade–they indicate a pulsing heartbeat and a lot of imagination behind their logos.

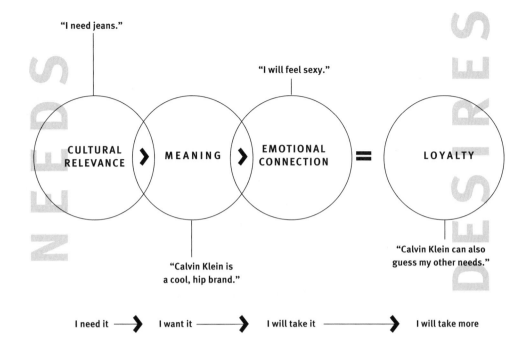

"I need jeans."

"I will feel sexy."

NEEDS

DESIRES

CULTURAL RELEVANCE > MEANING > EMOTIONAL CONNECTION = LOYALTY

"Calvin Klein is a cool, hip brand."

"Calvin Klein can also guess my other needs."

I need it → I want it → I will take it → I will take more

DEFINING A PERSONALITY

Commerce is, of course, all about selling more products and services, but people are all about desires and aspirations. We are constantly looking for brands that know what we want, and we are constantly considering the ways we may want to associate ourselves with brand personalities that possess charisma. We sometimes desire labels to express who we are (or, rather, who we want to be) to others, but most of all, we want brands that offer us a variety of experiences. So while commerce simply wants to own our minds and pocketbooks, we look for brands that understand our heart and soul in the exchange.

Once again, branding should not be about company nomenclature and obscure systems, but about flexibility and emotional reach. A lot of companies have logos but no soul. In those cases, a logo is a meaningless and unempowered visual element of a company's vision. It is critical for businesses other than fashion and retail to craft and define a clear emotional personality that will make them stand out (although for a Boeing or a Goldman Sachs it may not be as useful to be categorized by the good boy-good girl, bad boy-bad girl model –see sidebar). We all clearly understand Martha Stewart's message (classy, domestic know-how) and what Calvin Klein stands for (rebelliousness and sexy chic).

But, unfortunately, it is harder to clearly discern exact personalities for NBC or Winston cigarettes.

Emotional brands are most successful in extending their product offering to respond to their customers' aspirations. When you identify with a brand emotionally, you'll be more likely to buy varied products from it even if your emotional connection was first forged around one specific line. Rose Marie Bravo's magnificent turnaround of the Burberry brand was the right balance of emotion and product relevance. And if you believe in Virgin, you believe in its culture and meaning first and foremost, and in its products second; whether it is its airline, its cola, or its music stores, you are buying the brand first. Emotional brands have strong appeal that leads to growth potential through an extension of the company's offerings.

Bad Boy-Bad Girl Brands versus Good Boy-Good Girl Brands

When I am good, I'm very good, but when I am bad, I'm better. —Mae West

In seeking new ways to look at and understand identities, I have discovered a way of clarifying and decoding brand personalities that I find both helpful and amusing. When analyzing the effectiveness of Emotional Branding in the fashion and retail industry, it seems to me that there are clearly two separate camps into which these brands fall: what I call the good boy-good girl brands (GBGG)—think Brooks Brothers—and the bad boy-bad girl brands (BBBG)—such as Calvin Klein, for example). Based on the attitude—the rebelliousness and sexiness or well-mannered restraint—that companies project, it is often easy to place them in one camp or another. Gucci seems to fall squarely into the "bad" category, judging from its haughty ad campaigns that capture an on-the-edge urban lifestyle. Nautica certainly seems "good" in the sense of promoting conservative, good, almost family-oriented behavior.

This GBGG-BBBG polarity can also sometimes evolve over time for a brand. Did Estée Lauder buy a new product line or merely some much-needed sexy, bad behavior associations when it acquired the hip young company MAC, which endorses celebrities such as drag queen RuPaul and hip-hop stars Mary J. Blige and Lil' Kim? How about Lancôme, the fabulous multidimensional cosmetic company that recently injected some new life into its brand by rejuvenating the look of its line with new models and makeup artist Fred Farrugia? It updated an image that tended toward the staid and was beginning to seem dangerously too close to grandma's generation! But some brands lack clarity in terms of their GBGG/BBBG positioning. At first glance, the Gap and Tommy Hilfiger seem to be "GBGG" brands, since their brand imagery gravitates around neat, clean, wholesome images that keep any sexiness within certain boundaries. Yet, the Gap ads spoofing the world of *West Side Story*, a tale of gang warfare in New York, seemed to be a

stretch in the BBBG direction. And Hilfiger's clothing found an undisputed niche among the BBBG world of rough-and-ready hip-hoppers. Both Gap and Tommy Hilfiger appeared to want to play on both sides of the paradigm. Gap gave us the GBGG/BBBG "khakis/jeans" dichotomy of the *West Side Story* ads, but the "jeans" contingency seems like a kind of cleaned-up "PG-rated badness." I believe that taking a clear stand and being at one end of the GBGG-BBBG spectrum is more desirable.

Should Abercrombie & Fitch be categorized as BBBG? In its quarterly publication, *A&F*, it advises its Generation X readers to indulge in some creative drinking, portraying models in a frat-house kind of lifestyle—and very

naked! In the consumer brand business, is IBM "good" because of the perception of it as a serious, well-established business, and Apple perennially "bad" because it always finds a way to challenge the status quo? Is Coca-Cola "good" because it symbolizes Americana, and Pepsi "bad" because of its irreverent teen-driven communications? What about Victoria's Secret, the sexy lingerie brand, versus Playtex, the functional brand? Matching brands by association to a character classification is always an interesting way to identify the strength, relevance, and clarity of a brand. . . . Mae West, a very well-defined "bad girl brand," was definitely onto something!

GIVING MEANING TO A BRAND: VISUALIZATION AND PERSONALIZATION OF A BRAND CONCEPT

During a continuing relationship of more than fifteen years with Les Wexner, the chairman and CEO of The Limited, and Ed Razek, his WCMO (that's my title for him: "wizard chief marketing officer"),[116] I had the great opportunity to collaborate on the identity creation and repositioning of some of the most successful retail brands in the world. Brands such as Express, Structure, Abercrombie & Fitch, Bath & Body Works, and Victoria's Secret were projects in which our contributions had the most impact and where every drop of creativity was squeezed from us! Our goal was to reinvent corporate identity by infusing the elixir of emotion in order to reach an identity's most expressive limits. One of those assignments culminated in the creation of the emotionally driven name "Intimate Brands," when Bath & Body Works and Victoria's Secret were spun off from The Limited and introduced in a very successful public offering.

It was in our work for The Limited that we first tested on a grand scale our new concept of Emotional Branding. *We wanted to find an approach to branding that raised the bar on how far you could go in connecting with a consumer on a personal level by creating verbal and visual stories around a brand through an illustrated script everyone wants to read and believe.* Our initial attempt at utilizing this concept involved the repositioning of Limited Express in 1985 as a brand with European flair, at a time in America when everything European was desirable. I had been living in the United States for barely a month when Kevin Roche, a leading retail strategist (and one of the founders of FRCH, a well-known American retail design firm), heard of our company and asked us to meet with a firm I had never heard of–The Limited. My first meeting with Les Wexner was a lesson in humility and learning. I had never met anyone with such an intuitive feeling about brands, whose entire business model was brand driven . . . long before branding was a household word.

Our first assignment was to redesign the brand identity for Express, a new retail clothing brand they had just created. For research purposes, we traveled to Europe to observe the latest fashion trends. Once there, I realized that without some definite context in which the brand could evolve, I would never be able to direct my team of designers toward a groundbreaking solution. Frustrated and sleep-deprived early one morning in Paris, I went to Café de Flore, a wonderful place on Boulevard St. Germain, where generations of artists, poets, and writers seeking inspiration have met since the beginning of the century. On the way, I bought an issue of *Paris Match*, a French magazine (similar to *People* magazine in the United States) that publishes the latest gossip on the "famous and beautiful people." In it, an article on Princess Stephanie of Monaco reported details of her "unprincessly" life as a fashion designer and singer under the worried supervision of her family.

I was immediately seduced by the independent spirit of this young woman, the strength of her character, her creativity, and her blue-blood upbringing. This was a beautiful story, and I could not help but think that if we could attract someone like Stephanie to a new Express store, we would be communicating to the right aspirational customer. I felt I had a story that could propel the meaning of the brand beyond graphics and provide a great brief for my designers–design an identity to reach Stephanie! Which is what we did. But first, we created a visual board that conveyed in an imaginative way the lifestyle of this potential customer, this pseudofictional and composite character, as a foundation and inspiration for our work.

I was so afraid to have my concept turned down by the staff of Express that I hid this concept board until I could show it to Wexner himself. It was a risky strategy–if it didn't work, I risked being sent back to France for good! But it was the only way to make an impressive statement and distinguish myself from my competitors. This certainly was not standard procedure at the time, and anyone but Wexner would have been put off by my approach. Actually, at first, I started to show several logo designs and packaging applications, unsure of when or if I would present the "Stephanie"-inspired style boards. The meeting was going well, but I couldn't feel any great enthusiasm or commitment to the concepts. Even though the presentation was strong in terms of the work and probably would have been approved, it did not get anyone's adrenaline to shoot up to the point of making them true believers in the ideas presented so far. I had not reached the standard I had in other presentations.

I decided to show the "Stephanie" boards, and I could immediately see a sparkle in the group's eyes: the boards had made a strong and immediate emotional connection. It worked well, and Wexner foresaw in it great potential for the future of the brand. His immediate decision (in the very same meeting!) was to ask his brand group to make a huge poster of my board to be placed in the buyers' conference room and to print postcard-sized copies for merchants to take abroad so they could buy or design clothing with "Stephanie" in mind as the ideal customer. The stores themselves were later redesigned to resemble in a quirky manner the palace in which Stephanie was living. The story of Stephanie, and all the qualities that we projected onto her, became the idea behind the brand.

Conceptualizing a brand through personalization has become a very powerful way to build a brand identity.

This approach of inventing and romanticizing (or expanding imaginatively) a character as a "real person" and building details, characteristics, and emotions around them was subsequently modified and evolved into our SENSE® process, a unique technique for visualizing a brand, which that creates imaginary brand lifestyles to better help define a visual platform as a basis for the development of a branding program. The SENSE® process was successfully applied to other divisions of The Limited (for example, "Kate," a fictitious entrepreneur dedicated to making wonderful beauty products from natural ingredients culled from the American heartland, was created as the inspiration for the Bath & Body Works brand), and became the branding technique for which we were best known. This idea of conceptualizing a brand through personalization has now been adopted by other companies and has become a very powerful way to build a brand identity. It was reported to me that at some point, I was one of the virtual subjects of this branding game. I never probed further for fear of finding out more– it might have been a story I wouldn't have liked!

VICTORIA'S SECRET: THE MAKING OF A SUCCESSFUL CORPORATE IDENTITY PROGRAM THROUGH VISION, VISUALIZATION, AND EXPRESSION
In the early '90s, Victoria's Secret established itself as the premiere lingerie brand in the United States. The romantic English-inspired stores opened with great success all over the country, and the catalog became very well known among both men and women. Victoria's Secret had in fact given American women the

freedom to feel comfortable with sexy lingerie on their own terms, in contrast to competitors such as Frederick's of Hollywood, a California lingerie brand with a much racier attitude. Indeed, by 1995, Victoria's Secret was a successful brand that had achieved an enviably strong position as a catalog and store concept. But the modest price points that helped make the lingerie so attractive to shoppers also had a disadvantage: the line was seen as a mass brand. It had not yet reached the level of "status" symbol it enjoys today.

Vision

Les Wexner knew that in order to dramatically accelerate the business in terms of growth and profits, a fundamental element of the Victoria's Secret marketing plan needed to be changed. *He understood profoundly that the value of the brand was not in its product line, but in the emotional connection women had with the store.* By driving the business from an emotional perspective, he believed that the product lines could be evolved in a more meaningful way, that price points could be raised, and that women–younger women as well as the core customer base of women in their mid-thirties–would welcome a more meaningful in-store shopping experience with the brand. Wexner understood the potential of the brand and was determined to see it grow to its full potential. A team was immediately put together to create a new vision for the business: Ed Razek, Dick Tarlow (of Tarlow Advertising), Grace Nichols (president of Victoria's Secret), and myself (as the brand design consultant).

Visualization

From an Emotional Branding perspective, creating a story around lingerie can be fun and inspirational, but focusing on a good idea that is sustainable was difficult. Dick Tarlow, whose ad agency had been one of the first to capitalize on the success of the supermodels in its work for Revlon and Ralph Lauren, made an immediate connection between Victoria's Secret and the fashion credibility, modernity, and aspirational value of the supermodels. We all liked the idea. This was the beginning of a new and powerful brand story; the Victorian and slightly old-fashioned look of the existing identity was too narrow of a story and lacked the sex appeal star models could bring to the brand. What the brand needed was a major makeover!

In order to better define this new identity, we used the SENSE® process to bring to life the world of a supermodel. Not unlike the projective exercise we did for Express, we fleshed out in an idealized way what a typical month in the life of a supermodel would look like–where she lives, what her bedroom, bathroom,

and kitchen look like, the restaurants where she eats, the nightclub she hangs out in, the look of her boyfriend, the sports she enjoys, what she does in her free time, and so on. We also considered decorative materials and music that we felt fit the brand, and we listed key words that built a creative language around the brand's concept. The objective was to add a level of sensory experience to a brand that would affect the overall look and feel of the identity–through packaging and graphics–and express this new, younger identity. A new heart symbol developed, and the Victoria's Secret logotype was defined.

A particularly bright shade of the fun, feminine color pink, with its associations of love, was chosen as the corporate color, with stripes and the heart symbol to crystallize the whimsical, romantic character of Victoria's Secret. Wexner asked us to design the now-famous pink shopping bags to be seen a mile away–to be memorable and to act as advertising for the store in the street. The high profile of Victoria's Secret bags subsequently contributed to a general "coming out of the closet" for lingerie brands (this was around the time that Madonna was showed us all how lingerie could be worn as a fashion statement in and of itself). American women no longer had to be bashful about shopping for lingerie, and carrying the new Victoria's Secret bags was its own fashion statement. Eventually, the bags became a status symbol of their own—sending the clear message about the person holding them, "Look at me! I just bought some very sexy lingerie!"—and they became popular with men, as well.

Such a dramatic change for a business that was already wildly successful would have been terrifying for many. A lot of managers run companies based on numbers and past successes. Not so with Wexner, who manages his company based above all on the meaning of his brands to the consumers. He has the courage to change and alter that meaning to better match the consumers' desires as time goes by, even if it means taking bold steps in a new direction.

Emotional Connection

The full impact of all this effort could not be realized without sustaining a powerful cultural connection to the consumers. And that's where Ed Razek came in full force. Razek has an incredible ability to translate and elevate the emotional value of a brand to an ultimate level in the most brilliant and relevant ways. He is a true communicator. His idea was to test the power of Victoria's Secret through a fashion show—something he believed would also generate a lot of coverage for the stores. It sounds uncontroversial, but I still remember him telling me that he went out on a limb doing this project. "But it is right for the brand," he said to me in a conversation I had with him just before the first show—an attitude that demonstrated his passion and commitment to the business even though his job could have been on the line.

The enormous success of this initiative catapulted Victoria's Secret into the realm of the most admired companies worldwide. The event got more media coverage than any fashion show in the world, including the ones produced by the leading European fashion designers. This kind of exciting thinking certainly did not stop there. Through the years, up until the present, Victoria's Secret has continued to work hard to maintain this kind of unique edge in the market. Razek's 1998 Super Bowl ad that brought more than one million people to the Victoria's Secret Web site will

The enormous success of this initiative catapulted Victoria's Secret into the realm of the most admired companies worldwide.

be remembered alongside Apple's "1984" Super Bowl commercial as one of the most innovative and successful communication efforts of all time. This new awareness regarding the brand eventually fed into the success of the Victoria's Secret beauty division and its new hosiery business. Consequently, Victoria's Secret has been able to attract some of the finest executives in the world, such as Robin Burns, the former president of Estée Lauder, who now runs the beauty division. The catalog has also continued to be a phenomenal success, with supermodels now fighting to be in it. Razek's latest coup was to organize the "Victoria's Secret Cannes 2000" event to raise money for amFAR, a foundation which raises money to support AIDS research. In partnership with Air France, Victoria's Secret whisked a star-studded group of supermodels and celebrities such as Elizabeth Taylor and Elton John in a Concorde jet, custom decorated with Victoria's Secret identity details (such as Victoria's Secret logo decals on the aircraft doors and pink headrests and menus), to the French Riviera for a dinner and fashion show. This event, which was also Webcast, demonstrates not only the business savvy of Victoria's Secret, but also an important sense of social responsibility.

Emotionally driven corporate identity programs need to be visionary, integrated, visceral, and reflective of a true commitment from corporations to share their values with the consumers.

Emotionally driven corporate identity programs need to be visionary, integrated, visceral, and reflective of a true commitment from corporations to share their values with the consumers. Connected identities are culturally relevant and endorsed by people, consumers, and employees alike. They are flexible, imaginative, and attractive. Dictated identities are only what they are, only another logo on the door. In one of my recent meetings with Wexner, a new visual merchandising director for Victoria's Secret presented a new version of the striped packaging. The director mentioned that this look would forever be the new look of the brand. Sagely, Wexner replied, "As far as we can see."

Just Call My Name

Names are difficult to find and even more difficult to register. Just spend an hour on *www.uspto.gov* and you will realize that almost all of the words in the English dictionary and all the word associations have already been registered! Name research has become one of the most challenging (and frustrating!) projects for consultants and corporations alike.

At d/g* New York (my former firm, which I also cofounded) New York, our naming department has developed a unique technique that helps create the name of a brand. We have found that it is best to start out working with a name list composed by people of varying backgrounds—creatives, copywriters, teachers, researchers, and professionals well versed in languages—as a basis for a concept. As a parallel step, it is effective to have groups of people respond to visuals specifically selected to reflect the desired brand attributes in order to generate any relevant instinctual name ideas.

We are always surprised that very few people tend to like a name at first mention and generally have many rational, emotional, or personal reasons for disliking a name. The most important thing about naming is that a name takes on an entirely fresh meaning once it is associated with a business concept. Alone, it could have little appeal. Who today would endorse names like The Limited, or Nestlé, for example, all by themselves? They are not so great-sounding in isolation. What would we think of Chase today if it were taken literally and in isolation? A lot has been written about the Chevy Nova saga of a name going awry in Latin America, where "Nova" translates in Spanish as "does not go." Procter & Gamble launched the Pert shampoo in France. Not a great idea in a country where the hair product's name translates into "loss."

The objective of a name is to stand out and to distance itself from any formulaic or trendy expressions that could diminish the impact of the brand.

A name therefore needs to be viewed in its total context. We always recommend looking at names in several typographic fonts—they can take on entirely different meanings when expressed in different typefaces. Then, it is important to apply these varied looks to at least one element of the communications program, either a Web site, a storefront, or a letterhead. One test that really helps feel out a new name is role-playing: try being the receptionist and answer the phone by saying "Good morning, [New Name]," or repeat the phrase "I work for [New Name]." It really can lead to a different perception of the personality of the name when you hear and use it.

Of course, the objective of a name is to stand out and to distance itself from any formulaic or trendy expressions that could diminish the impact of the brand. In 1999, within a year of each other, these three companies appeared, all with the same suffix: Novartis, Lactalis, and Aventis. Sounds pretty old-economy to me!

Since the new economy has brought a new naming style to demarcate Internet brands from traditional ones, new possibilities in naming have opened up. Corporations are more willing to entertain concepts that would not have made even the first cut years ago. In this environment, risk-taking in naming is sometimes required for success. Computer Literacy worked with Interbrand to find a new, unusual name that users would easily retain for an e-commerce book site. They eventually came up with the controversial name "Fatbrain.com." Although it had an incredibly high recall percentage in focus groups (nothing less than 100 percent!), it was highly disliked by a significant number of participants. Some employees of the company even threatened to quit if the name was chosen. After much debate, the company took the plunge and went with the name despite the misgivings. The result was terrific: six months later, the average number of site visits was up 200 percent—and no one actually ever quit over the choice![117]

OTHER SUCCESS STORIES

I had the opportunity to discuss Lancôme, a brand that has benefited immensely from its corporate image, with the president of L'Oréal USA's luxury product division, Philip Shearer, who told me the fascinating story of this brand that clearly has the necessary components of Emotional Branding we mentioned before: cultural relevance, meaning, and emotional connection. The Lancôme rose and the accent on top of the *o* are two major signals that bring tremendous meaning and personality to the corporate image. The rose is obviously a symbol of femininity, but the circumflex accent on the *o*, which has no reason to be there from a purely grammatical point of view, connotes the French origins of the brand. The combination of both symbols brings a powerful cocktail of exoticism and promise, which have been at the core of a universal language that has struck an emotional chord with women worldwide for decades.

I have always been fascinated by Lancôme and followed the growth of this almost $2 billion brand with great interest. There is no doubt that Lancôme's success is based on the quality of its product line, including what most professionals and consumers perceive as the best mascara in the world. But this organization is also driven by its people. I have been told that annual sales meetings at Lancôme are major events, that company representatives dress up, bond, and show their pride in working for the company. People of different ages mingle together, creating an oral tradition that helps newcomers immerse themselves in the wonderful history of the company.

The most amazing thing about Lancôme is how it has evolved during its sixty-five-year history.

The most amazing thing about Lancôme is how it has evolved during its sixty-five-year history, always moving alongside trends and absorbing them into its brand identity without ever becoming dominated by them. The fact that Lancôme is as successful in Asia and the Americas as it is in Europe is another testimony to its great flexibility and ability to speak to women in a universal language.

LANCÔME 🌹
PARIS

Lancôme has always retained control of the voice, the reason, and the signature behind the products, regardless of who the company's ambassador is. Lancôme is warm and approachable, yet classy and elegant. It is about "la femme," the universal woman, and it crystallizes this universal woman's aspiration.

The Lancôme identity reflects this multidimensional brand character through its powerful visual symbols. The Lancôme identity is an identity that is "personal" and designed for "contact" through its flexibility. Myths need symbols, and Lancôme's layered graphic expression creates a bridge between the brand and women worldwide. It puts the final accent on a wonderful story . . . the eternal beauty of the rose.

The story I created with my team for Ann Taylor was the personalization of the fictitious "Ann." Sally Frame Kasaks, the president of Ann Taylor at the time

We updated the Bodoni typeface logo and added in handwritten script the tagline "Destination." Details, such as new box shapes, navy grosgrain ribbons, and a photograph of a purposeful, multifaceted real woman on a bag made from recycled materials, add character and personality to the total image.

(1992), was convinced that in order to turn around a retail brand that had lost a great deal of its cachet, consumers, as well as everyone in the organization, needed to be turned on by a new concept. Our SENSE® program this time was a collaborative exercise with the top twelve managers and buyers from Ann Taylor. It injected a new spirit and passion into the company and steered everyone involved with the brand in a clear direction. The story we built around the brand was so developed and realistic that people in the organization associated themselves in a very personal and emotional way with the independence, truthfulness, elegance, and approachability of the Ann Taylor character we created—even internalizing some of these perceived qualities. Often, managers reviewed products in the new collection and comment, "Ann would never do this," or, "This is very consistent with her voice"! On the basis of this visual strategy and story, we developed a new logo, a unique packaging program, the flagship stores in San Francisco and New York, and an ad campaign that resonated successfully with a new, younger consumer group of professional women who started to shop at Ann Taylor again. This identity program was one of the most integrated programs we have ever done, and it made Ann Taylor one of the premiere moderate-priced clothing brands for professional women in America.

Conclusion

People are usually afraid of change, and corporations most often hate change, but our lives are, of course, about change and human experience. The success of a corporate identity program resides in its flexibility; not so much to evolve and stay ahead of its market as to be meaningful—on many levels—to consumers and the company. Putting the word "forever" in a corporate identity program is like locking up the personality of a company that might not mean a lot to future generations. Some of my clients' major fears, I found, revolved around their questions "Is our logo going to survive trends?" or "Will certain graphics age gracefully?" The real question is, How can I ensure that my culture and consumer connection will stay relevant? The Apple logo was the antithesis of the "business-driven" logo, and it still lives. The Virgin Atlantic logo is still relevant, and the Bloomingdale's round letters seem to withstand the passing of time, even though they could have been perceived as trendy at the time they were invented. These identities are still relevant because they reflect a culture that is still relevant. The logo, again, is the badge and the visualization of an emotional reality, and as long as this connection exists between a brand and people, the identity will keep its positive meaning.

If the identity of your brand is not well defined, you may have visibility but no personality. A logo is but the tip of the iceberg in a corporate expression. If it is not supported by the passion of a corporation's leadership, if it is not about meaning and shared objectives, it will fast become generic and familiar, not loved. Through the process of vision, visualization, and expression that I have just described, identities with character and personality forge connections with consumers through unique, evocative, and multidimensional messages; the expression of the brand is without limits. If it is couched in these processes, it will remain relevant, almost updating itself.

If the identity of your brand is not well defined, you may have visibility but no personality.

12

Retailing with a Passion: Sensational Stores of Tomorrow

Raised in a family of retailers, I realized firsthand and very early on the truth of the age-old maxim that the key to continued success is the level of relationship you are able to build with your clients. The retail business does not stop at 5:00 P.M., but is an ongoing relationship process that continues long after the sale, which must constantly reinforce to your customers the idea that you are committed to providing them with the best products at the best value.

Retailing the Old-fashioned Way

My grandparents were clothing retailers in a small French village in the West of France. Since they met their customers every day in the street, at church, or during social occasions, their personal credibility was under close scrutiny at all times. They made sure that their reputation was one of integrity.

In those days, particularly in rural France in the first half of the twentieth century, traveling was very limited and done mostly on foot, on horseback, or in horse-pulled carts. Villages were mainly commercial centers in which every Monday an open market allowed farmers to sell their products, trade cattle, or buy necessary items such as clothing, agricultural equipment, or even food. Apart from the market, the other important gathering place was, of course, church on Sundays. The men packed into the back of the chapel in order to demonstrate just enough presence to be saved, and met afterwards at nearby cafés, where they tradeed or made business deals among themselves or with passing salesmen. In those meetings much was discussed, including arranging marriages and sharing human resources for harvest.

My grandparents understood the needs of this population intimately. One of the things missing from the community was the idea of a "general store," and my grandparents saw an excellent opportunity to make a decent living. Descendants of bourgeois landowners who had never worked, my grandparents saw their own version of a "new economy" with the advent of the industrial age and the flight of the rural population toward cities and new jobs in factories. This phenomenon literally wiped out the value of land and forced them to find another source of income. They created a retail concept that included a grocery store, a restaurant, a café, and a clothing store all under one roof.

In this clever idea that was ahead of its time, they saw the potential value in providing a place that would offer rest, clothing, and great food and drinks for a hardworking rural population. They created an environment that was relaxing, cozy, and cheerful. The restaurant and café was a place where people could find an atmosphere of friendliness and comfort and that enhanced their mood for shopping. They created the perfect state for potential shoppers to shop. In those days, farmers dressed up for Sunday church and special events such as christenings, communions, and weddings, and my grandparents' store offered not only the appropriate clothing for these occasions, but also the facilities in which to celebrate some of those events. My grandparents' store became an important place for social interaction and an integral part of the fabric of the village community.

There was an incredible attempt in the store to give every patron the utmost personal attention. My grandparents had a heightened notion of respect for their clientele. They felt, I was told, that if someone paid you for a service or for products, a moral contract existed between the vendor and the client—a contract that went beyond return policies to deliver the best level of quality on all fronts. It was a contract to never, ever deceive the client. The "brand promise" was made . . . and kept.

My grandparents felt keenly the significance of sharing what was important to their clientele on all levels. This is why they made it a point to go to church every Sunday. Similarly, they participated in all the village's seasonal fairs. They also were always available to meet customers at their own homes if work kept them there. This relationship with the town's people was reinforced further in times of crisis. The shop was used temporarily as a communication relay for the Resistance during World War II. They profoundly cared—and they showed it.

My family's retail history is a standardbearer of a responsive, interactive, and ultimately successful consumer relationship model.

I have always referred to my family's retail history as a standard-bearer of a responsive, highly interactive, and ultimately extremely successful consumer relationship model. Our lifestyles may have changed enormously, but people haven't, really. People still have urgent needs and beliefs stemming from our different social, cultural, and political backgrounds . . . and we still want to believe in a commercial landscape that will support and enhance those needs and beliefs. In a nutshell, we still appreciate when the people we do business with care about the same things we do! This means being able to find out what your customers really care about and telling them that you support the same causes they do and have the same interests. Tell them that you appreciate the same music, the same values, and the same dreams. In short, become a best friend. This is the way to create loyalty.

A Common-Sense Approach to Relationship

My grandparents' legacy was carried on as my parents entered the restaurant business. I vividly remember some of the business conversations they had around the dinner table with friends or family. Most of those discussions obviously seemed very abstract at my age, but they still fascinated me to the point that I would stay until I dozed off, when other kids or cousins had already left the table to play.

One topic that always was discussed with great seriousness when describing a competitor or someone's success centered on the *sense du commerce*–commerce sense . . . or business savvy. One either had it and was blessed, or did not have it and was destined to terrible luck–a life of hell, as I interpreted it. Having this "commerce sense" is, as I found out later, a quality that is very much overlooked in today's megaretail corporations. It simply means making the customer first in everything you do and constantly bridging the gap between your business and the end user.

The sense of commerce is about personal relationship, starting with the president of a company. It is about trust and commitment. Sally Frame Kasaks, the former CEO of Ann Taylor, when working on revitalizing the Ann Taylor brand with my company, implemented a card system that allowed each of her customers to communicate with her personally from the store, and she answered each card in person. The great Lee Iaccoca once said, "The dealer franchise system set up by Henry Ford is a damn good one. You want to buy from the guy who goes to the Kiwanis meeting and is part of the community."

In my business, I sometimes meet high-level businesspeople isolated in their ivory towers and incapable of making a real connection to the people to whom they sell their products. Some retailers won't even wear the clothes they sell! Maybe they are above the market or have a "superior" taste? But in reality they could be the best representatives of or ambassadors for their brands! At a time when hats were a must in church, my mother's role in my grandparents' store was the millinery business. She was a very elegant and beautiful woman, and always wore a fabulous hat to church in the most dramatic way, which was, of course, the best promotion she could have done. Her business became successful to the point that people traveled long distances to shop at her boutique.

I sometimes meet high-level businesspeople isolated in their ivory towers and incapable of making a real connection to the people to whom they sell their products.

Understanding the day-to-day life of your clients and catering to their wishes is the key to success and something that can be achieved today with the flexibility that new technologies offer. Meeting each and every one of your customers on a regular basis today is obviously impossible, but through technology companies can interface with them in some very unique ways–through personalized Internet sites or customized promotional initiatives. Basically, any sincere attempt to become involved in answering people's personal needs will help maintain this crucial emotional bond of human contact that can exist between companies and their audience.

Evolving Retail from Service to Relationship

In the Emotional Economy, there is little room for buying. True, buying takes place every day across the globe, but the Emotional Economy heralds a much more rewarding and engaging activity–*shopping*. Buying is an activity understood by economists. Shopping is a phenomenon of interest to anthropologists and sociologists. Shopping provides opportunities for dreaming and playing–it's an escape and, ultimately, an art. There is much greater demand, value, and, most of all, potential inherent in shopping than in its remedial counterpart, buying. Vendors who create atmospheres conducive to shopping give their customers a good reason to leave their homes and, in turn, create opportunities to buy.

We can learn a great deal about ways to inspire the art of shopping by borrowing ideas from the customs of age-old cultures. For example, in Marrakech, Morocco, the Souk, the Mediterranean Arabic version of our department store, brings magic to the shopping experience by awakening your curiosity and desires at all levels. It is recommended that you pay a guide to take you through this immensely complex amalgam of outdoor shops. The idea of a guide is already enticing, conjuring a mysterious world of shops. The guide coordinates your tour according to your desires, and he serves as both a translator and quality-control person. On your tour, music and exotic aromas constantly surround you. Each shop offers you a flavorful green tea that reinforces your sensory experience of the place. It is truly an experience to relish, on the same scale for tourists as visiting a monument or a famous site. Some years ago, we were doing a project for Ethan Allen, and Farouq Kawahari, their president, explained to me how much he enjoyed Oriental markets–similar to the open markets of Kashmir–and how his aim was to bring that sensation to his stores. His point was that the experience that people had there was so powerful that it sometimes bordered on the sacred. Even capturing a mere shadow of the richness of these experiences can transform most retailers into exciting destinations worthy of visiting simply for the atmosphere.

In contrast to this experience, consider the state of retailing in the United States today: a glut of offerings accompanied by the proliferation both of homogeneity and increased specialization. Department stores, most notably JCPenney, which have long been the mainstay of American families, are fighting to keep their competitive edge. This crisis mostly affects the fashion segment of the retail business–one fashion store after another offers almost the same merchandise and fights for each sale! In addition, today's brick-and-mortar retailer competes with online alternatives that operate all hours of the day and keep shop no further than the nearest computer screen. All these facts come down to one thing: *the rules of retailing have changed.* However, a select group of savvy retailers is spearheading a revolution in retailing that will make the art of shopping once again interesting and worthwhile to the American public.

> **Consider the state of retailing in the United States today: a glut of offerings accompanied by the proliferation both of homogeneity and increased specialization.**

WAL-MART AND TARGET REDO DISCOUNT

Wal-Mart, long condemned for pushing out local businesses and replacing them with one-stop shopping, has made a rapid turnaround in image by building an emotional connection with the communities where it operates. Today's Wal-Mart not only caters to consumers' value-driven buying needs, but also their indulgent shopping escapades and entertainment needs. It has fashioned a convenient and welcoming community-oriented atmosphere that combines diversity, efficiency, and quality.

But what exactly does Wal-Mart offer to shoppers, besides affordable goods? Well, for one, events such as the April 2000 bubble-gum bubble-blowing contest, which was held across 2,800 stores nationwide and awarded one winner a million-dollar prize while raising money for the Children's Miracle Network. It also provided countless families with an occasion for going out together for an afternoon's fun at Wal-Mart. By tying in with the *Rosie O'Donnell Show* and offering the winner an appearance on the show, the Wal-Mart bubble-blowoff gained a valuable presence in the homes of loyal viewers for whom Rosie is a trusted morning companion. Wal-Mart was also the exclusive home to the "Power Rangers Intergalactic Encounter Tour," complete with (at five thousand square feet) the world's largest moonbounce. Although the TV program that inspired it is aimed at young children, the show was geared to entertain teens and adults, as well. Other events have included Oreo-stacking contests and Garth Brooks's personal appearances. Combine that with quality merchandise, intelligently laid out stores, excellent prices, *and* convenient locations, and it is easy to understand why Wal-Mart has become the world's largest retailer. Although the Internet has made leaps and bounds in transforming shopping, it will be years before its entire retail industry can even hope to rival Wal-Mart's revenues. Estimates predicted that retail sales online would reach $184 billion by 2004, at which time Wal-Mart was expected to have $243 billion in revenue–domestically.

Wal-Mart's success is not only a result of business acumen—it is also a reflection of its devotion to aggressively redefining the concept of "discount retail."

Wal-Mart's success is not only a result of business acumen–it is also a reflection of its devotion to aggressively redefining the concept of "discount retail." At a time when stores such as Caldor's faltered, Wal-Mart realized it could dissociate itself from the drawbacks of "discount" without sacrificing value. At the heart of this change is an attention to the emotional state of its customers. Wal-Mart has set out a goal of meeting the needs *not* of customers but rather of specific shoppers–working mothers, excitable children, cash-strapped college students–both pragmatically and emotionally. Five years ago, discount was about second-rate. Shopping at Wal-Mart today reflects shoppers' intelligence and satisfaction. By tapping into values deep in the American psyche, Wal-Mart has quickly become the standard by which other retailers are measured, and

when others cannot measure up (which is frequently), Wal-Mart wins out. Wal-Mart has a real sense of community and an image that spells out all the values in which America believes. Sam Walton himself represented a new success story of integrity that was approachable, sensitive, and populist. The message is clear, the culture unique. Wal-Mart has, in fact, become such a cultural phenomenon that we even see the store as an inspirational setting for the characters in the book *Where the Heart Is* by Billie Letts, which was made into a movie starring Natalie Portman, Ashley Judd, Stockard Channing, and Joan Cusack, among others. The story is about a seventeen-year-old pregnant woman who is dumped by her boyfriend, with less than ten dollars in her pocket, in a small Oklahoma town on their way to California. Because Wal-Mart is the major community gathering place, however, it turns out she's in the right place. She immediately begins to meet some of the eclectic townspeople there who will help her change her life. The young woman secretly spends her nights in the Wal-Mart for several months, eventually having her baby there. After her creative use of the store as a home is discovered, Walton himself offers her a job, and she is on her way to building a normal life within the fabric of the store and the community surrounding the store.

Wal-Mart may dominate the scene in terms of sheer size, but Target's bull's-eye trademark has claimed first place in directing retailers toward a retailing future that is both fashionable and affordable. In the past three years, Target has revealed itself as the most innovative and interesting mass-market retailer. It positions itself as a culturally attuned discounter, and its merchandise takes the high road with style while preserving the affordability of its discounting competitors. Robert Ulrich, chairman of Target's parent corporation Dayton Hudson, explained to *Fortune*: "People's tastes are not determined by income, obviously. A lot of people want to be 'with it.'"[118] By drawing top-name designers such as Michael Graves and Philippe Starck, Target has produced whole lines of trendy and attractive housewares and furniture that transform kettles and knives into Kitchenware-extraordinaire and homes into a stylish metropolitan statement. By working harder to create a unique line of merchandise and drawing attention to that merchandise with flashy, youthful ads completely unlike its conservative competitors', Target has positioned itself as the hip and creative alternative to discount retail. Sure, Kmart is convenient, but its chief claim to fame is practicality. Target preserves that practicality and links it with "cool," and this allows Target to begin to compete not only with other discounters, but with the likes of Crate & Barrel and Banana Republic, as well. Its retail strategy has attracted customers from a broad stratum of economic and social classes, and other discounters are scrambling to decipher and implement Target's formula. Target's average customer is younger, more affluent, and likely to leave the store with a heftier receipt than are the typical patrons of other discounters. Target's success is an illustration of branding at its best. By developing true points of distinction that are valuable and relevant to consumers, it has developed an identity. That identity is propelling its profits and exciting consumers and investors across the country.

While Wal-Mart and Target may be the two largest players shaping retail of today and tomorrow, they are by no means defining it. In fact, their size and broad appeal may limit their ability to creatively challenge the standards of retail, and although they may be leading the way in certain innovations, their stores are still relatively tame. Their efforts at providing better service have been appreciated and have boosted sales, but twenty-first-century shoppers are adjusting to these changes quickly. In order to hold consumers' attention and continue inspiring shoppers to shop as opposed to buying, innovation and experience must be more thoroughly integrated into retail. In this realm, specialty retailers are often able to craft more moving and personalized stories to stir the customers' imagination and emotions.

Welcome to the Neighborhood

Kmart: Big K at Astor Place, NYC—when Kmart opened up a store in the East Village, a trendy neighborhood renowned for its bohemian, artistic past, many community members objected to its presence, and executives wondered how they might cater to this funky urban audience. In 2000, artist Paul Richard, a local resident, approached them wanting to display his art in their café. Management quickly secured approval from headquarters, and Richard's art moved in, including some that subtly pokes fun at the discounter. This was the first art display ever in any of Kmart's 2,000-plus stores, but in a community such as New York City's East Village, it made perfect sense. This is the kind of specific local community-bonding effort that, if done on a larger scale in all of its locations, could really help Kmart better compete with Wal-Mart and Target.

Remember that effective retailing interweaves social, emotional, and imaginative elements via the portal of an emotional brand. *Retail branding is about storytelling and engaging in a dialogue that connects your brand to a customer's heart.* Here are several examples of retailers doing this in different ways . . .

REI: GREAT MERCHANDISE IN GOOD HANDS

I visited REI, a Seattle-based provider of outdoor gear and clothing that understands that retail success is born in a story and led by a passion. In fact, its Web page explicitly tells that story, which goes like this:

It all started with an ice axe . . .

REI (Recreational Equipment Incorporated) began one day in 1938 when Seattle mountaineer Lloyd Anderson sent away for a new ice axe. Upon picking it up, he got an unwelcome surprise: The axe was nearly twice the price advertised, and about half the quality. Vowing not to be fooled again, Lloyd found his own source, buying a top-quality Austrian Academ Pickel ice axe at a lower price! His climbing friends begged him to get this ice axe for them, too. He did. Word spread, and here we are many years later, basically doing the same thing.[119]

What an inspiring basis for a brand! Based on that initial experience, founder Lloyd Anderson formed a cooperative venture with friends and acquaintances who pooled money to acquire the highest-caliber outdoors gear. Because all of the contributors were themselves outdoorsmen, they had a personal devotion to securing the best merchandise, and at the end of the first year of operation, eighty-two members of REI received dividends. Although their stores are open to the public, membership now costs $20, and REI has over three million active members, all of whom receive voting privileges to elect REI's board of directors, as well as a share in company profits through an annual patronage fund. However, it's not simply the membership policies or the history that distinguishes this chain of forty-six retail stores. REI's entire approach to retail embraces unique experiences, distinguished offerings, and personal relationships. Its Seattle flagship epitomizes the REI spirit. Every time someone enters the store, the door handles, fashioned from ice axes, recall the birth of REI. Once on-site, 2.1 acres beckon

Flashy effects and divine atmospherics are great, but in theater, as in retail, it is the people who really define the brand.

visitors' adventurous spirit. In addition to a comprehensive selection of gear for biking, hiking, canoeing, skiing, and other sports, REI boasts features like an outdoors mountain bike test trail, the JanSport Kids' Camp, the Gore-Tex rain room for trying out Gore-Tex rainwear, and the Footwear Test Trail featuring various terrain for shoppers trying out hiking boots. As shoppers tramp about on this path in varying pieces of footwear, educational sessions regarding camping and other activities may be ongoing in REI's 250-person meeting room. Most striking, however, is the REI Pinnacle—a sixty-five-foot indoor climbing structure manned by belay experts helping expert and novice alike enjoy rock climbing. However, the richness and quality associated with REI is not a function of the merchandise, the architecture, or the educational seminars. Rather, these are expressions of the REI identity that resides in the men and women associated with the brand. Just as its members are devoted to outdoor activities, so are its five thousand employees that form an in-house test crew. REI turns to them, avid outdoors enthusiasts, for field testing of products. When an employee tells a shopper this is the best tent for a given trip, that employee's advice may well be based on an REI-sponsored camping trip he took with that tent. If employees are dissatisfied with a product, then shoppers will not see it on REI shelves.

The exemplary outdoors knowledge of REI employees is in stark contrast to many other retailers that are saddled with poorly trained and often inappropriate salespeople. More brands must realize how crucial their employees are. I think of it this way—if a well-written play has excellent publicity, brilliant lighting, divine costumes, mesmerizing scenery, but unprepared actors, is the play a success? No, of course not. Flashy effects and divine atmospherics are great, but in theater, as in retail, it is the people who really define the brand. It's been said that if a play is cast right, 80 percent of the problems have already been solved. It is the same thing if a store is staffed right. I am sometimes shocked at the meticulous effort devoted to articulating brand identity through brand communications when that identity subsequently falls flat in the hands of incompetent salespeople. The importance of employees as the in-store living embodiment of a brand's identity cannot be underestimated. Employees should reflect the brand's intended identity and also have relevance to the shoppers. Finding a cashier should not be simply an issue of locating a reliable man or woman who will show up for work on time, work cheaply, and not steal from the register. Instead, it needs to be about choosing an individual who, in addition to the former qualities, will send shoppers out of the store not with a fake smile, but with a genuine brand experience. Perhaps that means a well-wishing, maybe it implies a sly comment about a cute guy. *From the CEO to the janitor, workers should be part of the brand itself, rather than people simply paid to dispassionately tend to its interest.* However, instinctual relevance to the brand needs to be supported with appropriate training. Salespeople need to be trained thoroughly on how to deal with customers in all their endless varieties: happy, hassled and hurried, picky, frustrated, nervous or excited, price-conscious, indecisive, depressed, and so on. Ideally, employees of a store will be drawn from the same pool as potential customers. For a little further insight into the state of retail service today and the potential (meaning consequence), I would like once again to turn to Peter Levine, the head of d/g* Consulting.

Love in the Age of the Vigilante Consumer: The Twenty-First-Century Empowered Consumer *by Peter Levine*

I attended a "destination wedding" several years ago in Florence, Italy. A woman I knew who was also a wedding guest had an emergency and had to return home to California a few days early. I overheard her on the phone with an American Airlines agent trying to rearrange her reservation. Her voice telegraphed tense frustration as she stated, "I have a full fare, first-class ticket, I'm a Platinum American Airlines cardholder—I belong to the Admirals Club, I have thousands of frequent flyer miles, I have an American Airlines credit card, and you still can't get me a seat on a plane out of Italy in the next day?!" she demanded. "Where's the love?" It was her plea, "Where's the love?" that seized my attention. I'd worked for several decades in a profession that aimed to create "emotional connections" between brands and consumers. Now I was witnessing firsthand a loyal customer begging a brand ambassador for "love." The response to her plight was a robotic, "that's our policy"-style solution.

Flash forward a few years, and my friend's "Where is the love?" plea has turned out to be a resonant consumer mantra. Of course, many brands out there are so shortsighted that they actually let consumers go away without even thinking about it. I would even venture to say many brands unknowingly usher loyal customers to the door—invisibly stating, "We are not especially interested in your business."

If we look back to the dawn of manufacturing, consumers were in the mindset of buying what was produced, shopping where that product was available, and paying the price the store asked. The manufacturer, company, and store were in charge. As products and consumers have evolved over the years, the concept of "brand loyalty" has emerged. A more even exchange or conversation between consumers and companies who had something to sell emerged. By the 1980s, there wasn't a consumer product out there that did not have qualitative and/or quantitative research behind it. Internal brand marketing teams had the ability to say, "This is what we learned from consumers and here is how we choose to incorporate some of their feedback." It was the era of action based on "consumer insight." As we progress into the twenty-first century, the Internet has changed all of that. Today, the consumer is not just providing insight. They are calling the shots. And they are also consumers who are out for vengeance.

Today, there is considerable data to support the notion that consumers have begun to curtail their spending. I have learned that consumers are not necessarily unwilling to spend just because of the struggling economy. They are also resistant to being "taken" in any way. Today's consumers are calling the shots and not waiting for "the love" any longer. The sentiment I hear most in consumer research is, "Here is how I need to be loved if you want me to remain a customer." They want rewards, discounts, VIP programs, samples, freebies, information, live contact, exclusivity, points, special treatment, personalization, customization, and on and on.

Today, consumers are savvier than ever before because they are willing to go elsewhere. They are willing to do the work to find what they want, how they want it, and pay what they feel is right and fair. This is the era of the "vigilante consumer." If brands are going out of business today because of a loss of consumer interest, connection, contact, and flexible policy, those brands are completely out of touch and have officially blown it!

We worked with the European car manufacturer Peugeot in the mid-2000s as they focused on bringing a new car-selling experience to consumers. Their biggest insight was that women don't feel fearful of or intimidated by a car salesman, nor are they merely seduced by a car's style or pretty color. These days, women come into a showroom fully prepared with a phone book-sized stack of information. They tell the car salesman, "Here is what you paid for the car, here is the markup you are asking, here is the profit you stand to make, and here is what my research has told me I should offer." It's all there on the Internet. Today's consumers are smart, informed, and prepared to fight or, even worse, disengage if you do not participate in a relationship with them. It is not so much an environment of brand switching as it is, "I can get it elsewhere the way I want it." Internet social networking sites have given consumers a collective power and a rapid force of information exchange. Blogs and chat rooms are loaded with real-life consumer feed-back. Who cares what you say about your brand anymore—today, it is about what consumers are saying to each other about you.

Someone once gave me an example I'll never forget. I was flying back home from a business trip and they said, "You know, I would bet that no two people on this full flight paid the same amount for their seat." When I thought about online deal brokers, frequent flyer miles, special promotional offers, people who bought long in advance, people who went through travel agents who knew how to get upgrades and discounts, people who were flying on package deals, people who bought tickets from secondary sellers, and on and on, it was true. The consumer had a hand in the deal they settled for. I put this notion into practice myself when I was having a problem with two cats I inherited when my mother died. Merging her two cats with my own two cats was not working. I had a cat sitter who suggested I try a product called "Feliway." It was a plug-in device that released a synthetic replication of a "feel-good" hormone that seemed to make cats content and happy. I began looking for the product at my local pet store. With the square footage of my home, I determined that I would need three of the Feliway plug-in devices.

Each vial of "feel-good" juice lasted one month. Committing to this proposition could really add up, as the refills at my pet store were about $40 each. Here is where my quest began. I jumped on the Internet to do some research. Lo and behold, the spread for the Feliway package of plug-ins and refills was all over the map. I investigated eBay, Amazon, Petco, and many other sites. I decided to call 1-800-Pet-Meds. A customer service representa-tive quoted me a price somewhere in the middle of what my research had told me. I said, "Thanks, I will mull it over."

The gentleman on the phone said, "Well, what would you like to pay?" Surprised, I gave him all the information I had uncovered from eBay (the cheapest opening auction bid) to Petco (the highest price). I gave him a fair number that was a great deal for me and he said, "Okay, we will sell the product to you at that price." I was amazed. I said, "If you will really stick to that price, I will also buy three more refills." He said, "I will guarantee the same price whenever you call back for future refills." OK, I was feeling my vigilante power—the power to walk away if I wanted to. I asked, "Can I also get free shipping?" He said, "Done." Now, I would never even consider going anywhere else but 1-800-Pet-Meds, because I felt "the love."

Today, I walk around with the empowered mindset of the vigilante consumer, and I urge everyone to do the same. The Dunkin' Donuts in my neighborhood still serves coffee in Styrofoam cups. I told the manager, "Those cups are unacceptable landfill," and I walked away. Staples gives valuable Staples dollars for returning any brand of used printer ink cartridges. I am loyal! I urge everyone to take serious note of who is "showing the love" and who is out of touch and could care less.

I had a broken humidifier that I paid over $150 for. It was less than a year old. I called the manufacturer. They asked, "Do you have the original packaging?"

"Sorry, No." I say.

"Do you have the original receipt?"

"No," again.

"Did you fill out and mail in a warranty card?"

"Huuuummm . . . I don't think so." They suggested going back to Bed Bath and Beyond, where I purchased the unit. I was instructed to ask them to look up my credit card record from a year ago. I thought that that was the most ridiculous thing I'd ever heard, but it was worth a try. If indeed they did have the record, the proposed action plan was that I would get that receipt and write a letter including the case number the manufacturer assigned to me. I would pack up the humidifier, go to a UPS Store, and return the unit to the company in Illinois for them to inspect and potentially repair, which would incur costs based on the problem. I went to Bed Bath and Beyond and sheepishly started to explain what I needed with the credit card record. Their response blew my mind—the customer service representative said, "Just bring it back and we will give you a new one." I walked in the door with the broken device and walked out with a brand-new humidifier in minutes. I did not fill out a form, give my driver's license, or show any receipt. Now I am their customer for life. Bed Bath and Beyond actually went beyond! They did not just help me out. They provided me with what I now call "heroic customer service." That may seem simple, but another incident demonstrates a brand that just didn't get it. I bought a bed at IKEA for my guest room. I managed to blow the "find the merchandise yourself in our warehouse" aspect of the shopping experience as I misread the Swedish name of the mattress. I ended up grabbing the wrong mattress off the shelf. When I got home and realized the error, I also discovered that I had no receipt for the purchase. Luckily, I was able to go online and download my credit card charge statement. I went back to IKEA with my statement and the wrong mattress in hand. They were firm: "No receipt, no exchange!"

"But it's a mattress that cost over $100. I can't use it—it's the wrong one." I begged. "Here is my credit card statement from online—it's from yesterday!"

"Sorry—no receipt, no exchange. That's our policy."

"Then, can I speak to a manager?"

"I *am* a manager," was what I got back.

Well, the newly empowered vigilante consumer I am thought, See ya, IKEA! Look for me on *ikeasuckz.blogspot.com*—if you even care.

THE SHAPE OF ANN TAYLOR

While service is of the utmost importance, atmospherics certainly still play a vital role as well in enhancing a brand's identity and elaborating the communications made through other mediums. Retail designers have the opportunity to impact society by bringing a renewed sense of beauty to all channels of distribution. People are looking for experiences of newness and excitement within stores. Furthermore, retail environments should be inspired by the products they sell in a way that brings total consistency to the brand image. Nike has delivered on this promise, particularly in its Chicago store, but car dealerships are still quite mundane.

Our goal at the time in designing the Ann Taylor store was to create on Madison Avenue and Sixtieth Street in New York City a forty-thousand-square-foot store that presented a feminine, sophisticated retail environment reflective of the Ann Taylor woman's dynamic lifestyle. Through our SENSE® process, we realized that the Ann Taylor woman is real, unpretentious, elegant, and practical-minded. To reflect her taste, the store we designed is warm, sophisticated, and refined. The townhouse-inspired façade clad in limestone was inspired by what the fictitious personage Ann Taylor's home would be like. The natural and relaxed interior is comprised of clean, refined spaces enriched by warm, tactile materials. The centerpiece, a staircase of glass and limestone, a vertical form spiraling up

five floors, welcomes visitors with its connotations not of selling products, but rather of an attractive and inviting home. Natural, monochromatic colors communicate the overall identity palette of the brand in a modern, unpretentious, comfortable manner, which plays off the navy blue of the brand's signature color. Sensual shapes rendered in a mix of warm and cool materials like bronze, stone, frosted green glass, and auburn wood create textural contrasts. Sculpted details on fixtures, door handles, and railings are unexpected additions that personalize the store design. We also created a "comfort zone," a sitting area for guests with a view of Madison Avenue, as well as a personal shopping area with a built-in desk that includes a place to plug in a laptop. The latter is part of Ann Taylor's commitment to service and a reflection of the multiple roles its customer fulfills in her daily life. If more brands undertake such pertinent design, our commercial landscape could become unimaginably uplifting and enriching. Until that happens, though, brands such as Ann Taylor will stand out among and above their competitors.

THE FACES OF MACYSPORT

One of the hallmarks of shopping is that it's easy to not even realize you are doing it. You sometimes show up in a store without even the intention of buying, and before you realize it you are leaving the store with shopping bags in your hands. Events are an ideal way to do this. For example, Macysport in New York City hosted a panel discussion sponsored by *Women's Sport & Fitness* magazine which featured pro volleyball player Gabrielle Reece, world champion surfer Lisa Anderson, nutritionist Heidi Skolnick, and other renowned figures in women's sports. Monica Bella-Bragg, vice president of special events at Macy's East, said: "It's hard to quantify an event like this, but we'll see some results in the next few months. Even if customers don't shop that night, when they need sports apparel, they will know they can find it here. It also makes women think different about Macy's as a place where they can get really good information and, in this case, inspiration."[120] These events not only positively reinforce Macysport's identity among consumers, but elaborate the identity far beyond that of a traditional retailer. For consumers in attendance, Macysport is no longer defined only by its products and price, but also by these speakers who have aligned themselves with the brand. Because working women and men have little in the way of free time, increasing stress, and never enough time for themselves, these efforts are doubly valuable. Any retailer that offers not only quality products but also rewarding experiences can expect to be rewarded in turn by consumers willing to pay a premium for that service.

DOMSEY'S DISCOUNTS FOR DEDICATED AND DEFT BROOKLYN DENIZENS

This vendor of secondhand clothing in a four-floor warehouse in Williamsburg, Brooklyn, is an interesting example of successful retailing to the Gen Y crowd that could be modified and expanded to other retail concepts. This inexpensive store has become a hot spot for the young and hip. What really distinguishes the store is its annex. An outlet on the side of the store, this space is where visitors find barrel after barrel, each some twenty-seven cubic feet in size, filled with unsorted clothes. Customers come with their friends and make a sociable afternoon of rooting through the piles of clothing in search of that one perfect item. But the real gimmick is that upon finding their items, the clothes are paid for by the pound! This store proves that creating a memorable and exciting retail experience does not necessarily require a massive investment. Domsey's has turned bargain basement discounting into an alluring point of difference for treasure hunting hipsters otherwise suffering from thrift store malaise.

GLIMPSING THE ASCENT OF TOMORROW'S MALLS

For all the changes inherent in the Emotional Economy, malls remain the most underrated vehicles by retailers and marketers alike. Taken for granted by the first group and misunderstood by the second, they are sadly underused, yet they remain one of America's favorite places to shop. Brands like Godiva, Aveda, Disney, or Warner Brothers have revealed that retail branding, particularly through malls, is a compelling way to bring a brand to life and the most thrilling way to allow a customer to enter the brand experience directly.

Tomorrow's mall will be a place where reality and virtual reality merge. Palm-held computers will scan the prices of items and, via cellular connections, quickly inform us if the product can be found cheaper nearby. Computer consoles and places to link into store networks will allow us to browse showrooms in the real word and order products immediately in the digital world. Most importantly, we will not live in a world of technology so much as technology will live around us. Shaped to the needs and well-being of consumers, technology will serve our needs and emotions in subtle and unnoticed ways with the same ubiquity as electricity. We will neither notice nor think much of this environment–it will simply be natural. In a world in which technology and its applications seem limitless, the decisive role will be played less by programmers with computer know-how than artists and visionaries with imaginative know-how. These women and men will develop the most touching and emotionally relevant implementations of technology, merging

Tomorrow's mall will be a place where reality and virtual reality merge.

the worlds of art, storytelling, and psychology within technologically enhanced design. Consumers of tomorrow will be likely to demand very sophisticated experiences. One place attempting to deliver this today is the Sony Metreon mall in San Francisco. This mall (if you can even fairly call it that) offers a cursory glance at what future malls may offer consumers: a fresh and innovative view of shopping. The Metreon mall is a perfectly suited platform for marketing Sony. After struggling with varying concepts for the mall, executives concluded it was technology that united their disparate ventures, from CDs to DVD players to the PlayStation. In the place of department stores, the Metreon has a dozen movie theaters and an IMAX theater. Attractions such as "Where the Wild Things Are," based on the Maurice Sendak classic of the same title, provide entertainment and a reason for whole families to come. While kids play in a field peopled by six-foot moving, mechanical, hairy monsters, parents can eat at one of the exclusive restaurants nearby that replace food-court fare with fine dining. "Wild Things" is one of two carefully designed indoor attractions, and kids can have access to both and play interactive video games in the super high-tech Sony-designed archives for one fee of twenty dollars–not too shabby, particularly for parents eager to escape the demands of child care for a few hours . . . Carefully selected stores, such as the Discovery Channel Store and MicrosoftSF, mesh with the interactive and technology-oriented theme of the mall, supplementing the Sony-designed stores. Most impressive is the architecture that unites elements such as soaring, suspended arches and video screens dangling from the ceiling to create a seamless and coherent structure. In the place of walls and doors dividing attractions are large open spaces that rely on more subtle atmospherics to guide the transition from one store to the next.

What's worth noting is that Sony and the other stores within the malls are not traditionally considered retailers. The San Francisco store is Microsoft's first, and the Discovery Channel Stores are offshoots of the cable channel. However, retail has proven an innovative and profitable way to market these brands. The mall of the future is going to be just the kind of place to do this. I predict that it will be a place where we come to experience brands, not just to buy products. Brands such as Lancôme and Microsoft will have boutiques alongside Coca-Cola, General Motors, and Canyon Ranch. Brands not traditionally considered retailers will make steps toward retailing as the future continues to blur the distinctions between branding, marketing, supplier/distributor, and entertainment. Marketers will have unprecedented opportunities to make a lasting impact on consumers by "three-dimensionalizing" their brands. Companies like Procter & Gamble and Unilever in the consumer brands category and IBM and

Apple in the computer industry will finally be able to free themselves from the restrictions of their traditional distribution systems to reach their consumers in markedly new ways. They will have the opportunity to bring to the consumer powerful sensory experiences of what their brand stands for through exciting interactive environments.

We will see more paid-admission "brand amusement parks," such as the LEGOLAND parks that feature a myriad of exciting hands-on interactive LEGO attractions, like the Imagination Zone, with its emphasis on exploration and creation through LEGO, and Miniland, with its astonishingly precise reproduc-tions of such famous landmarks as the Empire State Building–made from LEGO. It also has water and roller coaster rides, puppet and magic shows and restaurants, and, of course, an enormous LEGO shop.

We will see more paid-admission "brand amusement parks."

I foresee that stores will become part of advertising budgets and will be used as the best consumer-testing ground, perfect for new product launches or as a way of connecting the retail environment to the Internet for direct selling. Already, innovative malls such as Bluewater in England are considering charging an entrance fee to their leisure/amusement park-like atmosphere in order to lift the burden of rents for retailers who will begin to evolve their brand spaces into showrooms where visitors merely view the goods they buy via the Internet. Bluewater is an incredibly well-designed, innovative, and entertaining mall with three thematic sections of the mall that include a section designed around a pathway on the Thames River, and I would bet that Bluewater, if it chooses to charge admittance, will meet with success.

Several other groups have also aggressively challenged the definition of the mall, such as the Mall of America and the Forum Shops at Caesars, creating enormous "amusement park malls" that are successful in drawing huge numbers in traffic. The Forum Shops at Caesars have made an innovative use of lighting techniques with mechanisms that modulate the lighting and simulate the sky on the ceiling to give shoppers the impression of being outside and passing through the changes of lighting in a day. Caesars also has a fabulous electronics show with animated robotics.

Easton Town Center Mall in Columbus, Ohio, has found some very interesting ways to respond with greater sophistication and creativity than ever before to complex human needs that have little to do with checking off a shopping list. According to Barry Rosenberg at Steiner & Associates, the codeveloper of the

Easton Town Center project, the aim of Easton is to become a real community "city center" to replace an increasingly missing urban fabric.[121] The Easton Town Center model is perhaps even a sort of antithesis to our plugged-in culture, and, as such, just as important to the future of retailing, if not more so, than malls that make abundant use of technology. Easton has become a place to see and be seen in Columbus; it is a place for social gatherings where one might also pick up a pair of jeans at the Gap on the way to one of the restaurants, the thirty movie screens, or a concert. It has, in fact, become such a communal gathering place that the local baseball team comes to Easton to celebrate after winning a game, and the new hockey team picked the center as a place to unveil their jersey logo. Easton has a weekly farmers' market and paid jugglers, mimes, and artists, all of which contribute to the sense of a real, bustling, multifaceted downtown community. Therein lies the real power of retail–great products in an environment that enhances the buying experience by reaching out to our emotions.

Some Ideas . . .

As we approach changes in retail, the question becomes *What is a retailer? What can a retailer be?* In my mind, everything. For example, I think it would be interesting if a place like Home Depot had live theater inside its stores. Maybe a sitcom-inspired program based around a handyman's trips to kooky households. Of course, all the sets would be built exclusively with Home Depot merchandise, and the set designers would be available to advise shoppers on incorporating these looks into their own home. For that matter, why use commercials to introduce new product lines? Good street theater, I think, would distinguish a retail brand much better than good but ubiquitous advertising. Although the expenses may be higher in going the street-theater route, I would bet the news coverage and word-of-mouth publicity would compensate for these costs. Performers could even be put in front of the stores as a way of guiding passersby into the store, where the performances continue.

As we've seen, technology offers a great deal of potential for reinventing retail, as well. Earlier in this book, I mentioned the Acoustiguides, headsets that provide personal tours of the Museum of Modern Art in New York City. As I've said, I think megastores should consider emulating the MoMA Acoustiguides with headsets of their own. It would be fantastic for consumers to enter a large department store, such as Macy's, and pick up at the door a headset that would guide them through the store. The potential of such devices is immense. On arriving at the store, I could run my Macy's credit card through a scanner that would analyze my history of purchases and note my age and demographic data. Based on this information, it could draw from an existing database of customer profiles, accessing the one in tune with my own tastes, and immediately upload a tour tailored to my tastes and needs. Alternatively, customers could enter their own data to target their store search more specifically. This would be an excellent device for gift shopping, as well–enter in mom's info as well as a price range, and let the store lead you through a tour of possible gift items.

Shopping as an art and a passionate pastime is most definitely here to stay. While the Internet craze is offering new ways of "buying," it still has not reached the status of "shopping," so popular with not only computer-savvy Gen Yers, but most segments of our population! Consumers will continue looking for off-line fun in the shape of great experiential retail concepts.

I'd like to take you now on a quick tour of two of my own favorite stores—stores that I believe are great retailers because they don't just exhibit strength in one particular area, but score high

While the Internet craze is offering new ways of "buying," it still has not reached the status of "shopping."

in every important aspect necessary to create the kind of unforgettable retail environment consumers love, from imaginative retail architecture to high-quality service to imagination in creating vivid sensory experiences.

STEW LEONARD'S

> *Rule No. 1: The customer is always right!*
> *Rule No 2: If the customer is ever wrong, read Rule No. 1!*
> —Stew Leonard, Jr.

A consumer-oriented retail environment is a style of environment that always puts the customer first in the most fervent way. Stew Leonard's famous store of the same name in Connecticut is the ultimate retail experience both in terms of the unique level of customer service provided and the unbelievably enjoyable and innovative atmosphere.

Stew Leonard's is not just about groceries at the right price. It is about the physical experience of shopping: what you see, hear, smell, and taste. It is exciting and memorable. The more of this kind of sensory experience you create for your customers, the more you will be able to reach their hearts and make their shopping a pleasure. And why—unless it is a pleasure—should anyone today want to go through the trouble of shopping for commodities such as food, if they can buy all they need with a few convenient clicks on the Internet?

The service at Stew Leonard's is the friendliest you can hope to experience anywhere. Stew Leonard's really has an understanding of how to treat its customers right. As a matter of fact, it gives seminars on customer service to many of America's top Fortune 500 companies, such as Citibank, IBM, and PepsiCo! The store caters to suburban Connecticut families. These are, for the most part, hard-core commuters (to New York City) who want to enjoy their weekend time with their families. Stew Leonard's takes the burden of shopping and turns it into a family event.

You have to go there to believe it. It is very difficult to leave with an empty cart because the merchandise is so enticing and different every time.

At first sight, the look of Stew's store is reminiscent of a Connecticut country farm. This brings tremendous credibility to the overall concept of freshness. A small animal farm with cows, pigs, goats, ducks, chickens, and other domestic animals is located at the entrance to the parking lot—a thrill for children and parents alike. At the store entrance you are welcomed by a large stone engraved with Rules No. 1 and 2. As soon as you pass through the doors, your senses are immediately assailed by the delicious and relaxing aroma of freshly baked bread.

You have to go there to believe it. It is very difficult to leave with an empty cart because the merchandise is so enticing and different every time.

Stew is a master at making his customers feel good via different olfactory experiences as they tour the store. The tour of the store is guided and follows a well-established traffic pattern that exposes the customer to the total product offering, but it also offers several shortcuts to those who are in a hurry. Fresh coffee is brewed on the premises and offered to shoppers, and a kitchen prepares take-out food, keeping all those aromas we like so much in specific zones to keep our taste buds awake. A miniature milk factory with a sign saying "we churn our own butter" shows customers exactly how the milk ends up in those familiar cartons. This mini dairy factory, replete with a conveyor belt that carries the containers, brings authenticity to the concept of entertainment that is so much a part of Stew's.

The store executes many other amazing ideas with similar fanfare and fun. A miniature train runs around the store, as if to deliver the country's best brands and the farm products coming in on a daily basis. In the dairy section, you swing to the tunes of the three singing hens–Emma, Blake, and Sarah–or the Farm Fresh Five band (that is, a nice little group of singing milk cartons and chicks just hatched and still sitting in their eggshells). In the produce section, the Cindy Celery and Larry Lettuce Show makes you sing along with their "We're fresh vegetables and good for you" song, whether you want to or not! And let's not forget the Calypso monkey puppet show trio that is located on top of the fresh bananas. One of Stew's employees confessed to me that after awhile it can get a bit overwhelming. "Every time the music is on, people buy so many bananas, I can't keep up refilling the shelves! People really do go bananas!"

The Cindy Celery and Larry Lettuce Show makes you sing along with their "We're fresh vegetables and good for you" song.

"Homemade freshness from the source" is the message, and you are tempted to believe that a real farm supplying all that produce is right in back of the store. The original cartons are used for display, and you can read the address of the farm providing the products. You don't feel that any middlemen control the product quality and prices.

Stew's is a retailer constantly focused on providing all that we could possibly wish for in a grocery store: quality, freshness, abundance, and a friendly atmosphere. The customer is always encouraged to participate in the life of the store, even at home. As you leave, you can purchase Stew's easy-does-it cookbook *You Can Do It* or win a Stew's gift certificate by submitting a photo of yourself with a Stew Leonard's shopping bag, taken at any of the great landmarks of the world (the photos are then displayed in a special area of the store). But the last touch in this relationship store is the questionnaire offered as you leave, titled "What do you like? What don't you like? I'd love to know. Stew Leonard."

ABC CARPET
ABC Carpet & Home is another retailer that has created a special world of its own and clearly understands the consumer's desire to have a good time while

shopping. Although it houses one of the most extensive collections of carpets from all over the world, ABC Carpet is about a whole lot more than carpets. It is a shopping adventure . . . exploring Ali Baba's hidden treasure cavern!

Situated in downtown New York, this six-story Neo-Greco brick building circa 1881 offers on each of its floors one of the most comprehensive collections of furniture and home-furnishing accessories—from traditional to eclectic—you can find anywhere. The products are arranged to become part of the décor—a

Shopping at ABC Carpet nurtures socializing, visualizing, and discovering.

wonderful kaleidoscope of interlocking rooms or "sets" with a lifestyle presentation that creates a string of original fantasy worlds in which customers can envision their furnishing dreams. The product display encourages customers to touch, play with, and even rearrange the products. This store also engages all of your senses. Scents are prevalent in many areas and interwoven throughout the décor. Shoppers can take a break and eat in the charming, intimate Parlour Café decorated in an eclectic Victorian style (all the furnishings and decorations are for sale, too, so you can shop while eating!), or stop by the fabulous gourmet Food Hall for a snack.

Shopping at ABC Carpet nurtures socializing, visualizing, and discovering new and exciting products that smartly reflect many different price ranges in an extremely pleasant environment. In this store, the customer is the hero. Everything is done for his or her enjoyment; the store helps you to shop at your own pace, invites you for a rest, if needed (on the furniture itself or in one of their restaurants), and constantly challenges you with new arrivals from all around the world. The unique offerings and imaginative displays allow you to travel in spirit, something that is very much valued today.

Both of these models have successfully created the kind of retail spirit that used to make department stores so exciting. These retailers have a special sensitivity that allows them to reach customers in the most sincere and helpful way—by making them happy and transforming the otherwise demanding experience of shopping into a delightful walk in a "wondershop" that truly conveys the "art of shopping" at its best.

13

Brand Presence with Presence: A Fresh, New Approach

"The brand is the amusement park, and the product is the souvenir!"
–Nick Graham, former president and chief underpants officer,
Joe Boxer

What is brand presence? *Presence* is the science of creating or leveraging identities by connecting with different national and international audiences through the use of the appropriate visual and emotional stimuli at different points of experience. The Coca-Cola trademark, for instance, conveys different meanings depending upon whether it is used on the Atlanta headquarters building, on a can, at the Olympics, or in signage in the United States, in China, or in Venezuela. However, it is always consistent with Coca-Cola's core brand values.

From Ubiquity to Presence

Presence, unlike *ubiquity,* is an image-management process that transcends rigorous systems of applications to focus on communication that is targeted, personal, and always relevant, without compromising the integrity of the overall identity. *Presence expresses the emotional and sensory atmosphere that surrounds a brand.*

Brands are not static; they have many facets to their personality. In order to build up and retain equity as a preferred brand in the mind of the consumer,

Brands are not static; they have many facets to their personality.

a brand must evolve to stay connected to its target audience in its day-to-day, moment-to-moment existence. Brand presence at its best connects intimately to the consumer's lifestyle. *The challenge is to move a brand forward by understanding the consumer's level of receptivity and sensitivity to a message at a given time and point of contact.* In this regard, brands need to transcend a linear, primarily ubiquity-oriented mode of expression to connect with consumers emotionally in different ways at different times during the brand experience.

My company created a tool to do just this called the Brand Presence® Management system (BPM), which enables a brand to deliver the right emotional message to the right customer at the right time and place. BPM diagnoses a brand *from the consumer's experience perspective* and helps

Presence that is *felt*, as well as *seen*, is needed.

companies assess and audit a brand's total identity in the marketplace, providing solutions on how to manage and optimize the brand's expression emotionally. For more about BPM and an example of how we used this tool to develop the presence program for Coca-Cola for the 1996 Atlanta Olympics, please see chapter 17 in Section IV.

While it is true that "to be recognized, you must first be seen," a crucial part of a strong brand presence program must also be to build the relevant emotional experience the brand provides at different points of contact with consumers. Sending your logo up into space, as Pizza Hut did when they put a thirty-foot-tall Pizza Hut logo on the world's largest proton rocket, is not necessarily for everyone! A brand has many opportunities to reach consumers on a much more profound, personal level. Presence that is *felt,* as well as *seen,* is needed. It is necessary to manage a program that connects with and *engages the consumer with modular messages at different times, in different places in the consumer's lifestyle.*

Advertising is often a masterful way of speaking directly to consumers at different points of contact, but it is only one aspect of a strategy that includes a thorough understanding of all the possible places where a brand-consumer dialogue can take place, such as outdoor presence, Web presence, events, retail branding, or portable communication devices. A brand's outdoor-presence messages are generally very similar, sometimes for years and years. Advertising can (and should) change rapidly to adapt to new opportunities, but for some reason, outdoor signage is not usually managed in the same way. This is sort of like having an ongoing conversation with someone who says the same thing again and again. We tend to eventually tune them out! The key is to think like a consumer and to attempt to view your brand's presence from their perspective.

JCDecaux, a world leader in out-of-home advertising, is entirely based on the principle of understanding and responding to the needs of the public in creative and visually pleasing ways, while offering brands a privileged way to

communicate. The company's kiosks, bus shelters, bathrooms, telephone booths, and so on reflect an aesthetically appealing design with innovative solutions to daily city life. Their "street furniture"–present in forty-two countries and sixteen hundred cities–is designed by some of the world's best architects and designers, who seek to be sensitive to the particular cultural nuances of their native countries. JCDecaux transportation shelters and kiosks attempt to help build a city's contemporary image with flair, without distracting from its unique character. Similarly, in airports, innovative products such as their personal electronics charging stations provide in an elegant way a much needed public service. This is the best of all possible worlds: a brand presence vehicle that is visually attractive and highly useful to people in their everyday lives!

The element of surprise can also be very powerful in creating a bond with consumers through brand presence. Brand presence initiatives that exceed or play with our expectations can attain more emotional resonance. The first time I saw the "Absolut New York" billboard in Manhattan, I had that great jaw-dropping feeling of surprise, as did half a dozen or so other pedestrians who stood with me, pointing and staring in amazement at the incredible life-size

reproduction of a studio apartment (furnished by IKEA) stuck sideways up on a billboard! The billboard is replete with lots of real, fun details such as cartons of Chinese take-out food on the kitchen counter, toiletries on shelves, shoes on the "floor," glasses set out on the coffee table (martini glasses with Absolut vodka nearby, of course), and so on, so that looking at it becomes sort of a game and you can see something entirely new each time. This billboard is one of six super billboards Seagram's launched for Absolut in 2000. The others included such literally "off-the-wall" outdoor efforts as a fourteen-foot Absolut bottle on Sunset Boulevard in Los Angeles, where performance artists daily layer a thousand coats of paint onto the bottle, and letters spelling out A-B-S-O-L-U-T with a placard let passersby know which coat number the painters are working on. A field of flowers has been planted in Chile in the shape of an Absolut bottle (this outdoor display is called "Absolut Summer"). Richard Lewis, worldwide account director for the brand for TBWA/Chiat/Day, has said that Absolut is extending its efforts beyond magazine ads because these kinds of outdoor billboards can reach consumers in ways that magazines cannot. When he says of their efforts, "We're trying to create some kind of emotional connection to [a] market,"[122] he clearly has got the right idea about the potential of brand presence!

Brazilian city São Paulo banned all forms of outdoor media.

Can Less Be More?

The technique of billboarding can also go too far. In the world of emotionally branded presence, it is not quantity that counts, but quality. Consumers are so barraged by communications that finding a unique venue for a brand message can sometimes be more powerful than logos plastered everywhere. This is particularly true in New York City and other large urban areas, where modern computer technology has made the cost of oversized vinyl panels negligible and, therefore, 120-foot Gap models staring down at pedestrians from buildings are a commonplace sight and advertising clutter from bus stop ads to passing trucks is abundant.

In an age of hypersensitivity to some commercial messaging, there is a sentiment with people now in the age of social media that the overwhelming presence of pushed and unwelcome commercial messages has reached its limit. The creativity that was associated with the idea of visual presence has been replaced by a race for a massive implementation of outdoor venues. The idea of promoting while giving back to the environment and the community seems to give way to more and more intrusive media messaging that irritates people.

New brand experiences such as those called pop-up stores that allowed brands to rent, on a short-term basis, retail spaces in cities to share an emotional experience with people showed that there is a way to have presence without aggravating people's visual spaces. These are the types of solutions that truly bring a new way to reach people positively.

I wonder if the advent of electronic media has not given a boost to the outdoor industry and a new pitch to bring more marketers in. The medium in itself is possibly a powerful visual tool, but it is also laden with a lot of critics and rejections. One of those outdoor venues lit the bedroom of a teenager in L.A. all night. This is not acceptable.

Brands should really be aware of the negative perceptions outdoor media creates; grassroots movements have emerged worldwide against these intrusive modes of communication. São Paulo went radical in its mayor's decision to ban all forms of outdoor ads, associating them with visual pollution. Santa Monica has stringent rules that limit the proliferation of outdoor signs, and Vermont has told those billboard guys to go somewhere else. Well, they found Los Angeles, and for anyone curious to see how badly a city can lose its character when littered with outdoor media, visit this city.

To give you a sense of environmental communication gone weird, Kentucky Fried Chicken, at the beginning of 2009, took advertising to the streets to re-"FRESH" America's pothole-stricken roadways. They literally fixed potholes and painted their logo on top of the repaired work. Bob Garfield, the eminent and visionary columnist for *AdAge*, the trade magazine that loves anything advertising, wrote an article declaring "Branded Repaired Potholes Will Inspire Road Rage, Not Sales." Wow! Even Bob Garfield understood the cynicism behind such a campaign. Brands have to wake up to the fact that in a consumer-driven economy, even the choice of media, the frequency of commercials, and how those ads are displayed can become an issue with people.

There is every indication that in the future, no matter where you live, ads will be everywhere, including in your hands every time you take a look at your PDA and in your local grocery-store shopping carts. So why not make it smart and welcomed by people? Companies such as Hardware International Corp. are developing wearable video, and, apparently, we will soon have designer clothing with inlaid intelligent, changeable screens for ads! Many restaurants now even have ads that stare at you in the restroom stall (and, I might add, the tone of these annoying ads usually conveys a "let-me-grab-your-attention-in-this-private-moment-in-an-off-the-wall-clever-way" smug humor that I doubt is very successful).

Guerrilla Marketing

Long, long ago, in an economy far, far away, corporate empires and advertising oligarchs relied on big budgets to drive dominating advertising campaigns across the consumer landscape. As these behemoths gobbled up one medium after another, believing "bigger is better," small bands of rebel operations learned to make do with what they had. Using the weapons of creativity and resourcefulness, they succeeded in stretching their limited budgets far into unknown territory. And so, guerrilla marketing was born. Frugality was its hallmark and integrity was its trademark. Guerrilla marketing revealed a capacity to attract loyal niche markets that were inaccessible by mainstream ad campaigns, as well as crucial trendsetters turned off by the gloss and plasticity that characterize ad campaigns directed at the masses.

Guerrilla marketing provides the personal encounter that is so vital in the Emotional Economy–the consumer can see the face of a brand. Guerrilla marketing has now taken on a new life with the Internet. Buzz can be created there, reputations can be built, and through such rich media as videos, brands with little resources can become worldwide phenomena, albeit if just for a short time. Burger King, for instance, with a substantially smaller advertising budget than McDonald's, has come up with some of the best online videos of all time, such as the subservient chicken that brought million of viewers (for a more in-depth explanation, see my book *Brandjam*) or, recently, the drive to offer free hamburgers to Facebook users who decided to kick some of their friends out of their page (see chapter 15).

Barack Obama's campaign was an amazing "word of click" approach that proved that the interest generated by a blog can help you become a voice in your community. Alain Lambert, a senator from a region in Normandy outside of Paris and a former finance minister, understood the power of the Internet ten years ago when he was one of the first politicians in France to share his ideas and his work with people online. Understanding that clout in France was a Parisian thing, Senator Lambert sought out alternative ways to get his opinion heard and his region's best interest front and center despite his absence from the capital. As a fiscal conservative, he abhors anything that looks like a bad budgetary decision, and, by saying so, he has made a name for himself as a contrarian in French politics. His name has even become a verb! President Nicolas Sarkozy of France warned his close associates in 2008 not to be "Lambertized," a suggestion to them that they should not follow in the disciplined steps of this vocal former finance minister. Lambert's Web site (take a look, if you speak French) is a unique mix of local politics and national views. He speaks his mind, lashes out at the powers that be if necessary, and, in his blogs, welcomes politicians from opposite sides if they are doing something he feels is right for the nation. With 100 thousand unique visitors a month on his amateurish looking blog, he has become a voice to be reckoned with, and most politicians check his blog to see what Lambert's position is at any particular moment. With no personal fortune or staff support, he manages to be the leading voice in France on good management in government, and people adore him so much that they elect him to any position he deems fitting for himself. Alone with his laptop and a deceivingly little camera that captures the most precious moments of French politics, he pleases his audience with his genuine candor and sincerity. His outsider status gives him a rebellious image that the French love.

For some brands, what works best is to use guerilla marketing as a way of exploring the cretive possibilities for brand contact.

The authenticity of Alain Lambert's effort is what makes him special and a true guerrilla for change. When Pepsi-Cola, with its new redesigned logo (curiously close to the Obama campaign's famous identity), tried to crash the inaugural party in Washington by attempting to make people wear the Pepsi pins, hoping that people would confuse the Obama graphics with the new Pepsi logo, it was just plain silly. When alerted, people felt "taken" by this cynical approach, which is not a good way to start a campaign.

Physical presence can only be powerful if it is perceived as emotional presence. When people are hungry for quality, precious time, a better planet, and some fun in their lives, another billboard or pothole with a KFC logo might not be the best solution to make them enthusiastic. New interactive ideas or applications or entertaining programs can do a lot more good than spamming people with more fixed ideas that just offend viewers. Teen retailer PacSun uses its Web site to promote music festivals such as Coachella, Bumbershoot, Bonnaroo, Sasquatch, and Lollapalooza by giving visitors information on all the bands performing. This type of information draws people to the site and associates the brand with the coolest music festivals around–quite a good idea.

I read in the *New York Times* an article by Jesse McKinley about David de Rothschild, who went from San Francisco on a boat made out of plastic bottles named "Plastiki." His goal was to bring "eco-consciousness" to the world.[123] Propelled by the Sundance Channel, his and other initiatives like his reflect a new mentality and should be a clear sign to brands that when their products become vehicles for what's wrong, it might be time to think differently.

You can't forget what is most important right now for most generations: cost, responsibility, and engagement. Brands might have been ahead of themselves in thinking they would rule the game forever. The good news, though, is that it will be a lot more fun to promote your brands now that part of your brand's success will be in its ability to really bond with people.

When Hy-Vee, the Des Moines, Iowa-based supermarket, creates a dollar-a-day meal with all the minerals or vitamins that are necessary for healthy living for people who are facing hardship, they truly help and keep their customers—such a strategy is good business and a good contribution to society. When Weight Watchers gives people who reach their goals free admission to classes, they create incentives for people to better themselves, and those achievers become the best ambassadors for the brand and great witnesses of success for the groups. When Zappos sends a gift to someone who feels a bit upset on the phone to cheer them up, they gain a customer for life.

Another example of clever guerrilla marketing was the film *The Omega Code*, which was recognized by *Brandweek* as a "Guerrilla Marketer of the Year."[124] Taking inspiration from *The Blair Witch Project*, this film owed its giant success much less to quality product than brilliantly executed marketing. This Christian-oriented film, based on the Book of Revelation and filmed on a paltry $7.2 million budget, opened in October 1999 in the box office's top ten and earned the highest dollars-per-screen of its competitors. How? By enlisting the aid of Christian bookstores, ministers, media, and activists across the country. Congregation outings were planned, volunteers distributed flyers, and activists were encouraged by the prospect of speaking up not through boycotting but rather sponsoring a film that was in accord with their values. Producer Matthew Crouch told *Brandweek*: "It's not the best film in the world, but that's not the point. We've coalesced a consumer group that Hollywood and Madison Avenue didn't seem to know existed."[125]

However, the term "guerrilla marketing" remains elusive. Its strategies and

success stories are based not on formulaic executions but rather on savvy and intelligent improvisation. In chapter 1, in the section on Generation Y, I mentioned some effective campaigns targeted at that group, which included using trendsetters, clubs, and DJs to inexpensively spread the word. Other products may want to target urban basketball players or college art majors. Shows like MTV's *Fashionably Loud Spring Break 2000* are great venues for fashion brands to get huge exposure to Gen X and Y markets. But whatever the target, guerrilla marketing will determine the medium that draws the audience's attention and interests their passions. Tommy Hilfiger tried a new brand presence initiative in spring 2000 with a two-month promotion that offered Tommy-designed Motorola cellular phones as top prizes. This promotion, aimed mostly at Gens X and Y, brought about the first ever fashion-designer cellular phone. Only two thousand of the Tommy Hilfiger phones were manufactured for this promotion, but there are surely more designer phones to come in the future. He was ahead of the curve.

Conclusion

Well-thought-out, emotionally charged presence makes the customer want to join you in the brand story you have created. It is obvious that branded presence allows a product to rise above the competition by bringing a visual and experiential realm of the brand to life. We do not yet know what marvels the future may bring in terms of new venues and techniques to help us achieve this goal, but as interactive ads become more prevalent daily, and the technology behind them is quickly being refined, we will obviously soon have new creative outlets to challenge us in our quest for emotionalized brand expression.

A top ad creative even suggested to me that we might get to a point where a corporation like Target, along with their efforts for social causes, might raise money to contribute to the beautification of cities by buying back some of the worst billboard locations. That would be doing more with less and a cause worth fighting for.

14

Emotional Packaging:
The Half-Second Commercial

The bond between Heinz ketchup and our customers is essentially emotional and personality-based. The Heinz bottle is intrinsic to the brand personality.
–Bill Johnson, CEO of Heinz [126]

Packaging is a half-second commercial. It has to work instantly to catch your attention or establish your familiarity with a product. A package has half a second to be acknowledged and another half a second to be loved. The message needs to be instantaneous and direct–highly intrusive, yet emotionally connected. For a package to work, you need to have the following ingredients:

- Clarity of proposition as a product definition
- Proprietary visual expression
- Emotional connectivity–through an integrated sensory message and an element of surprise

From Impact to Contact: Packaging Is Concentrated Branding

Packaging has many practical objectives, not the least of which is that consumers don't want to waste time finding a product. Consumers are more comfortable with packaging that is easy to identify. But beyond the practical considerations, it is incredibly important to keep in sight the added value of engaging the consumers' senses to bring them into a different relationship with the product. *Packaging has to compete based on impact in order to be seen, but it must also create an emotional contact with consumers in order to be loved.* This alone can create product preference. Once the product is purchased, this experience of discovery can and should continue. The opening of a container or a shipping carton influences our brand experience; even the impact of the shape of a key holder for a car needs to build on the brand promise. Packaging is the ultimate communication tool, and the most imaginative ideas have emerged from the strict confines of the challenge of packaging products. To humanize, emotionalize, and tap into the senses a product needs to make the connection between perception and aspiration by translating the packaging forms and product graphics into a presentation that connects immediately to the end user.

Absolut Vodka is a great example. Absolut positioned itself as a unique proposition by initially targeting Gen X consumers with an alternative, more cerebral and contemporary packaging design that has become a badge for this generation. Absolut Mandrin, for instance, strengthens the flavor concept through an innovative proprietary visual expression that connects powerfully to our senses. By raising the bottom of the bottle in a half-mandarin shape sprayed with the color orange, Absolut is able to pull the mandarin color up into transparent vodka. The color glows softly in a diffused manner as we perceive it through the frosted bottle that also enhances the refreshing aspect of the drink. Bold orange letters in the Absolut typeface create a vivid impression. The proposition is clear and relevant. The visual expression enhances the overall theme (refreshing mandarin orange). The frosted and colorful treatment appeals to our senses by connecting with our need for beauty. And last but not least, the smooth, silky touch of the frosted bottle adds to the overall refreshing cue. These uses of glass are unusual in liquor bottles, but have been used in the fragrance industry in some very innovative ways, giving a new dimension to the possibilities of glass packaging.

Packaging has to compete based on impact in order to be seen, but it must also create an emotional contact with consumers in order to be loved.

The physical realm of a package is generally small, offering little space or volume for brand design expressions. Great packaging needs to work hard to stand out on the overcrowded shelves of stores and supermarkets and claim our attention. It is precisely because of these constraints that we see some of the most interesting innovations in this area—innovations that attempt to bring out sensorial elements to enhance our relationship with a product. Branded products are close to our hearts, and this allows them to have many functions and purposes in our lives. They can be used to simply fulfill our needs or to become instead a badge that expresses our personality, style, or status. All kinds of products are part of our home décor and therefore play a very intimate role in our lives. The Givenchy Rouge Miroir lipstick packaging is one of the most innovative lipstick packaging concepts I have found in the marketplace. It

incorporates a mirror into the packaging, a perceptive and elegantly executed solution to the problem of searching for a mirror when applying lipstick.

Packaging can also raise our expectations of a product and make us reevaluate an entire category. We expect superior presentation from any wine packaging, regardless of price, and an element of surprise and sensuality from a fragrance package. We feel that liquors should embellish our bar cabinet. Soft drinks strike our senses in the moment. Ice cream is about indulgence and fun, whether it is exclusive like Godiva or more accessible like Ben & Jerry's. Food packaging needs to have appetite appeal, and home products convey lifestyle cues. Packaging, like music, needs to tune in with precision to the consumer's desires. A wrong note can mean an immediate expulsion from the shelves.

Packaging can raise our expectations of a product and make us reevaluate an entire category.

PACKAGING IS SOMETIMES THE ONLY THING THAT MAKES A BRAND SING
Products with little support in advertising rely on the strength of their packaging to attract consumer attention and the favor of retailers, sometimes with great success. But packaging can also be the most powerful element of large-scale brand communication programs. As I mentioned previously, I am convinced that it is the iMac product design itself that has given strength to the Apple advertising campaign. In the same way, the Evian ad campaign relies heavily on the beauty of the product and its packaging to convey the message of purity and healthy lifestyle. *The Absolut Vodka packaging is the advertising supermodel that never ages. Packaging is the essence of a brand crystallized in a small space.*

L'original

This is why some marketers will go to great lengths to invest in packaging and why packaging agencies are, generally speaking, such great brand specialists.

PACKAGING IS EVERYBODY'S BUSINESS

Everyone has an opinion about packaging, and a packaging redesign never goes unnoticed. For certain products, we have a very strong perception of what the packaging should be like and will not forgive a marketer who makes the mistake of downgrading or even upgrading a familiar product's packaging. In fact, the emotional attachment people exhibit toward a particular design or element of design for a product demonstrates the tremendous and sometimes surprising equity packaging holds in the consumer psyche.

1999 was the year for Campbell's Soup to finally change its packaging–after 102 years! This event made the cover of the business section of the *New York Times*. Why such an interest from the press and the public? The changes in the overall look of the famous can are actually minimal, more of a "tweaking" than a redefinition. An evolution, but certainly not a revolution! But because of the emotional attachment people have toward certain brand "icons," we are interested–very interested–in what happens to that red and white can. Since Andy Warhol exalted the role of the Campbell's Soup can as a part of American pop culture, this commercial product has come to "belong" to us, and its fate concerns us all. It is truly an art to evolve a packaging design with this kind of heritage, to attract a new generation of consumers without alienating the loyal customer base. To boost their business, which was in need of some help, Campbell's Soup decided to show a new kind of responsiveness through their packaging redesign. The five new color labels are designed to showcase their newer products and help customers choose their favorite soup more easily from the selection of "classics," "fun favorites," "special selections," "great for cooking," and "98 percent fat free."

A lot of sophisticated research techniques have been developed around the impact of packaging on consumers' lives. While changing a TV campaign is accepted easily by an audience, a change of packaging could be unsettling, uplifting, troubling, or reassuring—but never neutral in the consumer's mind. Focus groups prove time and again that the emotional attachment to packaging is profound and powerful enough to puzzle any psychologist, even in the case of something as mundane as the design of a beer-bottle label or a soft-drink image. Given the impact of such communication, I am mystified by how little attention it sometimes receives from the top management of a corporation and how it is rarely integrated from the very beginning of a major communications program. If packaging is "everybody's business," it should certainly be the business of corporate CEOs. Heinz is a brand that has recently realized that one of its greatest brand-identity assets is the familiar, squat, octagonal glass bottle design which over the past few years has often been replaced in some of their markets by other, more practical bottle designs. Heinz is now spending a great deal of money to achieve a global standardized presentation of their ketchup in the iconoclastic bottle. Plastic imitations of the glass bottle are now being explored as well, thanks to innovations in plastic manufacturing technology that allows lower weight and higher durability and squeezability. Bill Johnson, CEO of Heinz, explains this renewed commitment to consistency in their packaging by saying, "If it keeps changing, if you can't rely on it, what kind of relationship can you build?"[127]

PACKAGING IS A MESSAGE . . . AND A CONTAINER

The primary functions of packaging are to protect stock shipped from the factory to the distribution centers and retailers, as well as to display and market a product on a shelf in a retail space by giving important product information and an overall sense of the brand's emotional attributes. Packaging as a container needs to respect quite rigid criteria, such as shelf space and the size of visual merchandising units in the distribution sector. Product packaging also needs to fit well into refrigerators or other storage spaces in the home. A product must be packaged for consumer use in ways that facilitate our daily usage.

Packaging informs us about product function and features and must often carry legal information, weight, nutrition facts, and the bar coding system, as well. Packaging that is destined to be international needs to allocate space for the translation of several languages and must be sensitive to the cultural values endorsed by different populations. It is crucial to keep in mind that overpackaging is often negatively perceived in markets where ecological sensitivity is very high. I have always worked closely with our clients on minimizing packaging waste and on the impact our work has on the environment. When you are working within all these constraints, there is little room to communicate your product's overall brand image and distinct advantage to the consumer, but this is what makes the art of packaging such a challenging and rewarding task. Despite all these practical considerations, it must also sell the product. It has a very big job!

> **Packaging defines cultures and periods of time and it is fascinating to see how a brand can evolve through packaging to stay relevant.**

I have always been a fan of packaging design and graphics from different countries because it is a very interesting indication of specific cultures and tastes. Here I will share with you some of the packaging innovations that I have found around the world and that have sometimes been used as inspiration for our work. *Packaging defines cultures and periods of time, and it is fascinating to see how a brand can evolve through packaging to stay relevant.* Recently, packaging has reached a new level of expression as technologies in printing and the treatment of materials have evolved to enable marketers and designers to explore new opportunities. The competitive pressure of today's marketplace has also challenged marketers to innovate by bringing a new level of communication into their packaging–one that is based on emotions.

Packaging Innovations in the Liquor, Fragrance, Beverage, and Food Industries

THE LIQUOR INDUSTRY

The success of Absolut Vodka has awakened a new set of competitors to the power of packaging, and these brands have begun to push the limits of innovation in glass packaging. The Polish vodka Belvedere has managed to achieve a stunning three-dimensional graphic presentation of their brand through an unusual bottle shape and by using the fact that the back of the bottle is visible through the front. What you see through the snow-covered tree branches design on the front of the bottle is Poland's presidential palace, magnified through the liquid. This tall, slender bottle is frosted all over except in the spot where the palace is viewed, which allows you to see the palace as if you were walking through the palace garden on a cold winter morning. This is a most compelling, refreshing brand expression that engages our imagination.

The Japanese liquor industry is obviously a great example of how to emotionalize packaging, since culturally the Japanese have always been highly artistic and have carried this sensibility over into the world of product enhancement. Each time I travel to Japan, I visit the food section of department stores for inspiration. The sake bottles are always packaged to invite the consumers to discover what is inside in a subtle yet dramatic manner that engages the senses and heightens our expectations. There are lovely, unique combinations of materials such as in the Tenzan sake packaging, which uses bamboo leaves and coarse rope ties to wrap the outer layer of

the bottle and covers the layer closest to the bottle with rice paper. The Mutsu Hassen brand covers the bottle in a transparent rice paper–type sheath, enfolding the cap in black paper tied with a burgundy rope. These colors and materials beautifully enhance the overall product presentation and express in a celebratory style the special moment of consumption. The Sho Chiku Bai, precious Giyo sake, uses a very interesting technique to package a collection of products using different colors. Liquors are bound by the legal restriction of a warning back label with long mandatory copy,

Packaging can tell stories and inspire us to make up our own stories.

and Sho Chiku Bai has found a clever added use for this label by printing the back of the labels in colors to bring a diffused coloring to the entire frosted bottle. This is a great usage of labels to enhance an overall package design.

Packaging can also tell stories and, most importantly, can inspire us to make up our own stories. Robert Mondavi's innovation of a clear wine bottle top that allows the cork and its information to be seen was a breakthrough concept in the wine category. The sensory elements are also well played out in the overall look of the Robert Mondavi bottles, such as the frosted 1997 Fumé Blanc wine bottle or the exquisite label of the 1996 Stags Leap Sauvignon Blanc that communicates the rich heritage of the brand and the pleasure of the drinking experience. Mystic Cliffs, another winery brand, has a 1997 Chardonnay label that symbolizes the steep coast of California and takes us to a place associated with world-class wine. Through the use of a clear label, the design is so well integrated with the bottle that you feel the spirit of California wines is embodied in that very bottle. An emphasis on heritage does not have to mean boring! Traditional packaging from the '30s and '40s was centered around storytelling, with a wonderfully enchanting use of color and style, such as the tin cases for Velvet tobacco that conveyed a romance and sensuality I sometimes miss. This kind of imaginative aesthetic could be translated into today's packaging beautifully.

THE FRAGRANCE INDUSTRY

Packaging is everything in the world of fragrance, where image is the only means of conveying the subtleties of the fragrance and differentiating one fragrance from another. The outer packaging, the bottle, and the name are often the only tools that convey to the consumer the invisible "genie" of promise inside. Fragrances need to deliver on an emotional promise to the buyer immediately. Fragrances are a fashion item that touches our most intimate romantic and sensual chords; they are strictly about emotions and sensations—not many real, "practical" benefits here. *The benefit is clearly in the psychological realm. So fragrance packaging needs to express an idea in the most emotionally potent way possible!* Textures, shapes, and materials have a critical role to play, and innovation is more than a rule—it is a necessity. The fragrance industry is a great source of inspiration for mass marketers, since this industry constantly pushes the limit of the "doable" in packaging. Fragrance packaging designers are known for challenging manufacturers to live up to their visions, which sets off new trends all around.

The most successful fragrances have always been about telling stories or sending messages, such as the tale of exoticism from Yves St. Laurent's Opium, the

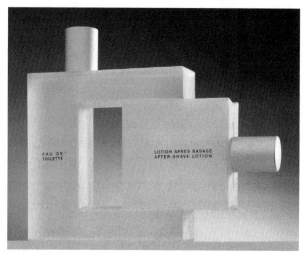

very personal message from Christian Dior's Remember Me, the Snow White/ Eve story told by Christian Dior's Poison, or the tale of eternal passion told by Calvin Klein's Eternity . . . I love the way the story behind Yves Rocher's fragrance Neblina is transmitted through the packaging copy that reads, "Between heaven and earth, in a sea of clouds high above the Amazonian forest, a shimmering mist releases a rare, delicate fragrance of nature. This is the essence of *Neblina*." Every year, there are hundreds of new fragrances, but only a few survive to become fragrance stars. These are the ones that strike a profound emotional chord.

Most fragrances are still designed for women, but the men's fragrance business is growing, and unisex fragrances such as cK One continue to have remarkable success. I have seen fragrances test well in focus groups but fail miserably on the market because of weak packaging and poor communication. In my experience with fragrances, the packaging and the communication *are* the product. This wonderful, modern

In the fragrance and beauty industry, everything needs to communicate.

puzzle-like bottle design for Issey Miyake's eau de toilette and aftershave lotion for men is so mechanically clever and compelling that you have to reach out and test the smooth slide of the way the bottles fit into one another—a beautiful solution to the practical problem of using two products in sync.

The need for innovation in fragrance packaging is also driven by the limited distribution channels available for fragrances. Most distribution takes place

through department stores, very challenging and static environments for the sales of fragrances. Specialty stores such as
Sephora are raising the emotional bar for fragrance
presentation, but this weak link in creating the right
environment for fragrance distribution is, I believe,
what has allowed specialty fashion retailers such as
the Gap to enter the fragrance business so successfully with unique packaging and retail environments
that enhance the sensual experience consumers can
have with the brand. What about MAC's fragrance in
a necklace? Is MAC selling a fragrance product, a piece
of jewelry, or just the attitude of a hip brand that makes
you hip by sharing its values? The answer is in our heart—where we will also
make the decision to buy or not to buy. I certainly like the idea of packaging
that you wear—a new level of intimacy with the brand.

In the fragrance and beauty industry, everything needs to communicate—the
container, the closure and application systems, the secondary packaging, and
the visual merchandising systems. All these elements need to work together
to heighten the emotional experience a customer has with the product and
provide a sensorial discovery. The Kenzo fragrance for men, Zebra, for which
my partner Joël Desgrippes designed the bottle, has simulated zebra hair on
the cap to make the concept more vivid. Another of Joël's famous designs,
the Boucheron Jaïpur bottle, is modeled as a bracelet and has transcended

its category to become a decorative item. In one case, I even heard of it being used as a home accessory! A Bloomingdale's salesperson once told me that a customer bought sixteen of them to use as napkin rings and gifts for a special dinner.

The Armani A/X DUO bottles, designed by Fabien Baron, clearly express the sexual nature of the product, and the outer packaging challenges standard approaches by presenting the product in metallic-finished sealed envelopes. The Ann Taylor fragrance bottle for Destination, which I designed, is meant to convey an invitation to travel. The mysterious name and jewel-like shape of the bottle for the Victoria's Secret fragrance Encounter, another of my creations, tells the story of romantic anticipation. Jean-Paul Gaultier's first fragrance, which is in a bottle shaped like a woman's torso, has a can as outer packaging, which communicates the concept in a very antichic, antistatus hip manner—one of the first expressions of the class-meets-mass trend. Another Gaultier fragrance, Fragile, is also a groundbreaking take on fragrance packaging design. The concept and the story behind this brand is the most important thing (and the more interesting the story, the better the fragrance). Taking inspiration from some of the fun, cheap tourist souvenirs one can find in Paris, Gaultier created a fantasy world of a "snowflake globe" with a figurine of a woman inside immersed in the perfume with gold flakes floating around her. The outer packaging of an old-fashioned shipping crate used to pack fragile and valuable items that opens like a flower to reveal the perfume inside, adds to the sense of discovery and wonder. This packaging breaks some of the traditional fragrance marketing rules, reclaiming the territory of fragrance that is about escape and fantasy. In this category, packaging moves product through emotions. It's as simple as that.

THE BEVERAGE EXPERIENCE

Beverages, from soft drinks to wines, are moving from an impact-only strategy to one that relies heavily on emotions and sensory experiences. A good example is Snapple, a once successful, then flailing brand under Quaker Oats, which is now a successful brand again. Snapple has reconnected powerfully to consumers through new product concepts and new primary containers supported by fresh and imaginative naming and graphics. Through its new product concepts and new primary containers with fresh and imaginative naming and graphics, *Snapple has challenged everything in the soft-drink arena. Something fundamental has changed when a ginseng black tea is called "Lightning," normal teas are called "Sun Teas," and fruit juices "Whipper Snapple."* Such innovations require a forceful packaging expression to work, and Snapple has integrated the emotional lifestyle core elements of these brands into its packaging well.

Snapple has challenged everything in the soft-drink arena.

The new labeling and packaging system we designed for Coca-Cola in 2003 provided a new look for the world's number-one brand. In reintroducing the historical but abandoned Coca-Cola "Dynamic Ribbon," Desgrippes Gobé elevated the brand perception from its functional image of refreshment characterized by the contour bottle to a new emotional language. Research told us that the new abstract graphics were perceived as an expression of energy, fun, and optimism without losing the traditional values of the brand as being

genuine, authentic, and real. But the best discovery in what turned out to be a two-year-long process was how an emotional strategy can bring a richer and deeper personality to a brand beyond its ubiquitous, rigorous expression. Emotional feelings toward a brand are indeed different if you are a mom or a teenager, if you are at the Olympic Games or in a supermarket. In the qualitative research that we did worldwide, we tested youth-driven, innovative designs to see if we could bring "cool" into the perception of the brand and connect with teenagers. We named those the "slim cans" in reference to their shapes. The cans were tested minus the famous Coca-Cola script to reduce its commercial look, relying only on the brand's historic icons. The result was beyond our expectations. The "slim cans" are now distributed in a very narrow and tightly targeted marketplace to create buzz around the brand and build an emotional connection with youth worldwide. Indeed, brands are not static entities with rigorous expressions but lively personalities capable of appealing to different audiences at once. One of the club cans was even auctioned off for $36 on eBay!

But the recreation of the ubiquitous and popular shape of the contour bottle on the cans is overall Coca-Cola's most interesting packaging innovation because the shape bridges the gap between this icon of the past and the all-too-generic can container. This is a reflection of Coca-Cola's commitment to striving to elevate the emotional brand contact through their packaging.

Gatorade, the sports drink par excellence and another one of our clients then, has gone to great lengths to cater to its demographic population segment of serious athletes. The lightning bolt of the Gatorade logo is one of the most

dynamic and compelling logos in the category and can fuel great impact in any presence program. The shapes of the containers are athletic and functional, and give the feeling of control when held in the hand. In 2001, we worked on repositioning the Gatorade brand image and evolved the packaging image to move the brand from the original refreshment concept graphics with a neutral green background and water drops to a variety of extreme sports graphics. These visual expressions bring the brand back to its core territory of "liquid fuel" for athletes. This new approach allowed Gatorade to expand more easily into new flavors. Gatorade Fierce Melon is an example of how far you can extend a core brand identity consistently through emotionally driven language and innovative packaging graphics.

FOOD PACKAGING

Food has always been the most conservative area in packaging expression. Most graphics are based on product description, historical or heritage cues, appetite appeal, and, except for youth-driven products such as cereals, do not engage in lifestyle, generational, or experience-oriented graphics. This is slowly beginning to change, and there are, of course, some exceptions. In Japan, for instance, the packaging of noodles is very appealing and creative, showing the product as a work of art. There is also a Japanese yogurt container that I love with a miniature plastic spoon encased in the lid for convenience. In France, an Amora ketchup dispenser in the shape of a cartoon-style icon with arms, legs, and a head represents a character they have named "ketchoupy." A brilliant idea. *Suddenly, this packaging can really come alive outside of the shelves—as*

a plaything, an animation on a Web site, a character in a children's book, and so on–and become a desired mascot that sells the product. Packaging that is designed with this kind of cleverness turns an otherwise commodity product into a communication symbol.

Pepperidge Farm also knows well how to balance quality and expectation. The packaging is reminiscent of an old deli bag, and this brings a homemade feel to the brand. The name supports this concept, and the cookie collection,

made up of famous city names such as Brussels, Milano, Bordeaux, and so on, takes it all a step further to the world of international delicacies, inciting our imaginations and taste buds.

The Lea and Perrins Worcestershire sauce packaging has always been one of my favorites; it communicates an added value to me in terms of taste expectation and special recipes just by the overall look of the packaging graphics.

Certain food categories are entrenched in a morass of "sameness." The cereal aisle, for example, could be a lot less silly in its effort to captivate kids, and instead reach for deeper aesthetic emotions. Why are all the cereals sold in the same printed cardboard boxes? Imagine the experience of actually picking a differently shaped box or container in the morning! Cereal brands could develop new unique shapes that integrate sound and toys into their packaging in this way and attract new customers. New concepts can be challenging for corporations—it certainly means risk—but surprising and delighting consumers with newness means desire . . . and market share!

Certain food categories are entrenched in a morass of "sameness." The cereal aisle could be a lot less silly in its effort to captivate kids.

Borrowed Cues for Packaging Inspiration

I have always used other categories as inspiration for packaging projects because they bring an element of surprise and discovery to consumers. Some brands have done this very successfully. For example, the deodorant brand Fa Body Splash has developed a package that looks like a soft-drink can . . . a refreshing symbol! When I designed the Gingham fragrance bottle for Bath & Body Works, which is based on the concept of honesty and quality from the heartland, I was inspired by the shape of an old-fashioned glass yogurt jar to communicate the integrity one expects in the milk products industry.

The bath line called Cottage gives us a delightful new take on bath salts that are packaged in a sugar dispenser. In the Gillette Series primary packaging, the grip inspiration came from tools, sports equipment, motorcycles, golf clubs, and other "grip" situations with which men are familiar. The Joyful Garden packaging we designed for Bath & Body Works was meant to reflect the shapes of the antique glass bottles that I collect. These bottles were used for medicine or drinks sold in rural general stores, and we found them to be a great inspiration for conveying the authentic and natural style of the line. The "down home," country style of this packaging gave it a charm that made the product line very successful in the stores.

Tropicana: Phasing Out the Old to Bring in the New

After the uproar around New Coke when Coca-Cola tried to tinker with the formula, half a century later, Tropicana created the same indignation with the public, this time not for a change in product formula but a change of packaging.

What happened? Well, in trying to update the packaging to fit a new trend towards simplicity, Tropicana threw away all the emotional cues that made this packaging unique in the first place, including the famous straw in the orange—a symbol of unadulterated freshness, direct from the source.

Most professional packaging designers will tell you about emotional equity and the power of imagery as it resonates with people in subconscious ways, particularly for brands that have had a long, positive history. We have a strong association with symbols. Carl Jung, the famed Swiss psychologist, told us that a long time ago. When the Mini Cooper and the VW bug were revamped, the designers made sure that the new design could still connect to the original iconic visual heritage.

Phasing out the old to bring in the new is sometimes necessary, and I would agree that the orange juice category needs a strong refresh, but unlike TV commercials, packaging has been appropriated emotionally sometimes since infancy. Therefore, our subconscious connection to the designs has a lot more to do with who we are than just what we are drinking.

The straw in the orange is one of the most powerful visual symbols in the history of branding, along with the Marlboro cowboy and the Coca-Cola dynamic

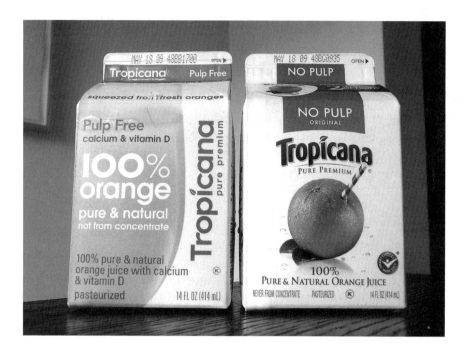

ribbon, so before changing it, one has to understand that they might change the brand meaning.

Packaging is psychology, not a strategy. When a packaging fiasco such as this one happens, it should not be taken as a reason to shelve all innovation but as an experience to learn from to move forward. Tropicana showed that people have a real emotional connection with a brand, and that they care. Tropicana should leverage that powerful learning and turn it into a commercial advantage.

CULTURAL INSPIRATION

Some products gain enormous credibility if they are associated with a specific culture. Russian vodka is still the authentic one, and we would have a hard time buying Irish pasta—even if it were the best in the world! Hershey's Ronzoni pasta brand communicates with its graphics and packaging the authenticity of an Italian product. The old-world typography and décor pictured is clearly European, and the name Ronzoni places the brand in the geographic area of the known specialists. Häagen-Dazs has a Scandinavian name even though it is made in New Jersey. Godiva, owned by Campbell's Soup, still trades on its original European aspirational image with stores and packaging styles that reflect the elitist nature of European gourmet foods. Most mustard presentations

reflect a French heritage. *Some might say that marketing is manipulative in this way, making false promises, but I doubt that anybody is really duped by these marketing efforts.* Instead, we are enticed by and want to participate in these aspirational stories that are more fun than a generic, utilitarian product experience because they help us dream. Most people are quite willing to let Ronzoni pasta be "Italian" in their minds!

Lifestyle Expectations

Each generation has different expectations and desires. New trends are constantly evolving, such as concern for the environment, the treatment of animals, a better planet, a healthier lifestyle, and our ever-growing need to explore new experiences in products. These trends encourage marketers and retailers to create alternative products that deliver

We are no longer eating food or drinking drinks; we practice "body management" and are buying convenience, escape, energy . . .

to new expectations. The Body Shop came up with "dressed-down" packaging as a response to the fanciful packaging used in the beauty industry at that time and to strengthen its point about environmental responsibility. Instead of expensive, glamorous-looking packaging, The Body Shop introduced us to the concept of simple, "undesigned" containers that were an antimarketing statement for a new group of young consumers looking for products with a cause and without all the hype. Many brands have been successful in communicating honesty and a sense of specialness through "dressed-down" packaging. This is part of the cultlike enthusiasm for the small "mom-and-pop" hair and skin-care line Kiehl's, which became so successful solely through word of mouth that it was just bought by L'Oréal, which plans to distribute the brand globally.

The current trends associated with health, vitamins, and natural and healing ingredients for mind and body have triggered a whole gamut of innovative products in the fruit- and tea-based drink categories, such as the Arizona line and the "New Age" Snapple line named after natural elements that I mentioned previously. Fresh Samantha, a juice company from Maine, manufactures real (not from concentrate) fruit drinks and smoothies blended with protein, vitamins, and plant extracts such as echinacea, the modern urban cure-all plant that builds up our energy and immune systems. *Clearly, we are no longer eating food or drinking drinks; we practice "body management" and buy convenience, escape, energy* . . . anything that conveys pleasurable, life-enhancing experiences. Gatorade is about winning, not thirst. Coca-Cola is about refreshment, not a cola drink, and Snapple is about elevating experiences having to do with the natural elements, not juice. The shift in the paradigm which makes products evolve from a commodity or need state to an emotional and sensory experience is the result of consumer demand for new, surprising ideas to nourish not only the body but also very human, emotional desires.

Whether the aspirational aspect of a product is primarily anchored in borrowed cues, based on culture or on a lifestyle concept, being relevant to a consumer is what is important, and many concepts can help you reach that relevancy. I have used all of these approaches for inspiration in packaging design, and they have helped me have a creative platform for new product development or rebranding programs, as well. The final goal is to build a unique and proprietary "dress" for your brand, a design voice that makes a tangible difference vis-à-vis your competitors and communicates powerfully to your consumer target. Packaging that has great emotional and sensorial messages creates an instant connection based on contact, not impact with the consumer in . . . half a second!

15

Emotional Advertising: Expressing Real Emotions Online

If you say it with a degree of sincerity and honesty and with a great love of the craft, it will come through.
–John McNeil, Advertising Creative Director

The Age of Excess

The most speculative economical growth the world had ever seen has brought trillions of new dollars to consumers for discretionary spending. This has sent brands and their marketing machines into overdrive to capture these very welcome extra dollars. However, for the past ten years, greed and hype (and not Emotional Branding) were the rules of the game. Greed, not creed, was what brands tried to achieve.

The result: Advertisers and advertising professionals accomplished something inconceivable. By losing their sincerity and honesty, they turned people away more and more from the commercial message. The reason: unchecked and massive intrusion on our private spaces with commercial messages fewer and fewer people want to see. According to Wikipedia, on average, American consumers will see approximately three hours of advertisements over the course of ten hours. In the '60s, you had fifty-one minutes of programming and nine minutes of advertising. In most cities, the amount of outdoor signage is so intense that it forces people around the world to rebel against what they perceive as a new form of pollution–visual pollution.

Resentment came to a tipping point in Brazil, where the mayor of São Paulo, Gilberto Kassab, resorted to banning all forms of outdoor media in his town. For the first time in the history of politics, this mayor was elected partly because of his decision to protect the town from what he called "visual pollution." (For more on this story, see our video on emotionalbranding.com.)

Advertising excess comes in all shapes and forms, not only with unbearable outdoor media but also with oppressively pervasive TV commercials of the worst kind. As broadcast media came to dominate our lives, so too did consumers become assets, "eyeballs" packaged without our knowledge into demographic groups that the media could trade for money to various brands. What did we get in return? Bad shows, elitist news, badly covered sports, and a constant barrage of commercials.

What brands lost during those years of greed was the trust they had earned in past years, the ethics they were associated with, and the authenticity of their promises. In 2008, the foundations of democracy were shaken when our banking and insurance systems collapsed, and the promises of our most cherished corporate brands turned out to be false. Who is going to believe "An American Revolution in the car industry" anymore? Let's not forget that a democracy can only work if it is based on the total integrity of accounting, banking, and insurance. Greed led pharmaceutical companies to advertise products not yet ready, car companies to hype products they should not have launched at all, and food or toy companies to offer untested dangerous products made elsewhere without proper control or supervision just to be first in the market. All that and a lack of consideration of how all the junk that was produced would be recycled or discarded. In short, we were piling up fake money and buying fake brands promoted by fake marketing that was making our own environment more and more unsafe.

WAITING FOR GODOT?

It is clear that we are living in a new age and are faced with new challenges, both global and local. The lower demographics of Gen X coupled with the Baby Boomer generation's loss of retirement funds will create a dip in consumption for many on a level we have never seen before. High unemployment will also take a bite out of people's wallets. Worse, with no jobs, millions will be left behind, and we'll see an ugly situation where the younger generation will have to fight against their parents' generation for employment. As unemployment spreads nationally and internationally, it will become a crisis that will force countries to go back to protectionism and close their borders to commerce. With the world's greatest consumer country, the U.S., at almost 10 percent unemployment in the manufacturing sector in 2009, we'll see a hard reality in how and what people buy.[128]

Some of those jobs lost will be replaced by new industries, but a large segment of the population won't be able to find a place in a job market that is shifting from their basic know-how. Corporations will hire out of huge candidate pools and people will enter the organization with only one ambition: to hang onto that precious job. Motivated only to please the boss, not rock the boat, large conglomerates will frown on any creative risks. This is the economical reality and the end of consumerism as we have known it. Marketing will have to do more with less.

From a media perspective, the radical changes brought about by digital media, the Internet, and the popularity of mobile devices has engineered the migration of billions of people worldwide from traditional media such as television to a multitude of other screens, including cell phones. For brands, this change will challenge the way advertising was done in the past and bring new opportunities for reaching a larger consumer base. Social media, with the emergence of sites such as Facebook and Twitter, take the lion's share of people's emotional time but don't offer an easy way to advertise. The increased predominance of social media thus signals the biggest shift in how brands will need to be built and promoted. Marketers will have to reinvent how to create promotional programs that can reach an audience that is now eclectic and amorphous. One thing is certain: in this new format—and this new economic landscape—consumers rule, and we'll see the end of corporate monopolies. Simon Clift, Unilever's chief marketing officer, is quoted in *Advertising Age* as saying, "This Internet-driven sea change that put consumers in control may at times threaten to overwhelm marketers and their agencies."[129]

This is the economical reality and the end of consumerism as we have known it. Marketing will have to do more with less.

Social media might not even be the place to promote a lot of traditional brands. As you will see later in this chapter, social media have been built by people for people where people control the game—they are platforms for the same people who, in the past, have had sour relationships with the hyped marketing messages of brands. The products that will thrive in these media are those brands with powerful emotional connections or brand-new technology applications that will enhance the experience of the media themselves.

New businesses will be created specifically for these new media and will prosper, given the low cost of advertising and distribution. Apple has already had one billion visitors to their online store selling "apps" for the iPhone!

Clearly, a new business model is in place and some brands will just die, not because they have no money to advertise, but because they will be shut out from the conversation.

WHAT DO PEOPLE WANT?

After the "shop 'til you drop" credo of shopaholics and the subsequent wallet sting, a bad economy is shutting down binge buying for a long time. In a time of crisis, some opportunities do still exist to motivate people to buy as long as the proposition fits their new budget criteria and personal values. We will see totally different types of products that will connect emotionally, products that people will really want.

Simon Clift, the CMO of Unilever, again verbalizes in *Advertising Age* what he foresees as the biggest hurdle for many brands: "Advertisers and their agencies are still rather partial to the idea that they define their brands." In the following examples, we'll see how brands can connect to people in a totally different way, and thus retain a consumer base.

People are not against commercial messages or advertising, but they don't want to be overwhelmed by it. They even want to be involved in the commercial-making process. The Burger King concept of "Whopper sacrifice," for example, encouraged Facebook users to "unfriend" ten Facebook friends for a free hamburger. JetBlue Airlines asked customers to pledge to do one green thing on Earth Day. These are two new strategies to engage people with their brands. In the case of JetBlue, the goal was to have twenty-two thousand people take the pledge, and they encouraged those who received the e-mail to pass along the message.

That kind of grassroots engagement with the people "à la Obama" is working well online and with social media. The powerful idea here is to encourage people to do things by themselves that help make the brand more popular. Increase volunteerism and let people promote the idea on their own terms. This way of thinking is a far cry from screaming in their ears about what you want them to buy. The best efforts, as we will see later, might not always come from the ad agencies but from public relations firms used to creating dialogues instead of the "beat them up over the head" model of advertising.

The elephant in the room is the question: What will happen to TV? Michael Hirschorn, an *Atlantic* contributing editor and founder of a TV production firm called Ish Entertainment, predicts "that the . . . concept of watching TV on-air is not as compelling as watching it when you want and where you want." He even suggests that "We are not far off from a time much like at the dawn of television, when, say, Procter and Gamble may lease a night on a major network and be free to do whatever it wants with it."[130]

One possible alternative future for television is that of Hulu.com, the brainchild of NBC Universal and News Corporation, which offers free videos of hit TV shows like *Family Guy, 30 Rock,* or *The Daily Show with Jon Stewart* online with a lot less advertising. Hulu places fourth in the pecking order of the biggest online video businesses, a list led by Google and YouTube. According to Beth Comstock, the chief marketing officer at GE, the owners of NBC and Hulu, the important element in the success of Hulu was for NBC to relinquish control of the content.

For advertisers, the money will have to find a way to reach people regardless of the medium, but for most brands still in the mindset of believing that more messages are better, they will have to do more with less, and it might not be a bad thing. While working on my documentary on the mayor of São Paulo's ban on all forms of outdoor media, I was surprised to see how marketers and advertisers who redirected that money to the Web or, in the case of Coca-Cola, with a better supermarket experience through imaginative displays did better than before.

There is still a major perception among advertisers from the age of excess that spending more on ads in the wrong media instead of bettering the product is not a bad thing. Venture capitalist Fred Wilson, at the 2009 *Ad Age* Digital Conference, has suggested a different tactic: "There are still some marketers out there buying their media when they could earn it, and earn it a lot less expensively." His point is that, by understanding the opportunities offered by social media, brands can really have a more emotional interaction with their audience.

Television as a medium is not going anywhere soon, but that doesn't mean it won't change. TV programs will be on demand, where and when we want to see them, with on-demand ads. Commercials that air on broadcast television will still function as one of the most powerful tools of branding, but only to a point and with a more integrated perspective. The new role TV commercials need to have, and how television will facilitate the interaction between people and brands, will be crucial.

From Push Communication to Push/Pull

Until very recently, advertising has been a "push" form of communication, meaning the sending of commercial messages without the benefit of any major interaction with the receiver. Now, with the help of the Internet, it is on the verge of a complete reinvention, perhaps even a renaissance. With these new media, advertising is becoming the multidimensional "push and pull" communication tool everyone in the business was looking for all along. Advertising can now instantaneously convey a brand message and actually help build a real dialogue (that will, in turn, affect the brand message) with people! Advertisers have been limited by the vehicles at their disposal to reach an audience: for the most part, the media of radio, TV, print advertising, and billboards. These "push" media were primarily used to target passive consumer groups. Today, the Internet is just beginning to reveal the tip of the iceberg of the vast opportunity for engaging people in a dialogue. "Pull" messages, or messages that encourage a response from people, help connect brands with the public in a very dynamic way. As this "push/pull" communication trend strongly influences advertising in both old and new media, it will be, I believe, an all-around very good thing for advertising!

On the whole, excluding the stellar work of a few, advertising over the past twenty-five years has become stale, and consumers, overloaded with a barrage of unexciting commercial messages, have become more and more impervious to these messages. When some of the old-world economy brands squeezed ad agency fees, organizing some of the most cutthroat competitions that were often handled through third-party consultants, it only encouraged short-term vision and compromise. To make things worse, advertising decisions were often made by people in corporations who, for safety's sake, preferred, above all, to remain unchallenged. When we first worked with Sergio Zyman, who at the time was chief marketing officer of Coca-Cola, he demanded that his ad agencies be only one thing: kick-ass creative! This was not a terribly popular practice when some of the major ad groups wanted to become "marketing consultants," envying the successful evolution of some of the "big seven" accounting firms into lucrative consulting practices. But he was, of course, absolutely right in making creativity the top priority with the agencies, because *who else can bring a brand to life, if not the advertising and brand-identity professionals?* He was an exceptional client for the times. Most clients remained in the "risk-free" zone, and the result of this was that overall, the creative life went out

Who else can bring a brand to life, if not the advertising and brand-identity professionals?

of the business and audiences disengaged from watching what had become cookie-cutter ads. Formula communication became the norm—a way to avoid presenting innovative ideas by showing snippets of other people's work . . . remember the overuse of rip-o-matics, the practice of recycling and splicing pieces of images from commercials to create a "new" concept? Fortunately, some firms such as Wieden and Kennedy, Crispin Porter, and TBWA/Chiat/Day continued raising the creative bar by avoiding compromise and became sources of inspiration for others. But for the most part, ad agencies became as bureaucratic as the people they were supposed to inspire with creativity, and executives from the top down started to speak, think, act, and look like their clients, offering none of the provocative ideas a brand needs to really stand out.

Now, however, as advertisers are forced to strive to meet the demands of a new economy and a newly empowered consumer, the paradigm is changing. I believe that the result of this will be a new infusion of creativity in the business. Innovation and breakthrough thinking will once again become the primary assets of an ad agency. As we have seen, in the new economy, entrepreneurship and innovation are accepted as the norm, so now we have an influx of new (and some old-new) companies who want . . . guess what? To take creative risk! Usher in a new breed of young communicators who are bringing a fresh outlook to the business and a new set of values! Ad agencies are once again taking control of a brand's communication strategy and are jumping on the creative bandwagon by empowering this new generation of fresh talent who are having a blast setting the tone for a renewed approach to brand messages. The stage is set to build a communications paradigm only available in and around a new medium: the Internet.

But first of all, let's take a look at Emotional Branding in traditional advertising and then move from there into the world of new media. Regardless of the medium, from the perspective of Emotional Branding, *it is essential to start any advertising endeavor with the acknowledgment that there is a new ad-savvy and marketing-Tefloned consumer out there* who is ready to act as a tough interlocutor. In-your-face visibility and brand dominance was a very '90s idea, but consumers in the new millennium expect more sensitivity and honesty from the brands they like and will appreciate those that respect their spiritual and physical environment. The McCann Erickson motto, "The truth well told," takes us back to the root of advertising and is clearly relevant in the current market environment. The old advertising tricks around a bad product will not work; a new approach and a large dose of responsibility need to be developed around brand communications. Cynicism is huge among the public, and certain generations (especially Gen Y, the first generation to be marketed to "from the crib") just hate advertising with all its excesses. Statistics tell us that we are, after all, barraged by close to three thousand messages per day. This is why the blogosphere has taken on the role of watchdogs for what is being communicated by the media. These blogs cater to people's desire to have a second opinion. Poised to respond to these consumer needs, but not yet highly visible, is a new generation of younger ad professionals, who have definite ideas about their personal impact on the world with the work they do. I believe that they will bring about a new sincerity reflected in the way they communicate. They know that only culturally relevant messages about great products will break the clutter of our overwhelming visual environment.

BUILD A COMMUNITY FIRST

In this new media world, building a community is the first step to gaining a welcoming audience. This means using a more segmented approach to look at people, understanding what that segment really likes and what type of topics are shared within that group. Desiree Gruber's PR agency Full Picture might be onto something with her ideas to build communities first in preparation for a brand interaction—the opposite of today's push advertising model.

Gruber is already the producer of the Lifetime television show *Project Runway,* a venture she financed with the help of the Weinstein Brothers. Her philosophy is simple and truly consistent with breaking the monopolies of a branded conversation down: "Go over the [heads of] fashion editors of traditional magazines and meet women directly by giving them the chance to make their own decisions."[151] Her consumer-first approach is based on the fact that women now are not afraid of technology and that they love to meet and share advice and secrets with other women.

"Beauty tips [are] a currency we trade with each other," she has said, expressing her powerful vision on how women relate to their lives. She has just launched Modelinia.com, a Web site that creates a community around the lifestyle of supermodels. On Modelinia, you find more than two hundred models telling you all about their personal and work lives in interviews and lifestyle snippets on video. You can follow the lives of supermodels at a level of detail never before possible with magazines.

With $5 million in seed money, this "magcom," a hybrid of a magazine and a sitcom, has the advantage of giving visitors total control over how they want to experience the site and the ability to share it with friends. If you want to find out about models based on their astrological sign, you can do that. Or, if you prefer to know where they spend their vacations, you can do that, also. This niche approach to a lifestyle site resonates with a specific emotionally engaged group of women and has already won the support of Maybelline as its first advertiser. On the site, Maybelline commercials are placed in an intuitive and relevant way. By offering tips on how to look beautiful, their content seamlessly fits into the site's programming.

By showing, as Gruber says, "how models are sharing their secrets, with their problems and imperfections, what they conceal and how, the dialogue is very genuine and authentic. It is more human and personal. . . . There is a big difference between us and Style.com where Anna Wintour is lecturing women about what they should wear." Modelinia is the type of idea that the Internet creates, and it integrates a community of fans who seek more intimate information on a subject they are passionate about. With relevant advertising that supports the overall style of the content, it is a way for brands to be more relevant and accepted. An added bonus: Rich information on the likes and dislikes of a distinct consumer group with amazing input on how you are doing with them as a brand, plus the added dimension of being part of the buzz. Women are great networkers—an exponential detail not to be forgotten.

This approach of content on demand does not guarantee success. Not unlike sitcoms that come and go based on their ratings and acceptance with an audience, brands will more and more be judged on consumer responses, and that might force certain brands off the consumer map, while others will flourish.

BREAK A FEW RULES TO BUILD A BRANDED COMMUNITY PEOPLE CARE ABOUT

I have been following Weight Watchers ever since I directed the design of their brand identity ten years ago. Their communication model is truly a symbol of what the future offers some brands and is a tremendous learning experience for others. One thing is fundamental to the Weight Watchers brand: it's a culture; it is built as a community and operates as a community. Unlike traditional brands, it puts people first in the equation. In order to do so, it had to break a few rules and be a contrarian brand.

- **Contrarian rule number 1:** When Weightwatchers.com launched in 1999 in the middle of the dot-com craze, the site was spun off from the main business and attracted the best technology minds of the time. The Web site was not just a second thought.

- **Contrarian rule number 2:** When everything on the Web was given away for free, Weight Watchers charged money to make money. This enabled them to bring the best service to online users.

- **Contrarian rule number 3:** Instead of coming up with a half-baked beta Web site model supported by ads, as most dot-com companies did, Weight Watchers spent close to $35 million to perfect its site with the most effective navigation system at its very launch.

- **Contrarian rule number 4:** The head of Weightwatchers.com ultimately became the president and CEO of the Weight Watchers brand; after building a real community online, he knew how to keep and grow one across the board.

- **Contrarian rule number 5:** All advertising Weight Watchers creates aims to bring people to the Web site, making the Web site the engine that fuels the brand's social engine.

Weight Watchers is now a $1.5 billion brand, and $200 million of these revenues come from the Web—what a return on their investment! The Web operation (acquired in 2005) is one of the most astute and sophisticated social media operations around, which is a necessity when you have four million unique visitors.

In speaking to several management executives at Weight Watchers, you get a sense of their passion and commitment to building the brand into one with a special social appeal—they let members take charge of the conversation. The brand has what one executive calls a "very light touch" on the site. "The members are very good at policing themselves" is the attitude.

This is what is missing in most traditional consumer-brand interactions. Most brands want to codify the relationship between their site and visitors to that site or control the message of the site.

The "oral" Weight Watchers business model is about emotions and conversations, about emotional engagement and a unique intimacy with the brand. The emotional fundamentals are just right in this company. For instance, people on the Weight Watchers program who achieve their goals are rewarded by being able to come back free to the groups and the program. Those who lead the Weight Watchers groups had to have gone through the program themselves, thereby engendering a human link and raw connection that inspires trust and makes this brand stand out.

Can any brand duplicate the Weight Watchers model and see similar success? Yes, but the bar has been set high, and brands need to work on fostering the following:

- A culture whose central mission is social, on doing good.
- A meaningful product that requires an emotional engagement.
- A core activity whose model is based on social engagement.

In short: to duplicate such an active community, you need to have a brand that people will find worth talking about to their friends.

OGILVY AND MATHER AND IBM: WHEN OLD BECOMES NEW AGAIN

Ogilvy & Mather, which was groundbreaking at its inception but had become kind of stodgy in the late '80s and early '90s when its brilliant founder retired once and for all to his castle in Toufou, is a great example of a successful turnaround for an agency as well as one of its major clients, IBM. This was a unique situation in which both parties' desire to succeed culminated in one of the strongest agency/client relationships in the business. Ogilvy & Mather offers some examples of campaigns that break all the rules in the best possible way. Their campaign for IBM has completely changed the way people perceive the brand. IBM has transformed its image of an old-tech, out-of-touch company to one of the most exciting companies in the world today.

IBM had been struggling for awhile against its Big-Blue image of a cold, high-tech machine that lacked a dose of humanity. This brand perception was, of course, made even worse by Apple, which had managed to communicate a very warm, consumer-friendly image and, most importantly, a culture of innovation that came through powerfully in its ad campaigns. Its now famous "1984" commercial, created by Chiat/Day for the launch of the Macintosh line, showed a woman breaking through the drab, freakishly uniform world of computerized big business (meant to symbolize IBM, of course) with a rebel toss of a hammer, shattering a huge computer screen. This was the expression of a company that seemed to own the future! Then came Lou Gerstner as the new CEO, who changed the brand from "Big-Blue Brother" into a brand that spells humanity.

I met with Steve Hayden, president of worldwide brand services at Ogilvy & Mather, in the course of writing the first edition of *Emotional Branding*, and I was certainly pleased to talk with one of the people who created the "1984" Macintosh commercial. Meeting with one of the few true creative visionaries in this business is always fascinating, and it reminded me again that advertising is about committed people. "You can contribute to the ugliness of the world or you can contribute to its charm," Steve told me, and he has made this motto a reality in his work. In his previous position at Chiat/Day on the Apple account, he mentioned to me how advanced he found the Apple internal culture. Steve Jobs and his people were committed to the democratization of technology, believing that sharing information would empower people and change society. With a corporate philosophy as strong as this, the emotional component of the brand can only come forward powerfully and become a great platform for branding strategies.

The idea for the "1984" commercial came from a headline in a newspaper lying around at Chiat/Day, "Why 1984 Won't Be Like 1984." Steve Hayden and Brent Thomas came up with the idea that the future was not about fear but hope, because the power would be in the hands of the people. The Cold War was real then, and the commercial that was aired during the Super Bowl resonated beyond its original intent.

Steve eventually came to Ogilvy & Mather to work on the IBM account because the challenge was great, "kind of like putting the Soviet Union back together," he says. On the trail of Bill Hamilton and Rick Boyko, Steve started to challenge the agency itself with the support of Shelly Lazarus, CEO of Ogilvy & Mather. They knew that history was in the making if they could turn IBM around, a challenge for both of these "formerly great" companies, which were now afflicted by bureaucracy. The return to greatness could only happen if people on both sides committed to changing the future. They did, and it worked.

Steve Hayden calls this attitude "the California style," which is "getting the work done and running before the bureaucracy could kill it."

The story is actually quite astounding, starting with the "Solutions for a small planet" concept for e-business, the idea that launched IBM and Ogilvy & Mather into the next century. The first letterbox e-business campaign commercials were shot by Joe Pytka as a trial concept, at the same time that the Lotus spots (a new IBM acquisition) with Denis Leary were being created. Both campaigns got thumbs-down from IBM management and would have been relegated to the lost archives of brilliant commercials were it not for Lou Gerstner's son, back home from college, raving about the Lotus campaign as being really cool. This saved the Leary spots and eventually created an opening to present the Blue Letterbox spots some weeks later.

Hayden calls this attitude "the California style," which is, in his words, "getting the work done and running before the bureaucracy could kill it." This is the signature of confidence. The success of these campaigns transcended the realm of "good advertising"; they succeeded in positioning IBM as a new economy force and a major player in the future of technology. Wall Street noticed, business began moving, and Ogilvy was able to attract the best talent to work on an account that had in previous years been a nightmare for creative teams!

Ogilvy & Mather has rightly steered IBM toward communication strategies that show how great the people of IBM and their clients are, establishing a visual vocabulary that resonates with a new level of sensitivity. The IBM print campaign shows real IBM customers and employees photographed in

a way that feels "real." The photographs are unpretentious and do not reflect any commercial setup. They are simple, amusing little vignettes about people striving and succeeding to do business on the Internet. They ring true to the audience and are successful in creating the kind of intimacy that is so important to Emotional Branding.

Today, Apple owns the emotional territory of innovation demonstrated by its innovative and friendly product design, but IBM has cornered an emotional territory around the strength of its people and a deep understanding of the concerns people have in a new economy. The message created by Ogilvy & Mather is powerful, taking the company from the message of "technology matters" to "man matters" and giving a new face to a brand that was previously unable to express its emotional character.

Good brands are generally perceived as the "good guys," and this emotional perception is sometimes overlooked for concepts that focus too much on product benefits and market dominance. In advertising and brand communication there is always a dose of intuition, a dose of magic, and passion for the business—a passion that is once again becoming part of the language with most professionals. Ogilvy is now going even farther in changing its culture, with a new identity program around the signature of David Ogilvy printed on a red background—very striking and elegant.

REAL ISSUES = VOLATILE EMOTIONS: NAVIGATING CHOPPY WATERS

I will now describe several examples of powerful Emotional Branding strategies that have led to different success stories. Benetton's strong communication program is an example of an ad campaign evoking negative emotions in a manner that got completely out of control, seriously damaging the company's image in the U.S. market. On the other hand, as we will see, Kenneth Cole takes on the exact same issues in his ad campaign with success.

Benetton, the Italian retailer, has been taking the stance of provocation since the late '80s, and in the end it seems to have alienated a lot of people from the brand. Provocation is not a brand strategy, just a short-term tactic to claim the spotlight. Brands are not in the business of changing society. Brands need to clearly express humanistic solution messages in line with their consumers' concerns and demonstrate that they are sensitive and supportive of the consumers' values. Benetton's visual of a black horse mounting a white horse to sensitize the world to racial issues is not necessarily the most effective expression of the

UNITED COLORS
OF BENETTON.

www.benetton.com/deathrow

SENTENCED TO DEATH

JAMES EDWARD THOMAS
BORN: 1/18/1956; PROVIDENCE,
RHODE ISLAND
CRIME: FIRST DEGREE MURDER
SENTENCE: DEATH BY LETHAL INJECTION

message of hope that was originally at the core of the Benetton brand identity. Benetton did it again in 1999 with their incendiary advertising portraying death-row inmates, another exploitation of a very touchy social topic for commercial purposes. These moralistic ads, steeped in pedagogy, seem more of a ploy to get their brand attention than a sincere attempt to either make a statement or build brand awareness. There are no facts given about the death penalty or the people on death row whom we are being confronted with visually through intense close-ups and, as usual with Benetton's advertising, no connection is made to the products or the people of Benetton. Unfortunately, the failure of these advertising campaigns has been reflected in a serious underperformance in the world's biggest market, the United States,[132] and Sears recently dropped the brand from its four hundred stores in the United States after having been picketed by victims' families. And now, Oliviero Toscani, the creative director for the Benetton ads, has made a quick exit from Benetton, ushering in perhaps a new era of more intelligent and emotionally sensitive advertising.

This is not to say that a brand cannot successfully make strong statements about the world. Kenneth Cole has made his mark in adopting causes as marketing tools, but with a different sensibility. The Kenneth Cole ad campaigns give the

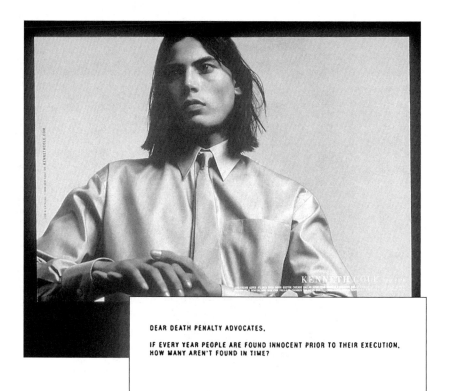

brand that sense of being current, which is so important to fashion brands, by addressing current events. Their 1999 campaign takes on the same issue of the death penalty, among others, in a way that I believe works. Let's take a look at the difference. The Kenneth Cole ads, which certainly do have an edge, handle this and other social issues in a more sensitive way by challenging people's beliefs through questions and facts and through the use of gentle, wry humor. By posing provocative questions, such as "If every year people are found innocent prior to their execution, how many aren't found in time?" and giving facts through the sardonic use of the "cc," the ads remain conversational in tone and attempt to create a dialogue. Rather than use a heavy, moralistic tone, the ads bring a fresh perspective that encourages an open-ended debate. Cole is positioning himself as being on the same side as his customers: the side of the truth. Another important difference here is that the Kenneth Cole ads show product and people wearing the product. It's as if the note, which is printed on a translucent overlay cutout, was written by the young person shown in the ad (and not necessarily by Cole himself) wearing the Kenneth Cole fashions, and in this way the ads create a rich and complete world of a brand image with a fully fleshed out personality. On his Web site, Cole expresses his values by stating that

Emotions can be exposed and shared in cyberspace in a personal way with people.

"To be aware is more important than what you wear" and lists the different causes his company supports. Best of all, though, he has a terrific chat section on this site which allows visitors to speak freely on topics such as "Violence in the media: Killer entertainment or killer influence?" "The Confederate flag: Pride or prejudice?" or "Selling supermodel eggs? Model society or ugly idea?" This is great because it gives a feeling of an open conduit of expression between the brand and the consumer. Cole is finding out, unfiltered, what his customers really think and feel!

One of the best things about the Kenneth Cole ads is their clever use of tongue-in-cheek humor. Humor should not be forgotten as a way to sell products! It is a bonding element between human beings: if you can make someone laugh, he will feel friendlier toward you and perhaps even remember you!

Old and New Media

Now, let's venture into the world of the Internet, where the results of the challenge of the successful promotion of a brand are immediate. As I said before, this is a medium that requires bold thinking. The Internet, which today exists as an extension of media strategies, will soon become the primary medium. The war between the old media and the new media is already settled before the fight. They are complementary–allies in bringing better, more truthful information and awareness to people.

Emotions can be exposed and shared in cyberspace in a personal way with people, and that is the most important element offered by this new medium. It is an opportunity to build an intelligent path to winning a person's trust and belief. Good-bye "push" communication, hello heart-to-heart, "pull" dialogue with people in cyberland.

GOOD GIRLS, BAD BOYS IN SOCIAL MEDIA: EMOTIONS THAT WORK
Secret: Because You're Hot!

I met Marina Maher a few years back when I was working on the Cover Girl logo. She then had a very successful public relations firm named MMC, and today it has become one of the most respected practices in the field of beauty, fashion, and pharmaceutical products. Marina believes that social media will change marketing before marketing will change social media. Why? "Women are more prepared for this type of medium," she says. "We are all about connections; we look at brands from a female point of view, from a 360 degree perspective." Her point is that women are not top-down or bottom-up people, but integrators. "At home," she adds, "women often manage the health of the family, the finances, or parenting responsibility. This makes them multitaskers and [they are thus] apt to see the world from a larger experience." Her comments emphasize that because of their enhanced responsibility, women are information seekers by nature, and the Web is the place where they can find answers.

Moving forward, the challenge for brands is to create brand communities with women who share the same values and aspirations. Women are shoppers, and the Web is the perfect place to compare prices and find products as well as the newest styles. It also allows them to seek the opinions of their friends. When 16-year-old young women try on prom dresses, for instance, they will most likely take a picture of the dress, send it to their best friends, and wait for their friends to chime in, instantaneously, with opinions.

This example helps illustrate the contrast between men and women. *Men and women use the Web differently, but it is always about who they are and what's relevant to that self.* Guys go to the Web to find the stats on products to then make purchasing decisions by themselves. "Women ask opinions; men gather information. Women don't ask questions, they want opinions," sums up Maher. This difference is not always reflected in many Web sites that forget why women love social media so much.

"The head knows but the tail is not there yet." Maher admires the resolve to look toward the future, but, she says, "the agencies are not there yet." In a world where clients need metrics and measurement, this is a challenge. What is my return on investment? The Web will bring more than its load of data on consumers and better profiles on who buys what, but everybody agrees that the tools to comprehend those social dynamics are not there yet for most marketers and advertisers.

"Advertising is about copywriting and PR is about dialogue," says Marina, and this is why she believes that PR agencies understand the Web better and will be more agile and creative in this format. "The Web gives you greater reach faster, a more targeted reach. General media tends to be broad. If I want to reach a left-handed redhead in New Jersey, I can do that," says Marina. "At MMC, we are about brand relationship, relationship with retailers, journalists, consumers, or all the redheads in New Jersey. We know the blogging sphere and monitor it constantly; we know how to connect with the right language in that medium."

That might be useful, since nobody can force anyone else to watch a commercial. Regardless, big brands are slow to respond to the new media; only 6 percent of their budget is spent on social media because of a lack of metrics. But the 18- to 35-year-old male has migrated from TV to the Web, and women that influence most buying are now online in a greater number than their male counterparts, so it might be time to think that in this Wild West of digital media a certain level of risk is still acceptable. Unfortunately, laments Maher, social media are often only looked upon by major brands as cause related when in reality they are a lot more.

A GOOD-GIRL SUCCESS STORY: LOVE!

I was intrigued by the way MMC promoted the fiftieth anniversary of P&G's deodorant brand Secret through social media. With such a great name and a focus on today's "tell-all" consumer culture, MMC launched the "Share Your Secret" online campaign. MMC believed that even though we live in a high-tech world, consumers and brands alike still have an emotional need to foster and cultivate relationships. The Ten Commandments of Emotional Branding, from service to relationship, become so much more interesting now that those tools are available to marketers.

Women were first encouraged to post their secrets on Shareyoursecret.com, via text messages, or even in good old Times Square in New York City, on a Reuters sign, with a live simulcast. The social media campaign drove both event participation and media coverage. Branded messages were posted on Gawker.com—a popular site for daily news and gossip—and other key blogs which, in turn, fueled traditional media coverage.

The campaign was a great success. After one month, Shareyoursecret.com hosted more than 104,000 viewers and more than 2.5 million page views, with five thousand secrets posted. It resulted also in twenty-one million plus media impressions on influential online and traditional media, including *Good Morning America*, CBS, *The Early Show*, FOX News, the *New York Post*, and Gawker. Positioned rightly as a "tell-all" story, the concept was properly created to match the values of the Web with a clear understanding of the interaction that exists there. This campaign proves it: People want to meet and talk without the oversight of a chaperone.

BAD BOY ONLINE: AXE

"Share your secret" was a great success, and it also spoke primarily to the good-girl qualities of women. The advertising campaign was a bit more daring with its "because you're hot" tagline. A powerful idea, because you do indeed need Secret most when you are hot, but it also had an unwelcome sexual come-on. To put any controversy to bed, the brand clarified its tagline by explaining that "because you're hot" was mostly about making a woman confident. Voilà!

They don't have the same problems at Axe, where "hot" is HOT! The confidence factor is also a big part of the brand's campaign: When guys wear Axe, the commercials would have us believe, they become irresistible to women who literally come on to them. Guys don't have to do anything that could impact their self-esteem; women just flock to them. For those who don't know Axe, how could you not? Axe is the Unilever deodorant that thrives on controversy. Indeed, it has had its fair share of adverse publicity, best described in Wikipedia's five pages dedicated to the brand's risqué approach. Comments such as "sexist and degrading advertising," "unsensitive to environmental issues," and "encouraging sexual promiscuity" all give you a sense of a longer list of negatives associated with the brand. In short, Axe has all the characteristics of the stuff that makes rebellious brands famous. And this works just fine for the brand: it targets the rebellious side of young men and clearly understands (what research has always observed anyway) that what's on those guys' minds basically comes down to one thing: sex.

Now, I am bringing up this brand not for its shock value, or to wake you up as you tire of reading this book. Rather, I am referring to it because of its success, which clearly is only possible because of the opportunities digital media offer. The Axe campaign online could not have been done with traditional media. For example, when, a few years ago, Abercrombie & Fitch tried to test the limits of good behavior with a racy catalog that–God forbid–showed how to mix drinks, the company was mauled on moral issues. With Axe, a clever use of social media such as YouTube allowed them to push into the reality of youth culture. On YouTube, you can review the "banned" Axe commercials that have become the most popular by making waves with a group of rebel wannabes who love underground culture. Among those banned commercials: "The Axe effect," with 1,206,170 viewers and "Horny babes get F. . . d hard," with 655,592 views. The brand strategy shows how controversial but also how relevant the language of the brand is for Gen Y guys. This is not a Baby Boomer world; this is a heart attack zone for parents.

Axe has leveraged new technology to reach its target audience and has even partnered with traditional media such as TV shows on MTV or SPIKE to have them create content or promotions for the brand. Kevin George, the VP-general manager of Unilever's deodorant and hair care brands, believes that "The goal is to create something people want to seek rather than trying to stick it in front of them." George's message clearly breaks the homogeneous way brands have traditionally worked in assuming that the same TV commercial would work across different venues. By evaluating the role TV, online, and print play emotionally in people's minds, Axe understands that the expectations are wildly different online from one community to another.

The chase for reaching an audience is becoming more complex, and getting people to sit down to hear a message is challenging.

IN SOCIAL MEDIA, YOU DON'T LOOK FOR CUSTOMERS—YOU SEEK FRIENDS

Nobody is glued to a TV set or listening to radio at home anymore. People now take the electronic equipment that used to be nailed to a wall or plugged into some outlet with them everywhere. Our cell phones and portable computers are always with us, and we are definitely on the go. Soccer moms are in a car most of the time, shuttling kids to different places, and businesspeople are always flying to destinations far away from home. As people spend less and less time in their living rooms in front of a TV set, computers are attracting more eyeballs than ever. Of course, we all want to know how this will change the world of advertising, because there is no question that it will!

The chase for reaching an audience is becoming more complex, and getting people to sit down to hear a message is, well . . . challenging! We have to adapt, and, fortunately, the rapid progress of technology, particularly in the wireless area, offers potential opportunities for reaching people wherever they are at a myriad of different points of contact.

The "push/pull" perspective is a helpful one, given this wide array of communication choices. This is a new, friendly way of speaking to people, based on the give-and-take principle. Yes, you're asking for something–the consumer's precious attention–but if your ad can also be helpful and receptive to the response, then you are giving something in return! Go to any open-air market in France and watch how the vendors sell foie gras, wine, cheese, fish, and poultry. It's one of the most delightful, amusing experiences you can have! Vendors talk, flatter, and jest with you in the most clever ways to lure you over to their stalls. They are so authentic, with the rural clothing, mannerisms, and accents that bring total authority and credibility to the origin of the goods they see and their quality. The products in these markets are presented in a way that tantalizes your taste buds, and even the brown paper bag in which they are handed to you adds to the charm of the buying experience. Has anything really changed? As the creators of myths and stories, we are only as good as the impact we can have on our audience, and only our passion, sincerity, and love of the brand will be able to create a dialogue and, eventually, a brand based on trust.

section IV:
vision

inspiration for change:
how to get there from here

E-motions

We tend to think of media as the conduits–the television or radio or Web site–that deliver some form of content. But the delivered content is, itself, a kind of medium. Content is just a medium for the interaction between people.
–Douglas Rushkoff, *Get Back in the Box*

In only a decade, the Web has dramatically evolved from a new-age transactional tool (eBay or Amazon) and electronic brochure for corporations to an experimental and alternative source of news (blogs) and locus of powerful search engines like Google. The Web has since opened itself up for user content–think Wikipedia, with its user collaboration, or YouTube and Current TV, where anyone can post content. Finally, it has exploded as a social tool with the advent of Facebook and MySpace. Not to be capped, Twitter pixelized our lives so we can share our reality even more effectively. The last frontier we'll see is the Web bypassing TV to become the dominant entertainment hub, an online multimedia platform, with services like Hulu.

One of the most powerful impacts of this modern revolution is how pervasive it is in how we live our lives. How many of us could live without Google to answer our every question? How would we feel without social media that question our answers? This begs the question: How will social branding based on emotions be put to use in the future, and what will the new challenges be in connecting brands with people in our quickly changing world? Skittles. com might be one of those approaches that crystallizes what will come next. A Web site is an overlay that gives consumers the opportunity to connect with the brand's different social sites (e.g., YouTube, Twitter, and Facebook). Social media are becoming social branding, in which the content is delivered by people.

In a consumer-driven "Time" civilization, as I explained in my introduction, very few decisions will be made on logic alone; instinct will supersede facts and data: what feels right when vetted by our friends will become everyone's dominant driver of choices. We feel together, experience together, and stimulate each other's imagination by being open to one another.

This is the age of genuine branding and emotionally connecting with people one on one. In this section, we will see how the Web has allowed for the emergence of a new generation of leaders like Barack Obama. With the emergence of online commerce, we will also see how in the future our most basic habits will be completely redefined. Even an activity as basic as shopping may one day save us time as we click a button to get goods delivered to our doorstep and protect our environment as we step away from the chain store to a more friendly, retro-commerce that emphasizes personal relationships with each individual customer.

16

Branding Emotions on the Web: From Social Media to Social Branding

The Web is a place where, in the greatest of paradoxes, freedom means that the whole world knows what you are doing in certain cases almost minute by minute. By voluntarily breaking the last walls of our privacy, our lives become an open canvas for our best friends or the people we trust.

It is impossible to look at this chapter without analyzing it through an audience lens. The Web is first and foremost the most emotional of all media because people made it that way; people gave social media their human substance and have expanded their context.

What do we want?

- To be listened to.
- A forum to share opinions.
- A blank canvas for creation.
- A bazaar for buying anything.
- A way to search or find most stuff.
- A place to change identities and become whomever we want.
- To know the people we are dealing with.

The Web has fast-tracked careers, turned unknowns into celebrities, built and destroyed brands and reputations, and—against all odds—helped elect a black candidate President of the United States. The Web simultaneously encompasses democracy, anarchy, megalomania, transparency, outreach, the power of numbers, and the end of privacy.

The Web as a change agent will conflict with the past, but the model is unstoppable and those who understand it will thrive. A new generation propelled and empowered by this new medium will find itself influencing votes, the way we do business, and how we interact with one another. It is a new emotional country created by people who prefer to be united rather than divided.

The world is adapting to the Web, and for those brands that think they can master or dominate this audience–good luck. In this world, people rule! This is a new world in which "xY" will thrive and older generations will become inspired. This is a new world that will stimulate and expand our thinking and creativity, bring forward new leaders, and unleash new forces, good or bad. Welcome to a new nation, welcome to the future and to the medium where brands will have to adapt and redefine their roles in connecting with people in this new environment.

From "You've Got Mail" to Social Media

In this book's first edition, this section was an investigation of the huge potential the Web has created for a more emotionalized brand expression. I focused primarily on two of the most visible examples of the progress the cyberworld had made at the time: commercial Web sites and what we called "e-commerce," or a new way to transact online. My focus was on how to bring the best of Emotional Branding to this new medium, but I also touched upon a new idea I foresaw as the most important opportunity for the future of this medium: social interaction. As I wrote then, the Web introduced *"the idea of unhindered communication between the brand and the consumer and among consumers themselves. Buyers can–and do–now communicate with each other, learn from each other, and help each other."*

The most important date in the history of social media may just be Friday, March 13, 2009, when Oprah Winfrey, on her hugely successful talk show, *The Oprah Winfrey Show*, anointed Mark Zuckerberg, one of the founders of Facebook, the "biggest thing" on American soil, proving without fail that Facebook had reached mainstream status. Oprah, a typical Baby Boomer, described Zuckerberg's success in terms of how rich he is, several times calling young Mark "a billionaire." But Zuckerberg, a member of a generation for which the status is about having less, emphasized that he was still living in his one-bedroom apartment and just got his first credit card. At the end of the interview, Zuckerberg very sweetly thanked the host by saying, "I never thought I would be on *Oprah*. I am so happy." Like others in Generation Y, he might not give too much credit to having money, but he does love the subsequent fame.

Oprah, like most of us, now has her own page on Facebook and Twitter, but, in my eyes, the most important development of her having the Facebook founder on her show was the vast differences it revealed between both in leadership style and values. For Oprah, Zuckerberg's great achievement was about having more money, whereas for Zuckerberg, it was all about the journey.

What Would Obama Do?

"Clinton may have won the bigger states, but Obama was garnering the votes that mat-tered." –Chuck Todd and Sheldon Gawiser, *How Barack Obama Won*

It would be impossible for me to avoid commenting on the successful campaign of Barack Obama, for it is the most important example of social branding of this era. *Obama's campaign was less about political issues or dogmas than about generational values.* Obama represented the emergence of "xY," and this is why this unknown candidate became the best-known brand in the world in less than two years.

What's mesmerizing about this election is that it expressed all of the values of the new generations and those on the margins. By breaking several barriers such as race, the lack of motivation to vote among younger generations, and how little technology was used to organize people, Obama hit all the sweet spots of younger voters and African Americans that do not normally turn out to vote. By connecting with them through the Web in a precise way from a "demographic" perspective, he was able to carve out his electorate in places that normally were considered outside of his reach.

I was in Washington in early 2009 to film Obama's inaugural address. Standing amongst two million other attendees, I saw firsthand the culmination of a campaign that started with a candidate with very few funds to speak of (especially compared to the others) and a reputation based on a twenty-minute speech he gave at the Democratic National Convention two years earlier. And here he was, being inaugurated as the most popular and visible brand in the world. The basis for his success was in his understanding of the type of message that motivates people to vote. From Obama's success, we can gain an extraordinary understanding of the emotional motives that unify people around an emotional promise. This is a valuable lesson brands can learn to achieve success.

By customizing his message around the belief that people are all different emotionally and that even in parts of the country with a Republican bent some people stand out with different political beliefs, Obama tapped into a completely new approach to campaigning. Traditionally, people who fall under the same general lifestyle would be classified by polls as belonging to a certain political group. Gun owners or fans of NASCAR racing, for example, would automatically be thought of as conservative voters. In reality, though, people view politics emotionally, or in a way that doesn't match polling pundits. While a majority of people might fall under stereotypical descriptions that link their lifestyle to a certain political belief, doing so overlooks the emotional nature of an election at a particular moment in time.

A CAMPAIGN FACEBOOKED

In April of 2009, *Fast* magazine ran a cover story titled, "Boy Wonder (The Kid Who Made Obama President)". The "kid" is none other than Chris Hughes, cofounder of Facebook, who engendered the most successful Web campaign ever to promote a candidate. In this article, Obama's campaign manager, David Plouffe, is quoted as saying, "Technology has always been used as a net to capture people in a campaign or cause, but not to organize."[135] The philosophy Hughes brought forward at Facebook, and for which he is credited as having had the most impact on, is in figuring out "ways that people would want to connect with one another."

It is easy to forget the emotional motivations that moved people to support the Obama campaign, but the emotional side of the campaign was very influential. Voters thought the United States needed to redeem itself for the previous administration's mistakes, and they wanted to both save the country's reputation around the world and be a part of history by helping to elect the first black president of the United States. Americans wanted to make history.

Expectations were high, and the desire for engagement strong, from some potential voters. Volunteers abounded, but this campaign's achievement was based on how the Obama campaign leveraged those average voters into foot soldiers. Most generations were involved in the Obama campaign, but how the campaign mobilized Gen Y–a generation usually prone to a passive attitude toward politics–shows its brilliance. It used the right people, like Hughes, to turn latent emotions into action.

By giving his supporters the tools necessary to help them take the responsibility to act for the campaign as individuals and affect change in their own neighborhoods, Obama's campaign broke the mold for political strategies. This concept rested on a combination of the "Space" approach of using the Web to fast-forward information, and the "Time" approach of relinquishing the control of the campaign to local volunteers and arming them with solid promotional material. The technology put in place by the Obama campaign and the programs made available to volunteers helped create a movement because the actors had the freedom to act and the tools to operate and subsequently impact communities.

This strategy worked, and Obama's amazing rise is one of the most phenomenal stories of recent history. Other American presidents, such as John F. Kennedy, Jimmy Carter, and Bill Clinton, have a similarly modest background, but what sets Obama apart are the expectations that he has stirred and the barriers he has broken, including race, which would have been thought impossible only a few years ago: He made the Web the core essence of his strategy.

THE TEN COMMANDMENTS OF EMOTIONAL POLITICS

Let's look at the Ten Commandments of Emotional Branding as applied to the Obama campaign. You'll see that unlike many brands, the Obama campaign hits on all the right emotional connections.

- **From consumers (voters) to people.** Not special interests, but people. As early as the second quarter of 2008, 258,000 people, with as many as 110,000 on the Internet, bring $32 million into Obama's coffers, effectively giving life to his campaign. Starting in February, $1 million per day was donated to the campaign.[134]
- **From product to experience.** Two books, two compelling stories written by Barack Obama. The Obama brand had a tone of gravitas and intellect, as opposed to the McCain camp's appropriation of Joe the Plumber, an attempt, albeit an unsuccessful one, to use a small business owner as the voice of the campaign on tax issues.

- **From honesty to trust.** Obama was "genuine." He made a tough call–"Don't go to war"–and never wavered from it. Obama stood up for consistency, sincerity, and transparency at a time when most politicians stood for nothing but focus group-approved strategies.
- **From quality to preference.** Senator McCain was a respected hero from the past, but Obama was seen as the future.
- **From notoriety to aspiration.** "Yes, we can." Obama shifted the message from fear to hope. The "Yes, we can" acceptance speech was viewed on YouTube by more than fifteen million people.
- **From identity to personality.** "We are the United States of America." Obama took pains to define a greater public call, not just the agenda of the Democratic Party.
- **From function to feel.** The Obama campaign avoided precise political issues, instead emphasizing "change" as the issue. This shift in thematic focus gave the candidate an emotional mandate to act on people's feelings.
- **From ubiquity to presence.** Total transparency. Sarah Palin, McCain's running mate and former vice presidential candidate, was ubiquitous but disingenuous, while Obama connected with authenticity. The choice of street artist Shepard Fairey to design Obama's official campaign portrait (titled "Hope") connected with youth. Watch our video interview with Shepard Fairey at Emotionalbranding.com.
- **From communication to dialogue.** The campaign talked to people on a personal level (a community of potential vote influencers estimated as close to two million people), with the Web as the rallying point and a channel for participation.
- **From service to relationship.** With the idea that we are all in it together, Obama created Organizing for America, a new group that will continue the campaign's grassroots momentum and give ordinary citizens a role in the changes ahead.

Barack Obama, as an "xY," understood more than anybody else the power of information that can be shared and leveraged emotionally. This campaign will forever change the ways in which political and consumer brands communicate. It starkly revealed the limits of the old (one-way) media and the power of the Internet as a way to reach out to communities. Successful brands of the future will be inspired by the novel, grassroots ways in which the Obama campaign went directly to people to create awareness, belief, and compassion, and infused voting intent in millions of people in a very short period of time. Obama has proved that we are now in an age of Emotional Branding, come to life through bandwidth and technology in the most powerful ways.

Hope and Fear: A Blessing or a Curse?

The Obama campaign played up three emotions—hope, urgency, and fear—to alter voters' choices and expectations. Its slogan, "Yes, we can," gave voters hope about the possibility of change. Fear, which usually deters action and lessens our ability to enjoy life, motivated voters to work harder in order to make "change" happen. And lastly, the campaign created a sense of urgency: Vote now so we can win the election and enact the change we all want.

This campaign strategy was brilliant and revolutionary; it was not about making the other candidate look bad but rather about fighting for a lofty goal with a candidate who had all the branded attributes of a leader.

This strategy also stands in opposition to the fear tactics of the previous administration that ultimately only led to its rejection. The Bush administration created what I call the "double negative." We are fighting in Iraq to prevent attacks on our soil (ouch!). Both the war and the threat of terrorism lack closure or winners (two negatives). When demanding sacrifice from a nation, you have to have a clear end goal. Not unlike Churchill asking the British people at the beginning of the Second World War for their " blood, toil, tears and sweat" as he promised his audience "You ask, what is our aim? . . . It is victory."

John McCain's campaign was also full of double or triple negatives. On the one hand, he countered the George Bush legacy with his culturally odd "maverick" image. A maverick is someone who not only can think independently but who is also a lone dissenter, a loner, not the open source candidate he tried to portray. Also, his patrician age, which could have been a plus—he claimed it signified experience that he could bring to a crisis—was undercut by his choice of a running mate. Choosing a perky young governor from Alaska only made him look older in contrast.

From a branding perspective, a brand association with a celebrity, for instance, can be a blessing or a miss if the fit is not there.

MOVEMENTS HAVE A LONGER LIFE

Supporters of My.BarackObama.com, an online community supporting the president, are kept in the loop. Subscribers receive regular e-mail from the president's staff and view the latest videos of speeches or activities they might have missed. For those eager to support administration policy, the site sends them the phone numbers of the offices of congressmen or senators in their district so they can call Washington directly and encourage support for Obama's programs. My.BarackObama.com has become a base for a new form of post-campaign activism that keeps people engaged and ready to influence others, including politicians and friends.

In 2009, a grassroots movement called "Organizing for America" was created for Americans who wanted to stay politically active and continue to promote the new administration's agenda on budget issues or economic recovery programs. As part of this organization, 3,587 meetings are held in 1,579 cities in America over 429 congressional districts in fifty states. The mostly Baby Boomer world of Washington should try to know what is going on, especially for the sake of their reelection, since their voters will be influenced by Obama supporters working under the radar.

While the Obama "doctrine" will impact future political campaigns by other politicians, more importantly, it will change the political process altogether by allowing newcomers a chance to get elected more easily than before. In the last New York state senatorial campaign, the amount of money all the candidates raised hovered around $200 million. Now, I understand that being a senator is a great job and many people would want to fight for the opportunity to serve in our government, but could that money not have been used in a better manner? To be elected senator, you need either your own fortune or the support of the well-off, who, as we know, might not have the voters' best interests in mind. This explains why our representatives, for the most part, represent special interests.

What the Obama campaign demonstrates is that this way of running a campaign may one day be less effective. Those who are elected in this manner will find having connections in high places not as valuable as before. One day, we might even see candidates with less money but solid computer "programming" in their background and an understanding of the communicative power of social media start a campaign on a shoestring and build a following that will actually understand and agree with their ideas. When shared, those ideas could inspire thousands more to show up at voting booths. If we can challenge those politicians flush with cash, we might see the emergence of a new generation of genuine people with a real calling for public service. Why can't an individual finance a campaign? Only then would we see a truly democratic process in action.

While Obama may now be the president, he keeps on upping the ante on individual involvement. On March 26, 2009, he set up, for the first time, an Internet town hall meeting that was Webcast directly to households, as part of his plan to sell a federal budget that defied history in terms of its size and impact. According to many sources, this online version of the traditional town hall meeting was Obama's way of getting his message directly to people, skipping over Congress and the Senate. Consistent with his campaign style, doing so mobilizes his advocates to influence their elected representatives and reinforces his image as an innovator and agent of change. This Webinar medium is consistent with his emotional brand.

The ingenuity of Obama is again in his ability to stand as a symbol of change, transcending the negative noise around the budget itself. According to the White House, close to 70,000 people watched the Webcast—a number good enough to fill a sports stadium. This number doesn't include the number of viewers who watched the Webcast on TV and the cable media that broadcast it. And viewers were also active participants in the meeting: individuals could send in questions through a Web site, and all told, the administration received 104,103 questions sent either as videos or in written form to the president. Four million people cast their votes on which one of those questions would make it live. Obama thus created a veritable dialogue.

This style of direct connection with citizens does have its critics; some liken it to the populist tone of *American Idol*. What everyone agrees with, though, is that this approach is innovative and truly game changing. This Webinar will have a lasting impact that signals a less dogmatic and more emotional way to reach people. "Getting perspective outside of Washington," claims the president, "opens [up] the White House to the American people." Transparency is a big "xY" value that Obama is capitalizing on.

The lessons of this political strategy could have ramifications for corporations—and how they operate—as well. The offices of top executives are often disconnected from the rest of the corporation. Many good ideas are not heard, and messages are passed down as written directives when a more interactive and emotional model is there for the taking. If you reach out to your consumers, you can develop an even richer dialogue and a powerful new platform that will enhance your brand reputation.

The new literacy is not our ability to read or write letters or our comprehension of words, but the ability to write "codes" to connect with the world online. The Obama administration is writing rules for a new dialogue in a vocabulary that is different from what we know now. What is taking place might just move our reality into the realm of ideas that make our civilization progress.

Asking "What would Obama do?" is the right question for many brands. It transcends any one political belief or what will be the legacy of this administration.

The farsighted communications campaign that brought a country together might well serve brands in need of a new interaction with their audience. This form of communication will become the standard for generations to come.

What brands will learn by observing the Obama campaign is that people, when motivated, flock to the ideals that will help them feel better about who they are. In the commercial world, most consumers will not stop buying, but they will be more selective. While buying less for personal, ecological, or economical reasons, they will still need brands that help them define who they are. This is why, despite the economic downturn, a million people spent hundreds of dollars to travel to Obama's inauguration.

Here are some cues brands can take away from the Obama campaign:

- The product is "authentic."
- The connection is "genuine."
- Don't broker your message; go directly to the people in order to build trust.
- Your consumers are not always where you think they are or those you think you have.
- The president of the company is on the front line of communication.
- It's a generational thing (Stupid).

Is it Tweetable?

The "nano" culture of Twitter is the pixelization of communication and, as a newcomer, is a case that stands out from the rest of all social media because it is a dream come true for "xY": a speedy way to save time, feel supported, and come up with on-the-dot solutions.

Twitter is becoming the Google of social media and the most defining tool of the "xY" generation. In a matter of months, "Twitter" has hit all the right emotional spots, as it symbolizes how to do more with less and gives users the freedom to connect anytime, with anyone. It has become the antithesis of a culture of excess epitomized by Baby Boomers. It is the ultimate symbol of the wider gap that is starting to form between Baby Boomers and subsequent generations. Let's not gloss over this divide, for it symbolizes a serious generational gap and suggests how the new generations will define themselves. For brands today, the most important question when launching a product or a branding program is: Is it Twittable? If it is not, start again!

Twitter resonates with the new generations because it is about doing more with less, and more often. It edits and simplifies connections at a time when the availability of information is out of control. Think about it: Twitter forces you to edit complex thoughts and ideas to their most succinct expression. Messages, when sent by people with a love for abstract concepts, can turn out to be the literary "essential oil"–no fluff, no hype, but just the raw truth. Sound bytes have power; word bytes even more.

Winston Churchill's "Iron Curtain" metaphor defined (another metaphor) the Cold War. Google's slogan, "Don't be evil," crystallized a culture, and Apple's "Think," a consumer. Advertising needs to take a page from Twitter: no hype, no dogs and ponies, but pure, raw, simple ideas. I still remember Les Wexner, the iconic chairman and CEO of Limited Brands, coming back from Italy and muttering two words that became a billion-dollar business strategy: "Dream Angels." Tweetable! When the former chief marketing officer of Coca-Cola, Sergio Zyman, would say, "It is first about the low-hanging fruits," everybody got it, and those words have become an industry mantra. When architect Louis Kahn tells his students to "ask a brick if it wants to be an arch," he is defining a revolutionary architectural philosophy that is unparalleled . . . and tweetable. When famous director Sidney Lumet says, "What do you hope your audience will feel, think, sense?" it defines a new way to think about movie-making, and it is tweetable.

WHAT ARE YOU DOING NOW?
In Los Angeles, a taco truck "tweets" to his list of clients that the truck is standing at their corner, which allows people to save the time they would usually spend worrying about when their favorite truck with the delicious tacos would come around.

When a famous European newscaster tweets that the only thing she is craving right now is a hamburger, she is just expressing a passing feeling. But if fifteen minutes later someone shows up at her building with a hamburger in hand, the connection takes on a different reality. Now, say she tweets that she cannot come down to pick up the hamburger because of the amount of work she has to do. That tweet then starts a flurry of tweets from fans who are spreading the word that she does not tweet herself but has someone do it for her, which undermines her credibility on the medium. If it were her tweeting, the thinking goes, then she would have come down to pick up the delivery of the innocent hamburger. And so the story takes on its own social drama.

In order to keep her credibility on Twitter, the celebrity then tweets back that if everyone watches her show, she will move her pencil in a certain way to prove that she is on top of her tweets. The thousands who watch her show then sigh with relief when they see her moving the pencil. Soon after, she meets the generous Samaritan and gets that hamburger she so craves.

Three things happened here: the hamburger brand, if mentioned, would've gotten a tremendous boost, the newscaster bolstered her own brand, and her show captured a greater audience. None of these are bad things. Most celebrities, such as Ashton Kutcher and even Oprah, have recognized the value of connecting through Twitter, no doubt propagating the hype associated with this new model.

The simple question that is the basis for Twitter, "What are you doing?" prompts countless responses that can all be brand-oriented. "What are you doing?" "I am eating at Demarchelier." Hundreds will remember Demarchelier, and a few might even show up and say hello in response to this tweet.

"What are you doing?"

"I have this offer with a company and don't know if I should quit my job."

In this example, the person could be unaware of the universality of Twitter, and after that tweet, can lose his job at both companies.

"What are you doing now?"

"Can't figure out my phone problem."

Someone from the phone company responds within minutes when it would have taken hours for this customer to get help using a phone. The immediacy of the information Twitter creates breaks down some of the bureaucratic walls that plague major brands by bringing back the old but so new notion of one-on-one service. For corporations, there is also a big warning: if you don't know the rules of the game, don't play the game.

Brands sell foods, communication, medicine, cars, trucks, and infrastructure, but the connection between brands and the people they target is littered with bureaucratic obstacles. Brands are set up bureaucratically, in a top-down

"Space" organization that prevents direct contact with the consumer or customer. A "Space" corporation only relies on its administration and staff and is inherently distrustful of anyone outside of its corporate walls.

Twitter, on the other hand, is all about the power of sharing knowledge multiplied by the number of connections. If you tweet "I am in the emergency room now," you will instantly get responses that could be potentially helpful, like "Avoid Dr. So-and-so at all costs." Brands need to understand the power of the number of people who will see and act on the information Twitter makes available.

Twitter represents a "Space" philosophy that is about basic human interest and trust and the understanding that there is always someone out there ready to help with answers. It is the power of goodwill and ideas—the power to reach out to a greater audience.

A New Technology that Defines New Leaders

Zappos.com, sold in 2009 to Amazon.com, is an online shoe seller with a map on their Web site of the United States, on which you can see live pictures of the products in real time as they are sold by Zappos all over the country. This map with all those shoes popping out in front of my eyes is magic to me. You can get a sense of what others are interested in, learn everybody's favorites, and vote your support for or against someone's order. You can also click on an item being purchased to buy it yourself. This is a magical, live consumer interaction that is totally captivating and engaging. I will admit that I spend an inordinate amount of time on this thing, so intrigued am I with the potential of this concept.

This is also a great example of what has changed in the e-commerce way of doing business: businesses can now leverage the power of the Web to bring total service and entertainment to shoppers.

Zapppos was launched in 1999 to be the Amazon.com of shoes (Amazon must have gotten the message), but it quickly became something more: a new model of distribution and consumer service based on a type of new-age management style that will revolutionize all businesses.

In a decade, Zappos has grown into a billion-plus-dollar company with a customer base totaling over 8.2 million, meaning that, as the company is proud to say on its Web site, almost 3 percent of the U.S. population have bought from Zappos. Customers are also extremely loyal to the brand; on any given day, approximately 75 percent of sales are from repeat customers.

I have worked with, written about, and talked to many business leaders who have been successful with their models. In most instances, the head of the successful company is a visionary with tremendous people skills and an eye for the customer. At Zappos, Tony Hsieh, the founder, is a youthful, thirtysomething member of Generation "xY" who sold his first company at age twenty-four to Microsoft for $265 million and who now, with his 1,500 employees and faithful customer base, is the manager who best embodies the Ten Commandments of Emotional Branding and the "Time" concept identified by Harold A. Innis.

Furthermore, Tony H., as he likes to be called, works on his own branding. His own ten commandments, which he calls "Zappos's Ten Core Values," are so great and relevant to the "Time" business model that I am replicating them exactly below in case you haven't seen them already on his Web site or blog–they are all dead right!

- Deliver WOW through Service.
- Embrace and Drive Change.
- Create Fun and a Little Weirdness.
- Be Adventurous, Creative, and Open-Minded.
- Pursue Growth and Learning.
- Build Open and Honest Relationships with Communication.
- Build a Positive Team and Family Spirit.
- Do More with Less.
- Be Passionate and Determined.
- Be Humble.

What is interesting about those core values is that they are mostly about the brand's culture, which privileges service. They don't use any words such as strategy, winning, market share, war, competition, goals, viral, ambush, or dominate. The company values are not about conquering more "Space"–that is, controlling the dialogue and imposing one's own terms–but in building "Time" strategies for the long term that embrace humanistic ideas. It is more about poetry than strategy.

These ten core values apply to the people the company will do business with and the associates that will interface with those people. And if you focus on the most important words from the value statement, they are strictly emotional in their concept.

- **On what you promise:** Embrace, open-minded, honest relationships, and "WOW."
- **On who you are:** Family spirit, passionate, determined, and humble, fun, weirdness, adventurous, creative, growth, and learning.

And all you have to do is read the site's comments from consumers to see that Zappos practices the values that it preaches. Tony H. and his employees believe in these ten core values, and the consumers benefit. Zappos has created a company that functions on a lot more than just a piece of paper put together by an elite group of consultants in a top-down company.

LEADING EMOTIONALLY THROUGH SOCIAL MEDIA

Commenting on the fact that his company made *Fortune*'s 100 Best Companies to Work For, Tony H. emphasized that management starts with what he calls transparency and values, reframing reality, helping others, and gratitude. For most marketers and retailers, the philosophy seems just the opposite: consumers should be grateful to be buying their goods in the first place, right? Tony H. stands out because he is connected to his team and his consumers. And how does he stay connected? Through Twitter, of course.

Twitter emotionally defines a generation of both leaders and fans who see in Twitter a new way of communicating and self-understanding that helps them in their work and relationships from a personal and business perspective. It also best shows the values of a medium that will jump-start the businesses of the future. If Blackberry, e-mail, and text messaging are the sure signs of Baby Boom leadership, then Twitter will define "xY."

Tony H. is quite articulate on his blog about how Twitter (he has more than 1.5 million followers) helped him become a better manager and person:

- "Twitter constantly reminds me of who I want to be and what I want Zappos to stand for."
- "Twitter encourages me to search for ways to view reality in a funnier and/ or more positive way."
- "Twitter makes me think about how to make a positive impact on other people's lives."
- "Twitter helps me notice and appreciate the little things in life."

He loves to think of what would happen if we were constantly on camera: What if our management style were a reality TV show? Would we act differently? Would we be more concerned? Would we care more about others? Would our personal values or how much we really care even be apparent? For Tony H., Twitter is like the dots in a drawing: by adding them up, you can see the big picture. Using Twitter, he can analyze his actions and remind himself that his customers are his best asset.

RADICAL TRANSPARENCY

One of the biggest transformations Generation "xY" has engendered is the end of secrecy. You see this openness with Barack Obama, an example of "xY" leadership: being true to your own values is fundamental to how others will perceive you. Google's slogan, "Don't be evil," for example, certainly signifies a change in the way the corporate world communicates. In a way, it is the end of hype and the beginning of sincerity. New media leaders like Tony H. are standing up for what they believe in and personally connecting with buyers. As a business leader, he is working hard to define and prove the values that the company stands for, a new paradigm for doing business online is emerging, aided by Twitter.

We will be moving from the faceless company to an emotional one with a human heart. What Tony H. has done is connect people all over the U.S. to him and his brand in the most intimate way regardless of distance. By putting his personal and intimate thoughts online, the leader of the company has personalized his brand and given it a human touch.

Online commerce will bring a human touch not unlike the one you get from that store around the corner that knows your name. At Zappos.com, service is even better than at the neighborhood store: associates at the call center are empowered to spontaneously decide to send your products overnight (for free!), or even some flowers if they sense that you are feeling sad.

Success with your online reputation starts by having nothing to hide. You can't delegate or fake it; it is you who is on the line and you who becomes the ultimate proof of your promise. You can't delegate likeability! It also forces you to face the music when in tough times you must tell your employees that you will have to lay off 8 percent of the company, explain why, and then wait for feedback. That's a tough call, but when you profess to be "a family company," your credibility depends on facing the reality of business without breaking people's will and motivation. Of course, delivering bad news is a lot easier if, like the president of Zappos, you make only $36,000 a year, which is a lot less than most executives. You can trust someone with that kind of commitment to do the right thing even if it is a tough call. Transparency is believing, and this is the stuff great brands are made of.

The conclusion here from an emotional perspective could be clearly articulated around the second commandment of Emotional Branding: from honesty to trust. For Tony H., his company is first and foremost not a shoe seller but an emotional company.

Interestingly, Zappos has combined its Web experience with an old-school tool to help connect emotionally with its customers. In an interview with me, Hsieh explained, "As unsexy and low-tech as it may sound, the telephone is actually one of the best tools for making a personal emotional connection with customers, one phone call at a time. Even though 95 percent of our orders come from online, we've found that, on average, every customer contacts us at least once sometime during their lifetime. We've found that if we get the interaction right, its something our customers remember for a very long time and tell their friends and family about."

The Power of Corporate Culture

"At Zappos, our belief is that if you get the culture right, like great customer service, or building a great long-term brand, or passionate employees, adding customers will happen naturally on its own," Tony H. is quoted as saying on his Web site.

To prove this point, Zappos offers its trainees $2 thousand after their first week at the company to quit. This is the company's way of making sure that every employee wants to be part of the company's vision for the long term. And guess what: less than 1 percent of trainees accept the offer.

Zappos is selling more than shoes–it is selling trust. Because their customers demanded more, at Zappos.com, you can now buy clothes, bags, housewares, electronics, and even kitchenware. Customers of the site even ask, "How about a Zappos airline?" a question that epitomizes how enjoyable they find their experience with Zappos. Maybe, in time, for the good of all of us, as Tony H. hones the good-service culture he has created and prepares for the next challenge.

As time becomes a rare and coveted thing, the Web brings a new set of ways to save time. Life has become so compressed that people are willing to pay extra for ordinary services to come to them in their homes, such as car washers, cooks, groceries, or DVDs. People today feel that personal time or time spent with family and friends is more important than money. It is no surprise that we are seeing a recent revival of doctor's house calls and success with online grocery shopping through brands such as FreshDirect or Netgrocer.

Building a branded store in the medium of cyberspace without the disadvantages inherent to maintaining a physical location opens opportunities to explore concepts that would not be feasible in a brick-and-mortar store. On the Internet, you connect with a different mindset and attitude, replete with a fresh set of expectations. Cyberspace is about imagination, fun, and discovery, and it is redefining our culture by forming a new, virtual community. Web surfers still view themselves as "cyber-rebels" of sorts; there is a pronounced sense of self-decision, exploration, and discovery. The attitude of nonconformity and empowerment is fostered with pride through the use of this futuristic medium. As management guru Tom Peters likes to say, "We are the CEOs of our own life." To be a brand in cyberspace, it is essential to understand this culture and work within the realm of the mind-set of this very demanding and savvy consumer. You need to bring a big idea!

In reality, the Web of today operates within a narrowly defined territory, where the expression of its branding potential is limitless through use of truly multisensorial elements such as sound, color, and animation, and even, eventually, scent (see chapter 9), which will lead to enhanced entertainment and connectivity.

These are the questions to start with in order to create that essential emotional bond with consumers on the Web:

- How can I ATTRACT people to sites?
- How can I best SELL my brands and keep a visiting customer in cyberspace?
- How can I DELIVER the kind of personal touch and service in this new medium that will assure user loyalty?

ATTRACT the Web Consumer by Making the Site "The Destination"

Since most decisions will be vetted online and given the fact that the Web is the most trusted of all media, doing commerce online needs to be the ultimate brand experience. For cyberstores, this is imperative, and for brick-and-mortars, doing business online creates a unique opportunity to not only marginally increase your business but also to build your brand. But with more and more businesses moving online and more and more brands emerging on the Web, the Web has become a very busy marketplace that presents challenges for businesses to attract people to their sites. Finding ways to bring people to your URL should thus form the backbone of any business's strategy for success.

As I mention in chapter 11, the highly successful Victoria's Secret 1999 Super Bowl commercial, which tempted a tidal wave of viewers to go online to watch its supermodel fashion show, was the first of its kind in making a brilliant connection between the Web site and the commercial. Ed Razek, president and chief marketing officer for Limited Brands and creative services of The Limited, Inc., has said that the main goal of this ad was not to create awareness for the Victoria's Secret brand, but to encourage people to log onto its site.[135] Why, then, if it was so successful, have so few cyberbrands tried this same dramatic formula? Nike has recognized the potential of this cross-referencing strategy with its "Whatever.Nike.Com" commercials, where viewers must log onto the Nike Web site to see the dramatic ending to a compelling story begun in its "teaser commercials." Once on the Web site, surfers are even allowed to pick and choose from various potential endings. This is a smart and truly interactive communication strategy.

SELL through Creating a Unique Brand Identity and Intuitive Navigation System

A strong visual and sensory identity is the most important element of brand differentiation. It can truly manifest the personality of the brand and set it apart from the crowd, and it is the only place to start. Designing a Web site for visual clarity and uniqueness will enhance the experience, increase buying intent, and create memorability. Besides content, you can often recognize a magazine simply by its cover and typographic style. *Vogue* has a photographic attitude that's different from *Elle*, and Martha Stewart's personal touch is all over her magazine. The points of view in the J.Crew and Brooks Brothers catalogs are totally different and relevant to each brand and the target group each wants to capture. The way Target uses its logo identity to communicate fashion and innovation is consistent with its strategy and demarcates it completely from competing stores such as Kmart.

On many of the most popular e-commerce sites, the point of entry with the brands is through a table of contents, with no introduction, no brand message . . . no foreplay! Could you imagine a magazine with no cover? Or a store with no windows? Or a catalogue with only product lists and bad visuals?

E-commerce brand identities must be multidimensional and multisensorial, and engage consumers in an emotionally compelling brand story in order to stand out from the crowd and attract visitors. Web sites have many communication opportunities at their disposal, particularly for telling a dramatic story that will add dimension and emotion to the brand.

WON'T YOU STAY A LITTLE BIT LONGER?

Once you have attracted a visitor to your site, the objective is to keep this potential customer from leaving and transform the visitor into a buyer, or a "brand fan." Everyone in the Web business knows that retaining that customer at your site is a very essential aspect of any branding strategy. But how do you do this? The answer is to give them a memorable experience based on great navigation systems, clarity of offering, and service that will make a customer stay . . . and come back for more.

DESIGN FOR NAVIGATION AND SPEED = SALE

Most leading sites are still about function, not emotion. Most sites do not yet have a clear, brand-centric hierarchy of information and content to help orient a consumer and provide him with a branded experience. Everything is thrown at the visitor at once, from inventory to information, and there is often no real, definite indication of what the brand stands for outside of being a Web-based commercial venture. Identity graphics and color, sound experiments, and interactive programs are not used enough to make site navigation a pleasant, easy, and emotional experience.

As an example of the kind of smart (and often simple!) differentiation that's needed, let's study a common but powerful shopping symbol: the shopping cart. This symbol has a reassuring psychological connection to physical, hard-core shopping. But there is a great opportunity here to define a different shopping cart expression on the Web, a more imaginative digital version. This could be done with symbols, typography, colors, language, or even animation. What if the shopping cart became a 3-D animated character of sorts, replete with a personality? The shopping cart could become a shopper's "friend," which would help customers make choices, answer questions, make fun suggestions, and so on, introducing some sense of the missing social element of "shopping buddies" into the cybershopping experience. Or it could be a graphic representation that shows items as they are added and becomes a game that would reward customers with surprise gifts or discounts when their cart reaches a certain undetermined point of fullness.

THE EXPERIENCE OPPORTUNITY

The second and perhaps most important opportunity is the potential for fostering a branded community atmosphere where people have the chance to engage in a dialogue with one another, recommending and discussing products, and sharing their favorite brand. Harley-Davidson has capitalized on this by organizing vastly successful rides for groups of its customers on its site. Lastly, you can bring enormous added value by offering information such as cookie recipes, travel tips, lifestyle recommendations, and so on. On the Web, this kind of content replaces the missing human factor. Most sites are beginning to recognize this very important element of their brand and the fragility of their connection to the customer. The best Web brands are responding by managing the consumer relationship and experience to the highest level.

DELIVER Personalized Service and Touch and Consumer Dialogue

Launched in 2001, Weightwatchers.com is a Web site that has broken all the cyberspace laws by making its model a paid one from the start. By offering powerful social interaction and visually compelling content based around opportunities to deal with weight loss, the site attracts four million unique visitors per month. Their over fifteen message boards hosting more than fifty topics demonstrate a thriving community that shares ideas and tips. For example, one member posted the question, "I'm curious about how many [gay] members [there are] in the Raleigh-Durham NC area? Being a gay, overweight male can be tough." One answer was "Come on out!!! I love it here! I guess I'm the only gay person in the area on Weight Watchers. Come on, there's got to be more!" This is just one example of how Weight Watchers's online community is bringing people together who were once isolated.

In good Web stores, shoppers get the kind of personal service that would be impossible to sustain financially in a normal store but that technology can provide easily. Amazon, for example, upgrades orders from its loyal customers to priority shipping or gives these customers coupons and recommends products that correspond to their previous buys via e-mail or every time they log onto the site. The *New York Times* Web site sends you notices about news pieces of particular interest to you. This makes business personal, and that's great service. The great e-commerce site Kidrobot, which was founded by Paul Budnitz, specializes in artist-created toys, and describes its brand as "planet Earth's premier creator and retailer of limited edition toys, clothing, artwork and books," and it is a fun way to launch toys. With one of their new toys, Munny, a toy you can decorate anyway you wish, they offer the customization that consumers want today and a short video to increase the appeal of the offer. Those toys must really be exciting, since a British corporate lad stole the equivalent of £780,000 worth of those toys to sell those precious little cuties himself. In a British press article, it is mentioned that the thief might have been "priming the market," to have a good supply for when the craze would sweep the U.K.[136]

New software programs are allowing companies to track consumers better even when they are shopping, helping them make pitches and anticipate their customers' needs. Companies like Pink Dot, the online grocery store that caters to Los Angeles, are enormously successful in using this kind of technology to suggest products to their customers, who invariably fall in line with the statistics and buy the product suggested to them based on their previous purchase. It's not about suggesting milk to go along with cereal, but knowing, for example, that 70 percent of your customers who order peanut butter also might need some diapers, or, in a further (and even less logical) refinement, that 60 percent of men who order peanut butter after 8:00 P.M. are likely to be receptive to a suggestion of beer. You get the idea; these statistics don't always make sense, but they work, which is why it is so brilliant to be able to make use of them!

WHEN THE DOORBELL RINGS . . . OR, THE LAST STRAW!
The final but often overlooked element of relationship on the Web is the actual, physical experience that the consumer has when the merchandise is delivered. The packaging in which the product is delivered immediately reflects the care a company takes in pleasing its customers. *The next sale starts the minute your customer receives the goods* . . . plain old common–or "commerce"–sense!

One of my clients, the president of a major cosmetics company, showed me a gift she had bought for a friend from the catalog of a top department store. The product was a collection of soaps for every month of the year, which came in a corrugated box and was wrapped in ordinary (and unattractive) paper–a far cry from the magnificent photo in the catalog. Her disappointment was so strong that she will not buy anything from this catalog again. Relationships on the Web need to be carried out to bring satisfaction to the consumer from beginning to end.

A WORD ABOUT WORD OF MOUTH

Before a customer leaves your site, you need to manage this parting of ways in a manner that will make the customer a positive ambassador for your brand–one who will tell her friends about your brand, because nothing works better than word of mouth as a promotion when the message is positive. We all know this. But word of mouth can also break the reputation of a brand. *Word of mouth has credibility–is trusted–because it is based on someone's personal experience. It is Emotional Branding at its best.* In today's cyberworld, word of mouth has taken on a different dimension; it has become global and immediate. It can affect millions of people in milliseconds.

In the course of the research for this book, people of all generations were asked for their impressions of brands they buy, and one of the consistent key reasons teenagers shopped in certain stores was because they had heard about them from friends. Traditional media, advertising, product and packaging design, store design, and corporate

Word of mouth has credibility—is trusted— because it is based on someone's personal experience. It is Emotional Branding at its best.

branding certainly do their job to create this kind of awareness for consumers. But I believe that nobody has sufficiently tried to understand how emotions are the main factor in the hard-to-control "word of mouth" link to the market. Word of mouth requires a real commitment from the messenger to pass on the brand message. This commitment can only come from strong emotions, the thrill of sharing good news with others, and sometimes the desire to gather support for stopping what we feel are injustices and abuses. And, in the last case, that is when word of mouth could become every marketer's nightmare: boycott! And boycotts are a very real threat; there are about 150 full product boycotts put in action per year.

In cybershopping, customers are increasingly able to speak with one another about the brands they buy online, as evidenced by the growing number of successful social media Web sites allowing disgruntled consumers an outlet to voice their concerns and objections. The Web is proving to be the biggest word-of-mouth forum ever created, and wowing your customers until way after the sale is done is good business and a powerful strategy. Social media are now more powerful than blogs and Web sites, with Facebook and Twitter bringing an added level of transparency and connection that will make online commerce the most trusted model.

- *In this medium, people do not look for products but for emotional connection.* In the "Time"-based new social media economy, how you portray your brand needs to be far away from blatant commercialism to be successful in the long term. You have to give your customers something in return. The opportunity is here for you and your brand to build a community of fans that will care about your brand more so than ever before.
- *In social media, everything can be checked and monitored but not controlled.* Brands have a hard time understanding that social media are more than a bottom-up movement but are rather an all-encompassing approach with people chatting in an open forum where transparency is key. The beauty of social media is not in people agreeing or disagreeing but in people being there, together, in the first place. The idea of losing control is unimaginable for a Baby Boomer brand, and knowing that a bad comment might appear or a critical video might be posted is beyond their appetite or culture. It is simply time to move on from this way of thinking about business.
- *The emotional reality of social media is the blueprint for a new business model.* The gap between the written culture that limits brands within the confines of their organization and the Greek oral tradition that shares the responsibility to promote the brand with consumers needs to narrow. Without such a narrowing, traditional businesses cannot survive. Using the Web is not just a placement game but also a relationship game. "From service to relationship" does not involve just one thing but a combination of events that solidify the brand connection with Generation xY. Brands need to understand this new dynamic and engage with it. People are no longer just targets for the taking, but can become your most influential partners and ambassadors.

17

Recipes for Emotional Branding Strategies

The Emotional Economy needs new yardsticks for discovering the real, emotional meaning of brands . . . and what is more interesting for this purpose than a sensory and visually driven research tool to bring to light how people feel about brands?

When I was copresident at brand design firm Desgrippes Gobé (which I also helped create), we designed three new proprietary research tools to better connect emotionally with the market. The first one is BrandFocus, which helps line up the management of a company behind a heartfelt brand vision; the second, SENSE®, is a visualization process that helps pinpoint the core attributes of a brand and build up an imagery around these attributes; and the third, Brand Presence® Management, is a tool that helps determine the most powerful places, times, and ways for a brand to express itself in the market. It is essential to define how people feel about a brand in the context of what corporations think their brand is and in what ways there are connections and where the disconnections may exist. Where does the brand hit the consumer the most? Through the head, the heart, or the gut? Maybe the head, like Aveda, or the heart, like Godiva, or the gut, like Prada? By understanding the emotional relevance of a brand, corporations can build an aspirational brand vision.

TOOL #1. BrandFocus: An Interactive Tool to Clarify a Brand's Positioning

BrandFocus is an interactive consulting tool used to clarify a brand's positioning and unlock its potential to communicate beyond its current message. The centerpiece of BrandFocus is an interactive exercise involving senior management and other members of the brand team. The BrandFocus goals are the following:

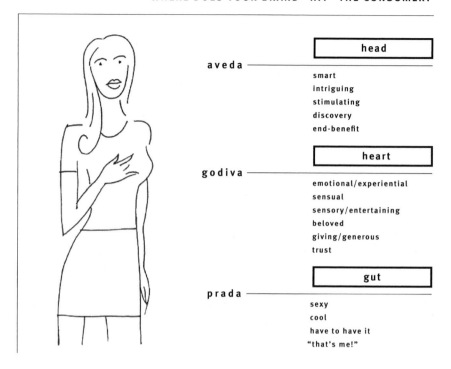

- Team alignment through interactive creativity and collaborative discovery of a strong vision.
- Visual definition of the future brand image.
- Dimensionalization of customer personality and brand emotional connection.
- Construction of key (pillar) attributes that define your brand through concise descriptive images and adjectives that craft your brand's unique DNA

The outcome of the exercise (and the synthesis phase that follows) is a focused brand positioning expression communicated visually and verbally. Implications for brand development and communication programs are outlined by integrating the results of the group's activity with cultural trends and opportunities in the market and beyond. The final presentation is multisensorial and can be used internally to brief creative agencies and to serve as a foundation for brand image programs in the future.

The following is a description overview of the BrandFocus process divided into phases:

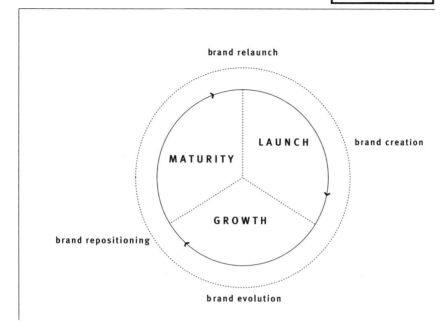

brand relaunch

LAUNCH

MATURITY

brand creation

GROWTH

brand repositioning

brand evolution

PART I. STRATEGIC FOUNDATION: INFORMATION GATHERING

Initiate assignments by gathering existing information from clients' management regarding current competitors, consumers, media, and any other relevant data. Meet with clients' management to receive a formal briefing and to discuss specific concerns, considerations, and requirements for the development of a cohesive brand vision. In this phase, through interviews with key executives and project directors and employees, explore the internal strategy and concerns of the company as well as initiate an investigative process into the company's overall spirit and culture. The brand's life cycle will be discussed to clarify the challenges ahead.

After the initial research and interviewing, execute BrandFocus sessions in order to accurately assess the range of input from all of the client's audiences. Do this either in one large session, or sometimes in several separate sessions for different corporate contingents. Once the BrandFocus sessions are complete, analyze all of the results and develop a single, cohesive, and relevant brand strategy that is effective and meaningful.

PART II. BRANDFOCUS EXERCISE

BrandFocus is set up and played as an interactive game. This format encourages a wide range of unfiltered viewpoints to flesh out hidden nuances within the brand that can be expanded upon in creative and strategic ways. Several visual categories for discussion are defined in advance. A series of images representing a range of attitudes and styles, all easily representing the brand, are compiled and placed on a board for the team to assess. Although the images selected by the group are used to craft a brand portrait, it is the words and vocabulary used to rationalize image choices that lead to brand opportunity discussions. The purpose is to find the images and cues that represent the brand's point of view beyond the product. An adjective brainstorm is conducted with the participants in order to explore a variety of meanings associated with the brand. Steer the group away from standard, prototypical brand descriptions. Each BrandFocus is unique, with images and categories chosen to gain insight into a specific brand's equity and opportunity. The first visual exercise is to define "the state of the team"; visuals are shown that immediately connote either positive or negative reactions relevant to clarifying a brand's strengths and weaknesses.

Because BrandFocus is interactive, and responses are meant to be spontaneous, comments arise like, "Picture number one is who we are today, but number

BrandFocus is set up and played as an interactive game. This format encourages a wide range of unfiltered viewpoints to flesh out hidden nuances within the brand.

moving away from what everyone says! | adjective sort

american
classic
genuine
authentic
heritage
established
original
international
service
quality

AN EXAMPLE OF A CLIENT'S ADJECTIVE SORT RESULTS

FUN

Humor
Wit
Surprise
Outrageous
Sexy
Quirky
Creativity
Entertaining
Color
Trendy
Fashionable
Young
Hip/Cool
Fresh
A Giggle

SPIRITUAL

Mind-Body-Spirit
Holistic
Vibrancy
Energy
Vigorous
Balanced
Whole
Free
Vital
Charisma
Self-Actualization

NATURAL

Organic
Earthy
Quality
Green
From Nature
Environmental
Healthy

DARING

Radical
Alternative
Guerrilla
Counterculture
Brave
Demanding
Challenging
Audacious
Break the Rules
Controversial
Antiestablishment
Unique
Provocative

SELF-RESPECT

Celebration
Women
Specialness
Esteem
Realness
Beauty
Multicultural
Confidence
Well-Being
Be Yourself
Self-Expression

PARTICIPATION

Community
Solidarity
Sharing
Social
Inclusive
Education
Local
Giftability

THOUGHTFULNESS

Friendly
Honest
Decent
Common Sense
Responsible
Care
Heart
Integrity
Compassion
Goodness
Decent
Worthy
Concern
Compassion
Service
Positive

PLEASURE

Sensuous
Fun
Love
Passion
Physical
Intimacy
Sensation
Femininity
Indulgence
Sensorial
Luxurious
Pampering

VISIONARY

Curious
Trailblazers
Storytelling
Inventive
Alternative
Innovative
Intelligence
Contemporary
Ideology
Instinctive
Leadership
Integrity
No Hype
Discovery
Philosophy
Solutions
Bravery
Values

MESSAGE

Campaigning
Respect
Animal/Human
Rights
Recycling
Activism
Awareness
Outspoken
Issues
A Stand
Advocacy
Concern
Anti-Cruelty
Issues
Opposition
Ethical

three feels more like who we want to be." All of the edited selections from the image exercise are collected and placed on the master board. The moderator leads a discussion about what we see emerging. The brand's unique personality comes alive as the visuals give insight into the look, attitude, mood, spirit, and usage of the brand.

Other categories of visuals are presented with questions such as:

- If (Brand) were a ride–what would it feel like?
- If (Brand) were a wedding–what kind would it be?
- If (Brand) were a kiss–what would it look like?
- If (Brand) were a dream vacation–where would it be?

under attack

 exuberant

sandtrapped

  strong spirit

playful

 leadership

The second part of the exercise focuses on the identification of core brand attributes that will support the visual voice created through the image exercise. Adjectives mentioned during the course of the exercise are recorded. At the end of the image game, each participant is asked to pull the three defining words from the board that speak to the essence of the brand.

Following this session, synthesize the selected visuals and attributes into a proprietary brand-positioning platform.

CONCLUSION

BrandFocus has proven to be a great motivator and team unifier, with the final result playing a major role in the clients' day-to-day brand development and management. BrandFocus allows teams to consider where a brand has been and where it is. Most importantly, BrandFocus defines where a brand can go. It stimulates creative thinking and motivates teams to break the traditional constructs of brand definition and brand communication.

TOOL #2. SENSE®: A Visual Territory Development Tool

SENSE® is a visual process that helps identify products' equities, profiles the customer, analyzes the competition, and develops a multidimensional, emotionally charged visual and sensual vocabulary that serves as the foundation for the design process. SENSE® helps brands establish a strong emotion-based sensory platform for the brand that can convey the brand's persona and character. An acronym for Sensory Exploration + Need States Evaluation, SENSE® combines the talents of observation, synthesis, and creativity with disciplined research techniques to assure that the premise for our ideas is grounded in the real-life experience of the target audience.

SENSE® begins with an analysis of a brand's inherent values—its equities—and encompasses the many ways it interacts with the consumer: intellectually, visually, associatively, and sensorially. A carefully illustrated customer profile explores the role the product plays in the consumer's lifestyle and pinpoints visual cues that establish brand preferences. An astute and trend-driven visual assessment of

SENSE® begins with an analysis of a brand's inherent values—its equities—and encompasses the many ways it interacts with the consumer.

the competition completes the preliminary audits and brings out the strengths and weaknesses of a particular business or product category.

As the final synthesis, presentation boards consisting of a rich palette of imagery are brought together to achieve a dynamic brand positioning and bring to life the emotional connection of the brand with the consumer.

Once a solid image-based strategy for creativity is established, move into full-scale creative exploration in any one of a combination of four design disciplines: graphics, industrial design, architecture, and interactive design. This unique proprietary visual methodology ensures that each creative solution is consistent, compelling, and strategically appropriate. The result is powerful, coordinated packaging, graphics, environments, and interactive design programs that generate an emotional response in the consumer and give companies a competitive edge.

SENSE® goes beyond the merely eye-catching to include the tactile, the psychological, and the experiential–all the things that generate excitement among consumers worldwide. SENSE® is a great way to build a powerful emotional brand territory!

CASE HISTORY: GODIVA, 1994

When Godiva management came to see us for an analysis of its retail branding strategy with recommendations for improving the performance of its stores, my firm then proposed that it use our SENSE® process as a way of determining the lifestyle of its existing and potential customers. We wanted most of all to discover more about the sensory experience people have with chocolate, and we had a lot of fun doing just that! Our offices became saturated with the pervasive, delicious smell of chocolate, and one of the most difficult parts of this project was to keep everyone from eating the samples! However, we discovered that the store was not about the sensory experience that we were having in the office, and we became motivated by the desire to recreate a place where the enjoyment of chocolate was paramount.

Baby Boomers, as we know, are interested in status and rewards, and Gen X

and Gen Y are more attracted by experiences. This insight at the time revealed that the existing Godiva store, with its heavy black and gold packaging and fixtures, with all the chocolates tucked away behind cold, unfriendly glass cases, communicated a very elitist message. This elitist message had helped establish the credibility of the brand originally, but today was too imposing for a younger customer who just wanted a little indulgence. SENSE® allowed us to visualize the trends in new potential customers' lifestyle and access the existing visual cues and codes of the store in comparison to those customers' aspirations.

The result of our audits told us that the stores were intimidating and that shoppers came only to visit for special occasions. Most products were out of reach in cases for refrigeration purposes, but we felt that this issue could easily be handled in another way.

The first sensory boards we presented to our no-nonsense client Cathy Green, general manager of global retail for Godiva, were screaming for indulgence, sensuality, the emotional reward of sharing, and just plain old good times! Cathy, who understands better than anyone the importance of emotions in retail, suddenly realized how much her stores lacked the pleasure that one feels with a chocolate experience and that Godiva's relationship with the customer was not focused on wetting their "chocolappetite."

During a trip to Düsseldorf, Germany, a few weeks before the presentation, as I was walking down the street with one of our architects, we stumbled upon a fashion retail store that was designed in the Art Nouveau style, the same style that is so popular in Belgium, Godiva's country of origin.

The style worked beautifully in this store, and we looked at each other thinking the same thought at the same time . . . this would be the perfect style for Godiva. Those luscious curves, which are so typical of the Art Nouveau look, seemed so appropriate for this project that we promised we would come back the next day to take some pictures. We almost didn't make it back to the store—in our excitement, we had forgotten to note the address of the place—and it took us a couple of hours before we passed it totally by chance. The style was very well received by our client, and we all knew that this distinctive look would enhance the brand perception. The final design of the store expressed the intimate relationship a store needs to have with consumers: an intimate understanding of their desires in the design folded into an overall framework that suggests a warm welcome, as if you were invited into someone's home. We found refrigerating wall units that limited the necessity of cases and used this opportunity to recommend some visual merchandising concepts that encouraged more browsing in the store. A station placed at the store window allowing personnel to dip fruits into hot chocolate brought a magical ritual into full view, encouraging more customers to enter.

In dollars and cents, this new concept increased sales by 20 to 30 percent in comparison to the old stores, and we have now rolled the idea out worldwide with great success.

Understanding your customer well and catering to the taste and the aspiration of that customer is the key to building a long-lasting relationship—and for us, the opportunity to keep enjoying those wonderful chocolates.

TOOL #3. Brand Presence® Management (BPM): An Assessment Tool to Explore the Many Facets of a Brand's Personality in the Marketplace

BPM is a brand presence assessment tool that allows for an expanded exploration of the many facets of a brand's personality in all its expressions in the marketplace, from "impact" to emotional "contact." In order to reach maximum efficiency, each brand-identity expression needs to be modular to reach people where and when they want to be reached. BPM is a tool that helps strategize what I call "proximity communication": the way to accompany or "escort" a consumer throughout his daily activities. BPM takes into consideration and measures levels of an audience's receptivity to this brand personality in the course of their daily lives. People's receptivity to a brand is obviously not the same at 7:00 A.M., when they are commuting to work, as it is at a club or a bar at night, or on the weekend at a ballpark, or on vacation. It is therefore critical to match people's

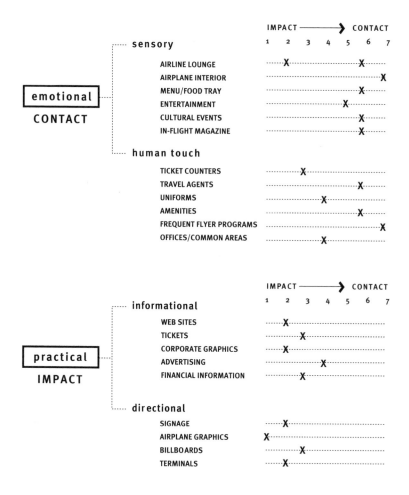

acceptance levels and expectations of a brand message through a multidimensional, sensitive brand dialogue. The chart above suggests the receptivity level of different venues at various points in time in consumers' daily lives.

It is by understanding these different "moments in time," and tailoring brand presence programs to interact with consumers with sensitivity and innovation at a particular moment, that memorable, emotionally relevant contact with consumers can be created. This is when a brand can become like a friend, neither shouting nor interrupting you . . . nor whispering so softly that you cannot hear what he or she is saying!

In the case of an airline, for example, the exterior of the plane, and the logo on the body and tail need to be highly visible from afar and are an "impact"-oriented mode of brand presence, but the interior of the plane, the menu, the in-flight magazine, and the uniform of the flight attendants should bring a heightened level of emotional comfort and be more "contact"-oriented to put customers at ease, since these visual cues and sensory elements will interface with a passenger before and during the flight. It is important to evaluate the balance between the emotional contact the company will have with a customer and the visual impact a brand needs to convey. The chart above, which uses an airline as an example, helps define balance of the level of emotional contact and impact a brand needs to convey in order to create the most positive experience.

On this numbered scale, you can evaluate the level of the emotional expression of the brand in different arenas. This chart helps audit and modulate the level of emotional communication a brand delivers as well as compare that analysis to the competition. By adding the numbers you have assigned to each area, you can reach an overall indication of where your brand stands in the emotional landscape. If you fall in the lower range, around one or two, it means your brand has a very *dictated* brand presence style, while ratings around six or seven lean toward a totally emotional and *personal* identity. Since the objective is to achieve a balance of visibility and experience, this tool can help format the emotional territory and identity of the brand.

CASE STUDY: COCA-COLA, 1996 ATLANTA OLYMPICS

Of all the work I have led, one company stands out from the rest: the brand presence programs we created for Coca-Cola for the 1996 Atlanta Olympics. Our goal was to create a program that was modular, targeted, and engaging. This brand presence program attempted to reach consumers through virtually every channel of communication throughout the city of Atlanta: information booths, vending machines, concessions, restaurants, and an Olympic City theme park that invited the fans to experience the Olympics from the viewpoint of the athletes through its fifteen-acre interactive amusement park and welcomed visitors for entertainment between the games. The Olympic City logo we designed was the cohesive element for all of these communications. We wanted to expand Coca-Cola's visual vocabulary into entertainment without losing the core character of the brand.

It is important to evaluate the balance between the emotional contact the company will have with a customer and the visual impact a brand needs to convey.

The strategy was to make fans and visitors the heroes of the games instead of focusing solely on the athletes by leveraging the concept of "Refreshment" inherent to Coca-Cola's core identity. This "Refreshment" concept was expanded to include refreshment of the mind, body, and spirit, which was translated into:

- Refreshment of the body: Consumption
- Refreshment of the mind: Information
- Refreshment of the spirit: Entertainment

Based on this multifaceted concept of "Refreshment," different messages were created to reach the Olympic visitors at different points in their experience in Atlanta. At the airport, visitors were welcomed by the billboard sign, "Traveling is thirsty work," and at the games and on the streets of the city, on buses, and on vending machines were brand presence messages saying "Cheering is thirsty work" to communicate Coca-Cola's passion for the games shared with the public. The paper cup with writing in different languages was part of the experience at the games and a welcoming gesture to all the international visitors by Coca-Cola as a global brand.

BPM helped us develop this complex presence program—which could have been a very homogenous "Let's throw the logo in everywhere" strategy—as an engaging and emotionally responsive program with the goal of enhancing the positive experience fans would have at the games—thanks to Coca-Cola.

BPM is one of the foundations of an Emotional Branding strategy and can also be used as a creative auditing tool that explores the many opportunities a brand has to engage an audience in the most meaningful way.

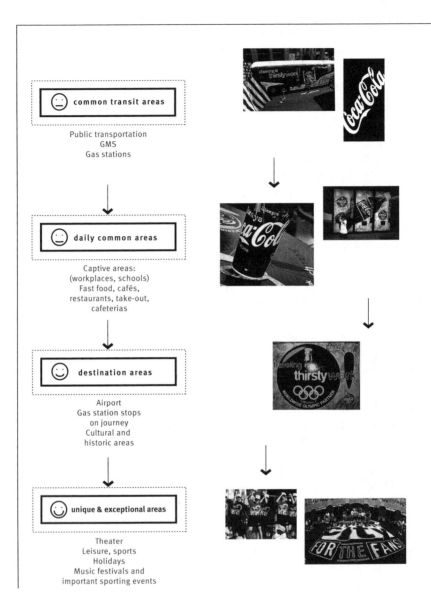

common transit areas

Public transportation
GMS
Gas stations

daily common areas

Captive areas:
(workplaces, schools)
Fast food, cafés,
restaurants, take-out,
cafeterias

destination areas

Airport
Gas station stops
on journey
Cultural and
historic areas

unique & exceptional areas

Theater
Leisure, sports
Holidays
Music festivals and
important sporting events

18

Key Trends for the
New Millennium

The most important commodity and the biggest luxury of all today is time. Americans are time-impoverished. In a study by Kurt Salmon Associates, a New York retail consulting firm, 60 percent of those queried said they had less time for leisure, and 44 percent confessed that given the choice, they'd rather have more free time than more money.[137]

Time Is (Even Better than) Money

We live in an era of less: less material wealth and less and less time. Americans have now surpassed the Japanese as the nation clocking in the most hours in a workweek. This change that has been gathering momentum for a while now is a fundamental shift in the fabric of our culture, and there are no references from the past to give perspective. While past generations may have been busy, there is obviously no comparison with our hyperdigitalized world today, where not only are we ourselves so busy but everything around us is moving at an incredibly fast pace. In this Information Age, we are constantly barraged with data and pressured to make important decisions and choices in a split second. What this means on the whole is that people are now keenly aware of the need to relax as well as the need to kick up their heels and really enjoy the free time they do have.

Instead of acquiring more material goods, people want to spend money to create quality time for themselves.

In this atmosphere, services win over products. Instead of acquiring more material goods, people want to spend money to create quality time for themselves and spend it with friends and family. Two polls, one conducted by Britt Beemer, founder of America's Research Group, and one conducted by the National Retail Federation and Deloitte & Touche, found that Americans are largely redirecting their gift spending to presents that enhance family life and personal well-being, such as vacations, massages, and golf lessons, at the expense of "gifts that come in a box."[138] Any brand that can either save consumers time or enhance the quality of an experience of time spent will do well in the future. On the one hand, people will be spending more and more on time-savers, such as financial advisors, personal trainers, housecleaners, dog walkers, and party planners. On the other hand, hotels, spas, casinos, restaurants, theaters, and other leisure-related businesses will do very well. Of course, the Internet will be hugely popular as a time-saving device as well as for its entertainment value.

Baby Boomers are a big part of this trend. They are now at the stage in their lives where they have acquired most of the goods that they need, and they are looking for quality-of-life solutions and services. Nearing fifty, they are ready to enjoy more of the income they have worked so hard for through the years to spend on leisure and recreational activities. As the number of Americans aged forty-five to fifty-four rose 34 percent through 2005, we have seen an enormous boom in services spending. But this trend is certainly not specific to the Baby Boomer generation. In our era of hypertime stress, people of all ages are looking for relaxation, entertainment, education, and adventure.

We see this trend in the enormous boom of products and services related to anything that helps people unwind and check out from their hectic pace for a while. The average hotel today often has a full-service spa, as opposed to just a health club. Resorts abound, such as Canyon Ranch, which offers, in addition to all of the usual spa amenities, treatments and workshops that emphasize the mind/body connection. Urban spas such as Bliss (purchased by LVMH and on the expansion trail), which offer a quick escape from the stresses of city life that have always been available to the wealthy, now proliferate on a mass scale. And, of course, this is also what is behind the explosion in the home spa–treatment category with aromatherapy, bath, massage, and facial products.

This trend is also the reason for the flourishing travel business, theme parks, and restaurants, luxury cruises designed to be multigenerational (so that busy families who rarely find that quality time together can reconnect), and mega-mall/entertainment complexes. For many product and service categories, it will not be difficult to fulfill the needs that the time deprivation trend is creating. For other, more traditional categories, the answer will be in their ability to innovate. Innovation in consumer products and appliances, for example, will be key for growth in these categories, since people are focusing their spending on services. The Sonys of the world must create new products that either save us time or wow us so much with their entertainment, aesthetic, or novelty value that we cannot resist purchasing them, despite the fact that they may not be necessary in our lives crowded with goods.

Retailers will also need to innovate, to better show their appreciation for the time customers spend in their stores in some very practical ways. Megastores are a great example. On a weekend, shopping with family or friends in these enormous stores can be a fun experience, but these stores are often extremely difficult to navigate if you are in a hurry and need to find specific items quickly. This problem could also be solved with computerized guides strategically placed throughout the store, equipped with product search capabilities, detailed store maps, price scanners, and more in-depth question-and-answer software. Any larger store, including more upscale clothing retailers, could use this kind of technology in addition to (but never ever replacing) helpful store employees. Department stores should also consider developing technology that would allow consumers to take a handheld store navigator along with them throughout the store. The device could be interactive, answer specific questions, and so on. These large stores have no idea how many customers leave the store in frustration after not being able to find the item (or sometimes even the department!) they came in search of. And who knows how many consumers dare not even enter a dauntingly large mega- or department store when they are pressed for time. I also can't begin to count the times I have abandoned an item I had every intention of purchasing at the sight of a long cashier line. One large grocery store that I know of in Connecticut has implemented a self-service checkout line with a scanner and credit card swipe machine to solve this problem. Another angle on the time-stress phenomenon is to lull shoppers into a more relaxed state, through either entertainment or an added-value experience, such as offering free in-store foot massages! There are many, many other approaches to the time dilemma for retailers to explore.

In the food sector, we see innovations based on saving time for consumers who don't even want to take the time to boil water, such as Lipton's Cold Brew, an iced-tea bag developed to infuse in cold tap water in just five minutes. Kraft Foods is marketing Handi-Snacks for adults, which include various elements of a snack-type meal in one ready-to-go package. Campbell's Soup has Soup to Go lunch packs that combine microwavable soups with other ready-made elements of a meal. To accommodate our on-the-run lifestyle, we now see even chips and dip packaged together. Kellogg's has a new line of Eggo Toaster Muffins that are portable, with no messy syrup. Chef America's Hot Pocket frozen sandwiches are advertised as "Real food for a busy life."

While time-saving devices and solutions are certainly a viable approach for brands to take, the opposite approach of coaxing consumers to indulge in spending time with the brand will also continue to work. One of the reasons that Martha Stewart is so popular is that she evokes an old-fashioned sensibility of taking the time to nurture things. She gives simple quick solutions and approaches to beautifying one's environment, which are essentially modern because they do recognize the need for economy of time. But overall, Stewart can be seen as almost a sort of rebellion from our rushed, prefab way of life that has us ordering Christmas trees sight unseen from the Internet. Stewart shows us how we can also luxuriate in taking the time to put our own individual touches on creating a personal, intimate home environment.

On the Internet, of course, many sites must be designed for speed of access to information and quick, easy purchases, but other sites succeed so well in capturing our attention and imagination that, invariably, we spend far longer than we'd planned surfing the site (probably when we should have been doing something else!) and walk away with a great brand impression or purchase. Whether a brand positioning is about saving time or convincing consumers to spend time with the brand, it is most important to be constantly aware of just how precious that time is for consumers. From an Emotional Branding standpoint, this means accentuating the positive. Because people experience so much stress in their daily lives, it is much less effective to emphasize the difficulties at hand. Much better to talk about the lack of time through humor and demonstrate that your brand has a wonderful solution. Or take people entirely away from their stresses with soothing brand imagery.

The Zenification of America: The Search for Meaning Is On!

In 1989, when the Dalai Lama spoke in New York City's Central Park, he addressed a crowd of about five thousand Americans. In 1999, when the Dalai Lama returned to speak in Central Park, he was greeted by a gathering numbering close to forty thousand.[139] According to recent statistics, seven out of ten Americans say they are religious and consider spirituality to be an

"SQUEEZED FOR TIME, HONEY?"

"BUSY AS A BEE? THEN GIVE ME A QUICK SQUEEZE."

Try these quick, low-fat recipes with nature's sweetener

important part of their lives.[140] Seventy-one percent of Americans still say they "never doubt the existence of God" (up 11 percent from 1987), 72 percent of Americans believe in heavenly beings, and 79 percent believe in miracles.[141] 69 percent of Americans now say that they are more interested in spiritual matters than they were five years ago, and there is an 80 percent increase in people participating in non-church spiritual groups.[142] There are now five thousand New Age bookstores in the United States.[143] Spiritual retreats have become a commonplace vacation alternative, and "spiritual travel," travel that involves seeking some form of enlightenment in faraway places such as Asia, is one of the fastest-growing segments of the travel and tourism industry, according

People are no longer embarrassed to speak about their spiritual affinities and private soul-searching.

to the World Travel and Tourism Council.[144] Richard Gere, an American icon, speaks often in the press about his practice of Buddhism and friendship with the Dalai Lama. From the media, we know that Madonna and Roseanne, among a long list of other celebrities, study Kabbalah.[145] Actually, it is extremely rare that we do not hear about a celebrity's spiritual journey.

People are no longer embarrassed to speak about their spiritual affinities and private soul-searching; it is now in vogue. It is so in vogue, in fact, that it is almost passé. America has mainstreamed spirituality.

The trend is one of openness and exploration. While traditional church-based religion has also seen a resurgence in membership, personal spirituality has largely surpassed formalized, practical religion. It seems that people are seeking direct experience as opposed to dogma and the freedom to take meaning where they find it, from a mixture of traditions. Buddhism has become one of the most popular spiritual traditions in this mixture. In the past few years, the number of English-language Buddhist teaching centers has jumped from 429 to 1,062.[146] Baby Boomers first embraced Buddhism as a way of protesting war and expanding the limitations of the "American as apple pie" culture of their youth. Gens X and Y now show a decided predilection for Eastern mysticism. These younger generations have been one of the driving forces to bring Buddhism back to the forefront, giving birth to the popular phrase "Tibet Chic," with hip endorsements like the Buddhist-influenced music of the band the Beastie Boys.

This trend has much to do with the time deprivation trend as it relates to stress and a fast pace of life. Eighty percent of all Americans are seeking to simplify their lives, and 78 percent want to reduce stress. Three million Americans actively seek tranquility (and improved health) by practicing yoga and Eastern martial arts such as Tai Chi.

Overstressed people everywhere today clearly look to soothe their senses and regain their balance. "Consciousness is not a state of doing, but a state of being," says Veronique Vienne, the author of *The Art of Doing Nothing*,[147] a wonderful book about finding beauty and peace in our everyday lives. People love this book because it recognizes our inherent need to get in touch with our deeper selves in the simplest ways: to lie on a beach and listen to the magical sound of the waves as they carve the sand around our feet, for example. Many corporations are now beginning to seriously consider the advantages of this perspective and the importance it has for their employees. Some companies, such as Acacia Life Insurance in Maryland, are actually building "Quiet" or "Meditation" rooms or zones for employees to take a break. To help spur creativity, the Austin-based advertising firm GSD&M has built a Zen garden and labyrinth where no cell phones or computers are allowed. As Vienne says, "Some of our best thinking happens when our mind is on sabbatical." She illustrates this point by

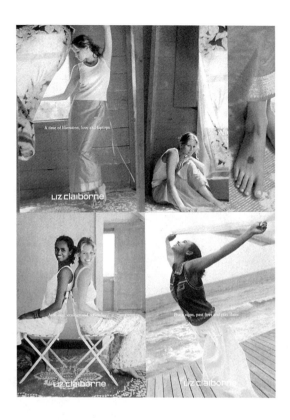

mentioning Sir Isaac Newton, who figured out the law of gravity while sitting under a tree, and Albert Einstein pondering the riddle of the universe with a cat on his lap. Companies such as Spirit Employed offer workshops, training, and individual and team consultation to help corporations bring a dimension of spiritual insight into the workplace. Large Japanese companies, regularly invite Buddhist monks to come and speak to employees about Zen principles and how they can be used to help management.

Consumers are, of course, bringing this newfound awareness of spiritual matters to bear in the marketplace. According to Marketwire.com (July 22, 2008), consumer expenditures in "inspirational" religious products (books, music, video, software, and gifts, with books capturing the lion's share) is valued at $6 billion. The overall market jumped 21 percent, or $1 billion, between 2004 and 2008. In 1998, consumers spent $27 billion on alternative medicine, according to a Harvard University study, and spending on holistic medical care such as acupuncture, chiropractors, and psychologists is up 36 percent in the past five years.[148]

In fashion imagery, Eastern mysticism abounds. The skin care, health, and beauty industries have also caught onto this trend and done extremely well incorporating the concept of products that also provide health benefits into the idea of products that reflect spirituality. Examples are plentiful. Aveda, the plant-based, ecofriendly cosmetics company, was, of course, one of the very first pioneers in this area with chakra products. Many others have followed suit. The Tony & Tina cosmetics brand has had immense success with their line of color therapy products designed to stimulate the body's chakra zones. Shiseido has a fragrance called "Relaxing Fragrance," designed to calm, and their lower-end company 5S is based on the "fundamental and mythical significance of 5." The brand Philosophy delineates its products according to the area of one's emotional life that needs attention, such as self-worth. Sally Hansen's line of nail and body art jewels has names such as *Mystic, Meditate, Harmony*, and so on.

Other manufacturers and retailers would be wise, I think, to pay attention to this particular trend in their approach to product and retail design as well as advertising. Brands as identity reflectors need to somehow recognize the need people have for deeper spiritual meaning in their lives. From an Emotional Branding standpoint, this means approaching this need with respect, as an open-ended dialogue. Whether a brand approaches this trend in an overt or a more subtle manner, it is important to exercise caution, not to offend people's sensibilities in this touchy area. This means that brands should not take themselves too seriously. The real objective is to simply show consumers that you are aware and responsive to the growing importance of this dimension of their lives. It is about recognizing who your consumers are and that their personal aspirations extend far beyond the world of commercialism.

People are most definitely looking for brands with more promise than simply "no more ring around the collar!"

Nostalgia: A Convergence of Eras

Retro-chic, cheesy, futuristic, sentimental, individualistic, kitsch, glam, geek . . .
Nostalgia/retro trends are all around us today. The VW beetle, the Mini Cooper, the retro look of the Jaguar, the success of Nick at Nite and TV Land, the '50s style of the Old Navy stores, the revival of Johnny Rockets hamburger restaurants, Walt Disney's Celebration, Florida—a real '40s-style community—Hollywood's espousal of retro-chic glamour (personified by Winona Ryder in a vintage gown twice as old as herself at the 2000 Oscars), and a veritable daily deluge of images and songs from the '50s, '60s, and '70s in advertising . . . these are just a few of many examples. The nostalgia/retro trend has definitely taken off and doesn't seem to be slowing down anytime soon. This trend is partly about soothing anxiety: a need to be reassured and grounded as we move forward

into a super fast-paced and seemingly uncertain future. It is also equally about a sense of excitement and empowerment—being at a vantage point in time when we are able to choose from the best of all eras. It is part of a global attitude of being able to have it all: having the freedom to cherry-pick and personalize things from all times, which means there's so much more cool stuff available!

This trend is partly about our need to be reassured and grounded as we move forward into a super fast-paced and seemingly uncertain future.

This is an important but difficult trend to utilize in branding programs. The nostalgia/retro trend so evident in our pop culture is complex because Baby Boomers and the younger X and Y generations all buy into it, but each for different reasons. In other words: a mix of current generations is pulling elements that resonate emotionally for them from a mix of previous generations ('40s, '50s, '60s, '70s, and now even the '80s). Baby Boomers are increasingly becoming nostalgic for cultural elements of the '50s and '60s, the decades of their youth, as they move into their sixties, and Gens X and Y are entranced by a mixture of past eras they did not get to experience firsthand, often flavoring their retro tastes with a dash of ironic irreverence.

Nostalgia began to take hold as a new phenomenon in the '70s, as a reaction to the tumultuous '60s, when the fallout from modern society was beginning to be very apparent in the form of the Vietnam War, warnings of pollution, rising statistics of violence, Watergate, great confusion in terms of gender roles, and the dissolution of the classic family structure (rising divorce rates). People were looking for the comfort of the simpler, more carefree times portrayed in the then–hit show *Happy Days* and movie *Grease.*

By the time we reached the safe distance of the '80s, Baby Boomers, fully morphed from hippies into yuppies, began to feel nostalgic for the '60s, and the music, images, and fashions of that era became rampant in pop culture and in branding programs.

For the past decade, Gens X and Y have added their twist to the nostalgia/retro trend. A big part of their approach to the past is to use elements from different eras to accentuate their individualism as a reaction against a cookie-cutter culture of lookalike stores and products.

They are looking to rediscover elements of an America they never knew. John Flanagan of Thermostat, a Connecticut-based marketing research firm that

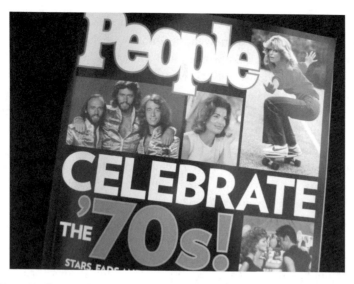

specializes in Generation X, says, "They are attracted to authenticity, to ties with the past, to the real deal. In a nutshell, that's why retro works."[149] As Gen Xers get older, watch for more nostalgia surrounding the '80s. Most of all, with the younger generations, it is a message of hope that they are looking for as they sift through the past.

In my opinion, the best branding programs using nostalgia borrow from the past, but infuse that past in an innovative manner with the present. This means a fresh, eclectic look at recycling the past.

In July 2009, *People* magazine came out with a new issue on the '70s and its innovative spirit. That same year, a film on Amelia Earhart's life hit the big screen, bringing back for women and men alike what it took to live an independent and adventurous life such as hers. If we add that Coke designed its iconic can with the stars and stripes of the American Flag in honor of the Fourth of July in 2009, you know that the brand is going back to its roots and its powerful heritage of happiness.

Emotionally, the amount of material goods that has spoiled us for the past decade is making us reconsider our reality, think about how those "things" we consume impact the environment, and look back for examples in our past history that are truly inspiring.

We love those people who stood for something larger and are in awe of the magic the old brands could share with us. Are we unsatisfied? I can't answer that question, but I know that we are missing something that is genuine and true. We are seeking more trust, authenticity, and truth.

Being nostalgic while keeping an eye on the future is a great strategy for brands. Keep on inventing, but make sure that you do it with the values most people associate with a positive, happy, and constructive outlook on life.

Almost any brand that has a branded relationship with consumers that spans more than a decade or so, or has an interesting story to tell from a historical perspective, can take advantage of this trend to revitalize the brand, because in our time-compressed age, retro is fast becoming "only a short while ago."

Both new and old identities should think of ways to serve this emotional longing that consumers have to experience our past alongside our present.

Cause Marketing: Stand for Something Bigger!

The trend of cause marketing has hit, and hit big. The list of companies that smartly support causes that accurately reflect their consumers' concerns is long: Apple, Avon, Wal-Mart, Procter & Gamble, Target, GE, Starbucks, Liz Claiborne, Toyota, Home Depot, and Coca-Cola, to name just a few! Ongoing surveys of consumer attitudes toward cause marketing confirm that these efforts pay off: 83 percent of Americans have a more positive image of companies that support a cause they care about, nearly two-thirds say that when price and quality are equal, they would likely switch brands or retailers to those involved with a cause, and 68 percent say they would happily pay more for a product associated with a good cause. In addition, the survey found that nine in ten workers at companies with cause

Get to know who your consumers really are, what really matters to them, and show them that you feel the same way.

programs said they are proud of their company's values, versus just 56 percent at firms not committed to a cause. Jed Pearsall, a marketing consultant, sums it all up quite well in an article in the *Wall Street Journal* by saying, "People are telling us they're tired of having advertising in their face. They want it to do something for them. Marketing will become a field that solves people's problems."[150] This is perfectly in sync with the premise of Emotional Branding; it has everything to do with getting to know who your consumers really are, what really matters to them, and showing them that you feel the same way. The effectiveness of these programs can no longer be questioned; done the right way, they can bolster a brand's equity and provide an open conduit through which the consumer/brand relationship will deepen. But what exactly is the "right way" to approach cause marketing?

Here are a few of the very best examples of cause marketing programs that work. (Many of these companies do much more in many other areas in addition to the particular effort I am choosing to mention here.)

Cause Marketing

What actions are brands taking to better their image and their environment through "Cause" Initiatives? This text is mostly imported from those brands' Web sites, with some editing. The idea is to keep the voice of the brands as intact as possible for your reading pleasure.

BONO'S (PRODUCT) RED WITH APPLE

More than 4,100 people die every day from AIDS in sub-Saharan Africa, and almost 2,000 children are infected with HIV each day. (PRODUCT) RED works with companies like Apple to create (PRODUCT) RED-branded products and direct up to 50 percent of gross profits from the sale of those products to the Global Fund to help fund AIDS programs in Africa. Since its introduction, (PRODUCT) RED has generated more than $130 million for the Global Fund. And now, you can make an impact by purchasing (PRODUCT) RED. Apple participates by donating a portion of the proceeds from RED Special Edition iPods and iTunes gift cards. Other (PRODUCT) RED companies include American Express, Gap, Converse, Starbucks, Dell, Emporio Armani, Windows Vista, and Hallmark. *www.joinred.com*

PROCTER & GAMBLE'S CHILDREN'S SAFE DRINKING WATER PROGRAM

The Children's Safe Drinking Water Program is a not-for-profit program founded by P&G as part of its global cause–Live, Learn, and Thrive™–aimed at improving life for children in need. The Live, Learn, and Thrive program provides clean drinking water in the developing world. P&G works with more than thirty partners and has committed to providing two billion liters of clean drinking water using PUR™ water purification packets within the next five years.

P&G's lifesaving technology uses small packets or sachets to disinfect water. Each sachet works like a mini-water treatment plant, removing dirt, cysts, and pollutants while killing bacteria and viruses in contaminated water in less than thirty minutes, ten liters at a time.

The World Health Organization estimates that more than one billion people around the world do not have access to clean, safe water. Every day, more than 4,000 children die from diseases caused by drinking unsafe water. These deaths are preventable, and there are proven, scalable, and cost-effective solutions such as the PUR™ packets that can dramatically improve water quality and potentially save a huge number of lives.

P&G also markets the PUR™ Water System to the public. The PUR™ water purification product is a powdered water clarification and disinfectant that comes in small, easy-to-use packets. In addition to CSDW programs in developing countries, PUR™ water purification packets have been provided to some of the most critical global emergency relief situations, including the tsunami in Asia, hurricanes in the Caribbean, and floods in the Philippines and Bangladesh. *www.csdw.org.*

AVON FOUNDATION BREAST CANCER CRUSADE

In response to the needs of women and their families, the Avon Foundation Breast Cancer Crusade has for more than a decade raised funds and awareness for advancing access to care and finding a cure for breast cancer. In the U.S., breast cancer is the most commonly diagnosed cancer among women, and it can strike men, as well. There is a new diagnosis every three minutes and a life lost every fourteen. From 1992 through 2000, the Avon Breast Cancer Crusade raised and awarded more than $585 million in fifty countries worldwide for awareness and education, screening and diagnosis, access to treatment, support services, and scientific research.

The annual main events: Avon Walk for Breast Cancer (U.S.) and Avon Walk Around the World for Breast Cancer. *http://walk.avonfoundation.org*

GE'S ECOMAGINATION

In May 2005, GE announced the launch of a program called "Ecomagination," intended, in the words of CEO Jeffrey Immelt, "to develop tomorrow's solutions such as solar energy, hybrid locomotives, fuel cells, lower-emission aircraft engines, lighter and stronger durable materials, efficient lighting, and water purification technology." But doing good has its own risks, bringing a heightened level of scrutiny such as the *New York Times*'s observation that "while General Electric's increased emphasis on clean technology will probably result in improved products and benefit its bottom line, Mr. Immelt's credibility as a spokesman on national environmental policy is fatally flawed because of his company's intransigence in cleaning up its own toxic legacy."

GE said that it would invest $1.4 billion in clean-tech research and development in 2008 as part of its Ecomagination initiative. As of October 2008, the program had resulted in seventy green products being brought to market, ranging from halogen lamps to biogas engines. In 2007, GE raised the annual revenue target for its Ecomagination initiative from $20 billion to $25 billion by 2010 following positive market response to its new product lines.

GE's renewable energy business has expanded greatly to keep up with growing U.S. and global demand for clean energy. Since entering the renewable energy industry in 2002, GE has invested more than $850 million in renewable energy technology. In 2009, GE's renewable energy initiatives, which include solar power, wind power, and Jenbacher engines using waste gases, employ more than 4,900 people globally and have created more than ten thousand supporting jobs.

TOYOTA'S "WHY NOT?" CAMPAIGN

In 2007, Toyota launched its "Why Not?" corporate advertising campaign, the "biggest, broadest corporate campaign in its history," according to *Ad Age*. Toyota will not discuss how much it will cost, but the spending on national TV, print, and online ads in America is expected to well exceed the $40 million the company spent last year on ads. The campaign focuses on three corporate pillars: environmental commitment, economic impact, and social responsibility. The ads were created by Dentsu America, New York; Toyota chose the "Why Not?" theme after six months of consumer research.

Toyota and Dentsu America launched a microsite at *www.toyota.com/whynot* to support Toyota's "Why Not?" campaign. The site engages users by allowing them to submit their own innovations in six areas—safety, water, land, air, community, and energy—while learning about Toyota's efforts in these same areas.

One person was chosen as the winner in the "Why Not? Innovation Experience," and received a week-long trip for a VIP tour of Toyota's plant in Kentucky and the opportunity to meet with top innovators in New York City.

"The goal in creating this 'virtual world' was to open a dialogue between Toyota and people across the country, while making it fun to use at the same time," said Mike Wilson, chief creative officer of Dentsu America. "Over time, the suggestions of users will 'grow' the landscape of the site."

Why might Toyota be doing this? Toyota has received a lot of bad press recently, such as being attacked by green groups over a proposed CAFE standard and losing a recommendation from *Consumer Reports* following a decrease in the

Highlander's safety rating and the 2009 Corolla's fuel efficiency. Steve Sturm, Toyota's vice president of strategic research, says there is no connection between the new ads and the recent bad press, and that the ads are just a way for America to better understand Toyota's corporate image.

The "Why Not?" Web site has two print ads, a video of the TV commercial, "Harmony," and the making of the TV commercial. The "Harmony" commercial features a car made by three people from twigs, mud, etc., that slowly fades in time-lapse images into the natural environment. The voiceover asks, "Can a car company grow in harmony with the environment? Why not?" and explains that Toyota is working towards cars with zero emissions and "zero waste" in everything they do. *Ad Age* is not amused, and writes that "striving isn't accomplishing, and it strikes us as a bit disingenuous to be selling some unattainable vision of the future." Toyota, wake up.

WAL-MART SUSTAINABILITY

Wal-Mart is the ultimate cost-cutting machine, and razor-thin margins are the reason for its massive success. How could that philosophy and strength be parlayed into a cause marketing program? As indicated below, Wal-Mart is working to gain traction on sustainability–but is it a cost-cutting goal, a genuine, an eco-friendly solution, or both?

While Wal-Mart only sources 1 percent of its power from renewable energy at the moment, it is still one of the largest solar installers in the U.S. The corporation is also working on organic clothing and food, sustainable seafood, and fuel-efficient trucks. Three prototype high-efficiency stores in Missouri, Illinois, and Texas were constructed with recycled building materials, use integrated water, heating, and cooling systems, contain low-flow bathroom faucets, and have energy-efficient lighting. Wal-Mart has also succeeded in diverting 57 percent of waste generated in its U.S. stores from landfills.

THE HOME DEPOT ECO OPTIONS

The Eco Options label makes it easy for you to identify products that make a difference, one choice at a time.

Every product with the Eco Options label has less of an impact on the environment than competing products. Specifically, Eco Options products offer one or more of the following benefits: sustainable forestry, energy efficiency, healthy home, and clean air and water conservation.

Eco Options also has a ready-made available magazine full of ideas, examples, and tips for making your environment more eco-friendly.

Eco Options Initiative examples:

- *CFL Recycling Program.* "As a part of our long-term commitment to the environment and sustainability, The Home Depot is pleased to offer free in-store compact fluorescent light (CFL) bulb recycling at all of our stores nationwide. Just look for the signs and collection units in our stores."
- *Plastic Bag Reduction.* "As of June 1, 2009, our stores will no longer provide complimentary plastic bags. To encourage consumers to reduce their use of plastic bags and protect the environment we will now charge 5 cents for each plastic bag. Please bring your own bag or purchase one of The Home Depot's reusable bags available in-store."
- *Canadian Green Home Index.* "First-ever Canadian Green Home Index reveals room for improvement in homes across Canada. Canadians score 60 out of 100 for green intentions and eco-action at home."
- *Wood Purchasing Policy.* "The Home Depot gives preference to wood that comes from responsibly managed forests."
- *Carbon Reduction Fund.* "On behalf of its customers, The Home Depot will offset 100 percent of the greenhouse gas emissions associated with the shipping of all online purchases. This means that shipping is carbon neutral. In conjunction with efforts to reduce emissions and increase efficiency, offsetting can be a useful and important part of our efforts to reduce the global effects of emissions caused by [our] activities."

COCA-COLA GREEN ENERGY

In 2002, The Coca-Cola Company and six of its largest bottling partners developed a strategy for sustainability. This plan focuses on the role and impact of the Coca-Cola system in four key areas: workplace, marketplace, environment, and community. They use this strategy to guide their approach to sustainability issues and to report their progress. To see how this strategy is adopted throughout the Coca-Cola system, visit the Web sites of some of their largest bottling partners.

Coca-Cola launched a multiyear partnership with WWF to conserve and protect freshwater resources. This $20 million commitment from The Coca-Cola Company to WWF will be used to help conserve seven of the world's most important freshwater river basins, support more efficient water management in its operations and global supply chain, and reduce the company's carbon footprint.

Introduced in 2000, the Ultra Glass contour bottle is designed to improve impact resistance and reduce weight and cost. The innovative Ultra Glass bottles are 40 percent stronger, 20 percent lighter, and 10 percent less expensive than traditional contour bottles. Use of the Ultra Glass design has eliminated fifty-two thousand metric tons of glass, resulting in a CO_2 reduction of twenty-six thousand tons or the equivalent of planting eight thousand acres of trees. *www.thecoca-colacompany.com*

Other Examples of Cause Marketing

YOPLAIT LIDS CAMPAIGN

Yoplait's "Save Lids to Save Lives" campaign is in support of Susan G. Komen for the Cure. The company packages specific products with pink lids that consumers send in, and in turn, Yoplait donates ten cents per lid to the Susan G. Komen Breast Cancer Foundation.

AMERICAN HEART ASSOCIATION

An example of a nonprofit certification of a product (or business) is the American Heart Association's (AHA) stamp of approval on Cheerios, the popular breakfast cereal. The AHA food certification program grants use of its "Heart Check" icon and name to dozens of cereals and juices, which signifies that that product meets the association's low-fat, low-cholesterol standards.

HAAGEN-DAZS HELP THE HONEY BEES

"At Häagen-Dazs® ice cream, we use only all-natural ingredients in our recipes. Bee pollination is essential for ingredients in nearly 50 percent of our all-natural super premium flavors. Our goal is to raise awareness of the honey bee issue so that our communities work together to bring them back. We've created a special flavor to make spreading honey bee awareness that much sweeter. Vanilla Honey Bee is our delicious tribute to these essential creatures. In recognition of our reliance on honey bees for our food, we're donating money to help fund honey bee research." *www.helpthehoneybees.com*

Other interesting initiatives that feature brands reaching out to show their responsible side:

- PNC Grow Up Great
- PNC Financial Services and Sesame Workshop, National Head Start Association and Family Communications. *www.pncgrowupgreat.com*
- *Lee National Denim Day.* Lee Jeans and the Susan G. Komen Breast Cancer Foundation. *www.denimday.com*
- *Volkswagen Fasten Your Seatbelts . . . Go Far!* Volkswagen of America and Scholastic. *www.teacher.scholastic.com/lessonplans/persuasivewriting*

The best cause-marketing programs integrate a social cause or issue into the brand's very persona. From the point of view of building a strong emotional brand strategy, it would be an interesting test to see if we could determine the name of the brand if we were given only the description of the causes supported. In many of the examples cited above, the answer is yes. However, in some cases, it seems that the honorable and very well-intentioned efforts of a company do not also reinforce the brand equity.

As with any other marketing endeavor, it never hurts to take an innovative, unusual approach to cause marketing. This can also make addressing serious, often intimidating or overwhelming issues more inviting for consumers.

A couple of examples of cause branding with a creative flair are:

- *The Body Shop.* The longtime activist company (and true trailblazer in the cause marketing arena!) has through the years found many inventive and powerful ways to not only support causes that are important to its consumers, but also to take the initiative itself in sensitizing the community to and involving it in human rights and environmental and political issues it feels strongly about. The Body Shop's "Make Your Mark" campaign is a great example. This campaign collected thumbprints of people around the world at sponsored store and public events which were used to create artistic portraits of human-rights victims and activists and serve as a petition for the causes connected to these people. In 1998, it collected approximately three million thumbprints!
- *Joe Boxer.* Joe Boxer sponsored a GM Chevy Ventura cab custom designed by Nick Graham, CEO of Joe Boxer. The cab, which sported the Joe Boxer logo and was loaded with lots of fun, wacky detailing, cruised the streets of New York for one year. All of the proceeds went to a breast cancer awareness program called Concept: Cure.

- *Also from Joe Boxer:* A Think-Pink in-store campaign to boost breast cancer awareness with a collection of "Think Pink" bras, panties, T-shirts, and so on.

An important result of this trend is that in supporting causes important to consumers, these companies are raising the bar for the expectations of social responsibility on the part of corporations. This means that corporations that are caught in the act of negligence or disregard in terms of social or environmental issues are largely taken to task by consumers. In this age of consumer empowerment, it would be wise to pay heed to this as a real possibility. Faith Popcorn has identified a trend on her Web site called "Vigilante Consumer" that is all about consumers taking matters into their own hands with protests and boycotts when brands disappoint them. Using Nike and Kathie Lee Gifford as examples, she talks about how consumers really do care about the truth of what's behind the brand. The Internet makes consumer outrage all the more powerful, and Internet activism is on the rise.

After episodes of picketing, protests, and pressure from environmental groups for marketing products made of wood from endangered forests,[151] Home Depot announced in August 1999 that it would begin giving preference to vendors that provide wood harvested responsibly. Home Depot has also recently made its first commercial touting an environmental theme, starring two giant pandas and showing the volunteer efforts of Home Depot employees to build a habitat for the animals in their new home at the Atlanta Zoo. Apparently, Home Depot is now wisely attempting to expand its effort at being a socially responsible corporation beyond its work in the housing causes to include the environmental concerns of its consumers. Given the fact that in a poll conducted by Environmental Research Associates in 1999, 87 percent of adults say that they are "concerned" about the condition of the environment in the United States and 44 percent say they are "very concerned," almost 50 percent of consumers look for environmental labeling on products, *and* the upcoming Gen Y group is highly sensitized to environmental issues;[152] they are wise to do so!

Conclusion

Although this book is meant to share my own branding experiences and could be interpreted as a sure way to reach the "promised brand," it also supports the theory that Emotional Branding is not for everyone. Unfortunately, Emotional Branding has become such a buzzword that it has transcended its own meaning.

Almost overnight, everyone and everything wants to be an Emotional Brand, an environment that is emotionally compelling, or an institution that connects emotionally from a branding perspective. It now seems we can't buy, enjoy, or do anything that's not emotionally branded; countries, states, cities, and even people are presented to us as emotional brands. Sometimes I am even tempted to look at my cats and try to understand which emotions they might feel that would make them a brand!

Captains of industry now believe that Emotional Branding is the only road to success. They even are welcoming and paying for the greatest and most expansive hoax in marketing today: putting people through MRIs to see how their brains respond to luxury or supermarket brands.

Is everyone mad? Is this the only savvy way to approach the world of business today? Is it only "brand smoke"? In a conversation with Nick Graham, formerly of underwear company Joe Boxer, he and I pondered the current branding mania and its inherent meaning (if any). We discussed how the Swedish clothing store H&M, which opened in New York at the beginning of 2000, has had one of the most successful entries of any store in this country.

Emotional Branding is about cultural relevance and emotional connection, not hype!

People lined up to shop there. Is H&M a brand or is it simply a popular store with low prices? And why have "brand darlings" like Nike and Tommy Hilfiger lost their branding edge? Why are brands like Guess, Gucci, and Apple able to make turnarounds? According to Graham, effective branding is about cultural relevance and emotional connection, not hype! I couldn't agree with him more.

The cause for this speculative "brandmania" is that most corporations confuse awareness and emotional connection. How much a product is known does not make it relevant to a market, nor does it make it esteemed or preferred by consumers. K-mart is a well-known brand, but Target has an emotional aura; Microsoft is a major player in the computer industry, but Apple and Google strike a chord with users; Folgers is a great coffee brand, but we love Urth!

Powerful brands only work if the people inside the company really care for their customers. Branding is a people-to-people business, not a factory-to-people business. A brand needs to have human qualities and emotional values–it needs to have a personality. Branding should define corporate culture and express it through imagery that engages people. If you can make consumers desire a partnership with your brand, you have created a unique emotional connection that spells long-term success.

I hope that this book has demonstrated to you the power of this emotional connection and given you new insight and inspiration for ways of creating, recreating, and sustaining this connection through the Emotional Branding process. Having a truly emotionalized brand means constantly reevaluating the strengths and weaknesses of the brand. I would like to leave you with three final thoughts that are essential to remember in managing a successful, emotionalized brand and keeping it connected to the marketplace.

- **First:** Brands have life cycles. Popular brands today are not necessarily the winners of tomorrow. The future of a brand is defined by its relevance at any given time and by how well it can protect the values that made it great in the first place.

- **Second:** Brands are made every day based on their emotional relevance with the public and its commitment to quality. The biggest enemy of branding is overexposure. Consumers quickly tire of the "buzz" and begin searching for something new.

- **Third:** Real brands are about dialogue and trust. Brands have to stop being "wowed" by social media and move onto social branding to establish an emotional connection with customers. A brand's success is now based on how many followers it has and how many times it is shared.

The biggest misconception about branding is that it does not need to evolve. Even this book is a work in progress, in the truest meaning of that phrase. We all have a perennial need to search out magic formulas, but it is actually much more interesting to look for the evolving dynamics of the market, that fascinating brand/market interplay. In any market, there are products you need and products you desire; to get people interested in a long-term relationship, keep your ear to the ground and always be ready for any market changes.

Change is good, but predicting change is better–the answer is within people's hearts. Have that discussion.

notes

Notes to Introduction

1. Herbert Muschamp, "Seductive Objects with a Sly Sting," *New York Times* (July 2, 1999).
2. Thomas Perzinger, Jr., "So Long, Supply and Demand," *Wall Street Journal* (January 1, 2000).
3. Sarah Larenaudie, *W* (January 9, 2000).
4. John Huey and Geoffrey Colvin, "The Jack and Herb Show," *Fortune* (January 11, 1999).
5. Gina Kolata, "More than an Exercise in Vanity," *New York Times* (May 13, 2008).
6. Aimee Lee Ball, "*O* Interview: How Daniel Goleman Is Changing Our Ideas about Living Green," *O, The Oprah Magazine* (April 2009).
7. Glen Thrush, "When I'm 64," *American Demographic* (January 1999).
8. Richard Lee, "Stew's Changes with Hard Times," *News-Times* (April 14, 2009).
9. "Boomers Plot Exit Strategies: A Generation Checks Out New Ways of Checking Out," *USA Today* (May 15, 1999).
10. Lev Grossman, "Generation Gap," *TimeOut* (January 20, 2000).
11. Kemper Scudder, cited by Robert Scally, "Gen X Grows Up," *Discount Store News* (October 25, 1999).
12. Elena Romero, "Urban Outfitters Successfully Caters to the 'Newly Homeless'," *DNR* (December 28, 1998).
13. Jane Levere, "BBDO New York Breaks Down Why, When, Where, and How Young Adults Get Information," *New York Times* (December 9, 1999).
14. "Event," The National Campaign. Accessed August 26, 2009 (*http://www.thenationalcampaign.org/media/press-release.aspx?releaseID=23*).
15. Alexei Barrionuevo, "In Argentina, a Camera and a Blog Make a Star," *New York Times* (March 13, 2009).

Notes to Chapter 2

16. "African-American Marketing in the U.S." Packagedfacts.com. Accessed February 1, 2008.
17. Graham Stedman, "Marketing to African-Americans," *ANA–The Advertiser* (December 1997).

18. *New York Times Magazine* (May 7, 2000).

19. Graham Stedman, "Marketing to African-Americans."

20. "Ethnic Hair, Beauty, and Cosmetics Products in the U.S." Packagedfacts. com. Accessed November 1, 2008.

21. Eugene Morris, "The Difference in Black and White," *American Demographics* (January 1993).

22. "African-American Black Market Profile 2007." Magazine.org.

23. Graham Stedman, "Marketing to African-Americans."

24. Ibid.

25. Geoffrey Brewer, "Spike Speaks," *Incentive* (February 1993).

26. U.S. Census Bureau. April 20, 2000. Accessed August 26, 2009 (*www. census.gov*).

27. Excellent information on this subject is available from Strategy Research Corporation, "Population & Demography," U.S. Hispanic Market Survey (1998).

28. Ibid.

29. "The State of the Hispanic Economy," *Hispanic Business* (April 1999).

30. Christy Haubegger, "The Legacy of Generation N," *Newsweek* (12 July 1999).

31. Helene Stapinski, "Generation Latino," *American Demographics* (July 1999).

32. "Minority Phone Users Make Different Demands," *Wall Street Journal* (April 7, 1999).

33. "Asian-Americans Fastest Growing Minority Group," *Retail Ad World* (October 1999).

34. Wei-Tai Kwok and Vicky M. Wong, "Tapping into the Asian-American Market," *DMA Insider* (Winter 2000).

35. Stuart Elliott, "Ads Speak to Asian-Americans," *New York Times* (March 6, 2000).

36. Becky Ebenkamp, "Ancient Chinese Secrets?" *Brandweek* (November 8, 1999).

37. Jonathan Boorstein, "*New York Times* Targets Chinese-American Market," *Direct* (August 1999).

Notes to Chapter 3

38. Karen Epper Hoffman, "Internet as Gender-Equalizer?" *Internet World* (November 9, 1998).

39. Kate Sayre and Michael J. Silverstein, "The Female Economy," *Harvard Business Review* (September 2009).

40. Gerry Meyers, "Selling (a Man's World)," *American Demographics* (April 1996).

41. Beth Fuchs Brenner, "Plugging into Women," *Brandweek* (March 15, 1999).

42. *www.women-drivers.com.*

43. "New Twitter Research: Men Follow Men and Nobody Tweets," *Harvard Business Publishing* (June 1, 2009). Accessed October 16, 2009 (*http://blogs. harvardbusiness.org/cs/2009/06/new_twitter_research_men_follo.html*).

44. 2009 Women and Social Media Study. Accessed October 16, 2009 (*http://assets3.blogher.com/files/2009_Compass_BlogHer_Social_Media_ Study_042709_FINAL.pdf*).

45. "Women CEOs Slowly Gain on Corporate America," USA Today online (January 1, 2009). Accessed October 16, 2009 (*http://www.usatoday.com/ money/companies/management/2009-01-01-women-ceos-increase_N.htm*).

46. "What Would Happen if Women Ruled the World?" MSNBC (March 1, 2009). Accessed October 16, 2009 (*http://www.msnbc.msn.com/ id/29445093*).

47. Lahle Wolfe, "Women in Business." About.com.

48. Jennifer Shu, "SAS Institute: An Employer that Redefines 'Family-Friendly,'" *Women-connect.com* (March 9, 2000).

49. Michael Wolff, "Waiting to Exhale," *New York Magazine* (February 14, 2000).

50. Ibid.

51. Lisa H. Guss, "Targeting Women," *Supermarket Business* (May 1999).

52. Judith Langer, "Focus on Women: Three Decades of Qualitative Research," *Marketing News* (September 14, 1998).

53. Diane Harris, "Why Can't a Man Invest More Like a Woman?" *Investor* (February 2000).

54. "A Man's Place," *New York Times Magazine* (May 16, 1999).

55. Lisa H. Guss, "Targeting Women."

56. Kathleen Sampey, "This Is Not Your Mother's P&G," *Adweek* (March 13, 2000).

57. Hershel Sarbin, "Claiming Ownership," *Folio* (September 15, 1999).

58. Judith Langer, "Focus on Women: Three Decades of Qualitative Research."

59. Mary Lou Quinlan, "Women: We've Come a Long Way, Maybe," *Advertising Age* (February 22, 1999).

60. Anne Jarrell, "Models, Definitely Gray, Give Aging a Sexy New Look,"

New York Times (November 28, 1999).

61. Mary Lou Quinlan, "Women: We've Come a Long Way, Maybe."

62. Ginia Bellafante, "Feminism: It's All about Me!" *Time* (June 28, 1998).

63. "Twentysomething Women Declare Themselves Primary Purchasers," *Quirks* (May 1997).

64. Wayne Friedman, "Barbie Is Working Harder," *Advertising Age* (March 6, 2000).

65. Scott M. Roy, "Marketing to WWWomen," *Digitrends* (Winter 2000).

66. Ibid.

67. "Same-Sex Couples and the Gay, Lesbian, and Bisexual Population: New Estimates from the American Community Survey" (2006).

68. *http://forrester.com/er/research/brief/excerpt/0,1317,17004,00.html.*

69. Mark Dolliver, "Out of the Closet," *Brandweek* (August 23, 1999).

70. Richard A. Oppel, Jr., "Exxon to Stop Giving Benefits to Partners of Gay Workers," *New York Times* (December 7, 1999).

71. Michael Wilke, "Ads Targeting Gays Rely on Real Results, Not Intuition," *Advertising Age* (June 22, 1998).

72. Ronald Alsop, "Cracking the Gay Market Code," *Wall Street Journal* (June 29, 1999).

73. Ronald Alsop, "Web Site Sets Gay-Themed Ads for Big, National Publications," *Wall Street Journal Interactive Edition* (January 17, 2000).

74. Grant Lukenbill, *Untold Millions: Marketing to Gay and Lesbian Consumers* (New York: Heyworth, 1998).

75. Ronald Alsop, "Web Site Sets Gay-Themed Ads For Big, National Publications."

Notes to Chapter 5

76. Morris B. Holbrook and Elizabeth C. Hirschman, "The Experiential Aspects of Consumption: Consumer Fantasies, Feelings, and Fun," *Journal of Consumer Research* 9 (September 1981): 132–140.

77. Michael Tuan Pham, "Representativeness, Relevance, and the Use of Feelings in Decision Making," *Journal of Consumer Research* 25 (September 1998).

78. Morris B. Holbrook and Elizabeth C. Hirschman, "The Experiential Aspects of Consumption: Consumer Fantasies, Feelings, and Fun."

79. Gerald J. Gorn, "The Effects of Music in Advertising on Choice Behavior: A Classical Conditioning Approach," *Journal of Marketing* 46 (Winter 1982): 94–101.

80. Ibid.

81. Jane Bainbridge, "Scenting Opportunities," *Marketing* (February 19,

1998).

Notes to Chapter 6

82. Laura Ries and Al Ries, *The Twenty-two Immutable Laws of Branding: How to Build a Product or Service into a World-Class Brand* (New York: HarperCollins, 1998).
83. Mr. Talley's statement from *www.pantone.com/allaboutcolor/guru2000.htm*.
84. Pat Brillo, telephone conversation with author, February 2000.
85. Lesa Sawahata, ed., *Color Harmony Workbook* (Beverly, Mass.: Rockport Publishers, 1999).

Notes to Chapter 7

86. Patrick D. McCarthy and Robert Spector, *The Nordstrom Way* (New York: John Wiley & Sons, Inc., 1995): 145.
87. Ibid.
88. Ron Lieber, "Super Market," *Fast Company* (April 1999).
89. Ibid.
90. Paco Underhill, *Why We Buy* (New York: Simon & Schuster, 1999).
91. Paul Rozin, "The Importance of Social Factors in Understanding the Acquisition of Food Habits," *Taste, Experience & Feeding: Development and Learning*, ed. Elizabeth D. Capaldi and Terry L. Powley (Washington, D.C.: American Psychological Association, 1993).

Notes to Chapter 8

92. Phyllis Berman and Katherine Bruce, "Makeover at the Makeup Counter," *Forbes* (April 19, 1999).
93. Paco Underhill, *Why We Buy: The Science of Shopping* (New York: Simon & Schuster, 1999).
94. Ibid.

Notes to Chapter 9

95. Allaine Cervonka, "A Sense of Place: The Role of Odor in People's Attachment to Place," *Aroma-Chology Review* 5 no. 1 (1996). Also see Rachel S. Herz, "The Relationship between Odor and Emotion in Memory," *Aroma-Chology Review* 5 no. 2 (1996).
96. Susan Fournier, "Consumers and Their Brands: Developing Relationship Theory in Consumer Research," *Journal of Consumer Research* 24 (March 1998).
97. Gail Civille, in a telephone interview with the author, March 2000.

98. "Decorating with Fragrances," Happi.com, August 1999, *http://www.happi. com/special/sep991.htm.*

99. Reuters, "Aroma Sofas Come Up Roses in Latest British Home Trend," Indian Express Newspapers, January 25, 1999, *http://expressmedia.com/fe/ daily/19990125/0255215.html.*

100. Linda Dyett, "Something in the Air," *House Beautiful* (October 1996).

101. Susan C. Knasko, "Congruent and Incongruent Odors: Their Effect on Human Approach Behavior," *Compendium of Olfactory Research* (Dubuque, Iowa: Kendall Hunt Publishing Company, 1995).

102. Robert A. Baron, "Of Cookies, Coffee, and Kindness: Pleasant Odors and the Tendency to Help Strangers in a Shopping Mall," *Aroma-Chology Review* 6 no. 1 (1998).

103. Atmospherics, a company that specializes in in-store scents, implements these devices, among others.

104. "Dollars and Scents," *Success,* April 2000, *http://www.successmagazine. com/issues/dec97/hottopps.html.*

105. Ibid.

106. Allaine Cervonka, "A Sense of Place: The Role of Odor in People's Attachment to Place," *Aroma-Chology Review* 5 no. 1 (1996).

107. James Fallon, "Urban Renewal," *W* (April 2000).

108. Ibid.

109. Ibid.

Notes to Chapter 10

110. Catherine McDermott, *20th Century Design* (Woodstock, N.Y.: The Overlook Press, 2000).

111. Veronique Vienne, *The Art of Doing Nothing* (New York: Clarkson Potter, 1998). Veronique Vienne, telephone interview with author, April 23, 2000.

112. Frank Gibney, Jr., and Belinda Luscombe, "The Redesigning of America," *Time* (March 20, 2000).

113. Ibid.

114. Bob Garfield, "VW: Best of All Media," *Advertising Age* (May 31, 1999).

115. *Wallpaper* (May 2000).

Notes to Chapter 11

116. Ed Razek's current title at The Limited is president and chief marketing officer for Limited Brands and Creative Services.

117. *Red Herring* (January 2000).

Notes to Chapter 12

118. Shelly Branch, "How Target Got Hot," *Fortune* (May 24, 1999).

119. REI, *www.rei.com* (accessed April 12, 2000).

120. Rosemary Feitelberg, "Conversation Spurs Commerce in Active," *Women's Wear Daily* (February 10, 2000).

121. Barry Rosenberg, telephone interview with author, May 2000.

122. Hillary Chura and Amanda Beeler, "Absolut Bolsters Outdoor Budget," *Advertising Age* (July 17, 2000).

123. Jesse McKinley, "After the Silver Spoon, a Green Life," *New York Times* (April 17, 2009).

124. T. L. Stanley, "Bringing Out the Faithful," *Brandweek* (March 27, 2000).

125. Ibid.

Notes to Chapter 14

126. Ken Banta, "Message in the Bottle," *Metropolis* (June 1999).

127. Ibid.

Notes to Chapter 15

128. Richard Florida, "How the Crash Will Reshape America," *The Atlantic* (March 2009).

129. Jack Neff, "Lever's CMO Throws Down the Social-Media Gauntlet," *Advertising Age* (April 13, 2009).

130. Michael Hirschorn, "The Future is Cheese," *The Atlantic* (March 2009).

131. Desiree Gruber, in interview with author.

132. Benetton gets only 5 percent of its $2 billion annual sales in the United States. Silvia Sansoni, "Capital Offense: Benetton Ads Act as Live Bait," *Forbes* (October 19, 1998).

133. Ellen McGirt, "How Chris Hughes Helped Launch Facebook and the Barack Obama Campaign," *Fast* (March 17, 2009).

134. Marc Kravetz, *Obama* (France: Dalloz-Sirey, 2008).

Notes to Chapter 16

135. Ed Razek, in telephone conversation with author.

136. BBC News Channel (February 12, 2009).

Notes to Chapter 18

137. Lauren R. Rublin, "Too, Too Much!" *Barron's* (March 9, 1998).

138. Ibid.

139. Charlie Hess, "Women Lead Way in Profound but Quiet Revolution,"

Advertising Age (January 24, 2000).

140. Richard Cimino and Don Lattin, "Choosing My Religion," *American Demographics* (April 1999).

141. Ibid.

142. "Spirit Employed: Hire a New Employee–Your Spirit!" *PR Newswire* (October 15, 1998).

143. Becky Ebenkamp, "Celestial Season," *Brandweek* (November 16, 1998).

144. Shirley Brady, "Spiritual Journeying: Om Away from Om," *Time* (July 6, 1998).

145. David Van Biema, "Pop Goes the Kabbalah," *Time* (November 24, 1997).

146. Jeanne McDowell, "Buddhism in America," *Time* (October 13, 1997).

147. Veronique Vienne, *The Art of Doing Nothing* (New York: Clarkson Potter, 1998).

148. Heather Chaplin, "Gen X in Search of a Drink," *American Demographics* (February 1999).

149. Dick Silverman, "Every Going Concern Should Get Its Concerns Going," *DNR* (July 21, 1999).

150. Jonathan Kaufman, "Marketing in the Future Will Be Everywhere–Including Your Head," *Wall Street Journal* (January 1, 2000).

151. Brent Israelsen, "Environmental Groups Picket S.L. Home Depot," *Salt Lake Tribune* (October 15, 1998). Allan Dowd, "Green Groups, Firms in Talks on Canada Rainforests," Reuters (March 16, 2000).

152. Lisa E. Phillips, "Green Attitude," *American Demographics* (April 1999).

index

Books from Allworth Press

Allworth Press is an imprint of Allworth Communications, Inc. Selected titles are listed below.

Brandjam: Humanizing Brands Through Emotional Design
by Marc Gobé (6¼ × 9¼, 240 pages, hardcover, $24.95)

Branding the Man: Why Men Are the Next Frontier in Fashion Retail
by Bertrand Pellegrin (6¼ × 9¼, 224 pages, hardcover, $27.50)

The Art of Digital Branding
by Ian Cocoran (6¼ × 9¼, 272 pages, hardcover, $24.95)

Branding for Nonprofits: Developing Identity with Integrity
by DK Holland (6 × 9, 208 pages, paperback, $19.95)

Design Thinking: Integrating Innovation, Customer Experience, and Brand Value
edited by Thomas Lockwood (6 × 9, 304 pages, paperback, $24.95)

Corporate Creativity
edited by Thomas Lockwood and Thomas Walton (6 × 9, 256 pages, paperback, $24.95)

Building Design Strategy
edited by Thomas Lockwood and Thomas Walton (6 × 9, 256 pages, paperback, $24.95)

AIGA Professional Practices in Graphic Design, Second Edition
edited by Tad Crawford (6 × 9, 320 pages, paperback, $29.95)

Green Graphic Design
by Brian Dougherty with Celery Design Collaborative (6 × 9, 212 pages, paperback, $24.95)

How to Think Like a Great Graphic Designer
by Debbie Millman (6 × 9, 256 pages, paperback, $24.95)

Design Disasters: Great Designers, Fabulous Failures, and Lessons Learned
edited by Steven Heller (6 × 9, 240 pages, paperback, $24.95)

Creating the Perfect Design Brief: How to Manage Design for Strategic Advantage
by Peter L. Phillips (6 × 9, 224 pages, paperback, $19.95)

Designing Logos: The Process of Creating Logos That Endure
by Jack Gernsheimer (8½ × 10, 208 pages, paperback, $35.00)

Advertising Design and Typography
by Alex W. White (8¾ × 11¼, 224 pages, hardcover, $50.00)

The Graphic Design Business Book
by Tad Crawford (6 × 9, 256 pages, paperback, $24.95)

Business and Legal Forms for Graphic Designers, Third Edition
by Tad Crawford and Eva Doman Bruck (8½ × 11, 208 pages, paperback, includes CD-ROM, $29.95)

To request a free catalog or order books by credit card, call 1-800-491-2808. To see our complete catalog on the World Wide Web, or to order online for a 20 percent discount, you can find us at ***www.allworth.com***.